THE BUCCANEER EXPLORER

WILLIAM DAMPIER'S VOYAGES

WILLIAM DAMPIER:
'Pirate and Hydrographer'

THE BUCCANEER EXPLORER

WILLIAM DAMPIER'S VOYAGES

Edited and with an introduction by
GERALD NORRIS

THE BOYDELL PRESS

First published 1994 as *William Dampier: Buccaneer Explorer*
The Folio Society, London

New Edition 2005
The Boydell Press, Woodbridge

Transferred to digital printing

ISSN 1743-4769
ISBN 978-1-84383-141-9

first person singular

For Sally Norris with love

The Boydell Press is an imprint of Boydell & Brewer Ltd
PO Box 9, Woodbridge, Suffolk IP12 3DF, UK
and of Boydell & Brewer Inc.
668 Mt Hope Avenue, Rochester, NY 14620, USA
website: www.boydellandbrewer.com

A CiP catalogue record for this book is available
from the British Library

Library of Congress Catalog Card Number: 20040227727

This publication is printed on acid-free paper

CONTENTS

ILLUSTRATIONS

(Reproduced from the 1699 editions of *A New Voyage
Round the World* and *Voyages and Descriptions* by William
Dampier)

INTRODUCTION

In Room IV of the National Portrait Gallery, off Trafalgar Square, is a painting by Thomas Murray of the only buccaneer allotted wall-space among Britain's worthies. Until recently this canvas, painted around 1702, bore the legend 'Captain Dampier (1651–1715): Pirate and Hydrographer', which must have halted even the briskest gallery-goer. 'Pirate' has now been changed to the somewhat tame 'Circumnavigator', but the subject's piercing, steel-blue eyes probably still, like the Ancient Mariner, 'stoppeth one of three'.

William Dampier is the most remarkable seaman that England produced in the century and a half between Francis Drake and Captain Cook. He circumnavigated the world three times – twice more than Drake or Cook. He commanded the first government-funded voyage of discovery to investigate matters of geography and science. In his treatise *A Discourse of Winds* he made a lasting contribution to hydrography and meteorology. He wrote the first great English travel book, *A New Voyage Round the World*, seasoning a pungent narrative with vivid descriptions of places, people, animals, plants and much else that was wholly fresh to his readers. These achievements would be striking enough for someone who was not also a legendary buccaneer.

Born into a Somerset farming family at East Coker, he was baptised on 5 September 1651. While still a boy he was orphaned, but was cared for by relations, who gave him a sound education and eventually apprenticed him to a Weymouth shipmaster with whom he visited Newfoundland and Java. After service with the Royal Navy against the Netherlands in 1673, he went to the West Indies as assistant manager on a Jamaican sugar plantation. Finding the work uncongenial, he joined logwood-cutters in Campeche, Mexico, where he had begun to establish himself when the hurricane of 1676 destroyed his business and put everything three feet under water. He spent the next year with buccaneers and around this time started making notes of what he saw and learnt. Having recouped his fortunes, he went back to the logwood trade. Ten months later he returned to England.

Early the following year, 1679, he headed again for Campeche, having meanwhile married a girl called Judith, who worked at Arlington House, Euston, perhaps as handmaid to Isabella, Duchess of Grafton: alas, we hear no more of her. He broke his journey in Jamaica, where he negotiated the purchase of 'a small Estate in Dorsetshire'. If, as seems possible, this property was bought in partnership with his older brother George, it may have been at North Poorton, near Beaminster. Soon afterwards he fell in with another band of buccaneers and embarked for Panama. Having raided the rich fortress-town of Portobelo, they marched across the Isthmus of Darien, acquired boats from the Indians and made forays along the Pacific coast of Central and South America. He next sailed for a year with French and English buccaneers in the Caribbean before settling for an equal length of time in Virginia. He resumed buccaneering in August 1683, when he was almost thirty-two, serving under several captains in assorted vessels that cruised the west coast of South America. Reaching Mexico in March 1686, he threw in his lot with Captain Charles Swan, who proposed crossing to the East Indies, which was, says Dampier, 'very agreeable to my inclination'. They arrived at the Philippines in June and stayed there for six months, during which time Captain Swan, fêted by local chieftains, subsided into sybaritic lethargy. Dampier and others finally stole his ship and, abandoning any pretence of being privateers, who solely attacked England's foes, turned to straightforward piracy. Their progress through the Philippines and Indonesia, with a fruitless excursion to the arid north-west coast of Australia, proved increasingly aimless, and in the spring of 1688 Dampier parted from them at the island of Great Nicobar. Over the next two years he worked aboard Sumateran ships, making trips through Malaysia and to India, then serving as master-gunner at Fort St George, Bengkulu. He returned to England in September 1691 at the age of forty, after an absence of twelve years, having, in multiple stages, circumnavigated the globe.

Nothing is known of his life during the next five years. In March 1697 he was appointed a 'land-carriageman' with the Customs in London – not a particularly important post – and in the same year his first book, *A New Voyage Round the World*, which he must have spent much time assembling, was printed. It became an instant success, running to four editions in two years. Not since Drake and Cavendish had there been an account of a British circumnavigation, and never before in the first person, which was presently imitated by Defoe and Swift in *Robinson Crusoe* (1719) and *Gulliver's Travels* (1726). Dampier's book offered more than the Drake and Cavendish chronicles: there were buccaneering adventures, descriptions of foreign lands and customs, strange animals and plants, and, above all, an account of the dogged survival of one ordinary (or not so ordinary) human being who chose to exist on the fringes of civilisation.

A New Voyage brought Dampier to the attention of the Royal Society, founded in 1662 to promote scientific research and foster inquiry into the natural world. He went to dinner with Samuel Pepys, a past President of the Society and Secretary to the Admiralty. The Council of Trade and Plantations asked his advice on the Darien Scheme. Then, despite his buccaneering past and inexperience of naval command, the Admiralty appointed him leader of an exploring voyage to Australia, still largely uncharted and known as New Holland. Meanwhile he produced his second book, *Voyages and Descriptions*, comprising three parts: *A Supplement of the Voyage Round the World*, *The Campeachy Voyages* and *A Discourse of Winds*. By the time this appeared in 1699, he had set sail for the Far East, as Captain Dampier of the *Roebuck*.

The voyage was unhappy and mainly unsuccessful. Dampier's lieutenant, George Fisher, resented serving under a former pirate and made trouble. When publicly rebuked, he bellowed at his captain, 'Old Rogue! Old Dog! Old Cheat!' Dampier thwacked him with his cane and clapped him in irons; then, while revictualling at Salvador in Brazil, he persuaded the Portuguese governor to hold him in the city gaol. It took Fisher three months to gain his release.

The *Roebuck* reached its destination in July 1699. The object of the mission was 'to meet with some fruitful lands . . . productive of any of the rich fruits, drugs or spices (perhaps minerals also, etc.) that are in the other parts of the Torrid Zone', and to make a survey of the coast, investigating whatever might seem 'beneficial for navigation, trade or settlement'.

Little of this was achieved; during a mere five weeks in Australian waters nothing was discovered, and scarcely anything charted. Running out of provisions, Dampier went to the island of Timor, some 500 miles north, then cruised round New Guinea for five months. When the *Roebuck* showed signs of breaking up, he set sail for England. He was just able to make Ascension Island before the ship sank, fortunately in shallow water. Six weeks afterwards he and his crew were picked up and given passage home. A year later, in June 1702, he was court-martialled for his treatment of Lieutenant Fisher, docked his entire pay for the trip and stigmatised 'not a fit person to be employed as commander of any of Her Majesty's ships'.

Yet out of this failure and disappointment came *A Voyage to New Holland*, the last of Dampier's three books, published in two parts in 1703 and 1709. Here, in addition to meticulous and picturesque accounts of faraway people and places, was a deepening scientific awareness, which sometimes led him to recount facts that perplexed him, but eventually proved of great benefit to 'better qualified persons who shall come after me'.

Court-martialled he may have been, but Dampier's stock remained high. Ten months after his apparent disgrace the erstwhile pirate was presented to Queen Anne and kissed hands on receipt of a Letter of Marque that entitled him to command a privateering enterprise funded by Bristol and London businessmen. He had charge of two ships, the *St George* and the *Fame*, the latter captained by John Pulling. An old shipmate, Edward Morgan, who had just completed a prison sentence, joined the *St George* at Dampier's request to represent the interests of the consortium as purser and agent. The expedition began disastrously. Pulling quarrelled with Dampier and sped away to the Canaries in the *Fame* while the *St George* was still provisioning. He then went to Bermuda, where his cook set fire to a brandy vat and blew up the ship. Dampier, meanwhile, sailed to Kinsale, near Cork, and finding there another vessel, the *Cinque Ports*, ready for a privateering voyage, agreed with the captain, Charles Pickering, to band together. They planned to cruise along the coast of South America and intercept Spanish shipping.

The *St George* and *Cinque Ports* left Ireland in May 1703, reaching the Cape Verde Islands by October. Here, Dampier turned his first lieutenant, Huxford, off the ship. When the *St George* arrived at Brazil, he put Huxford's replacement, Barnaby, ashore, with a further eight men. Shortly afterwards, Captain Pickering died, and his lieutenant, Stradling, assumed command of the *Cinque Ports*. In their first engagement, he displayed such lack of resolve, firing his guns only a dozen times, that Dampier withdrew from the attack.

While the two ships were being cleaned at the islands of Juan Fernández, off Chile, forty-two sailors went ashore and refused to continue. After they were persuaded to return, Dampier and Stradling parted company, their assorted seamen choosing to sail with whichever captain they found less obnoxious. Alexander Selkirk, the prototype for Robinson Crusoe, gladly quit Dampier, but soon realised he could not stomach Stradling either and had himself marooned at Juan Fernández. Stradling went north and wrecked the *Cinque Ports* on deserted Malpelo Island, 250 miles west of Colombia. After surviving for several months, he was captured by the Spanish, taken to the mainland, marched 900 miles south and chained for five years to a dungeon wall in Lima.

Dampier moved to the Gulf of Panama, picking off local craft and making brief sorties ashore. His few engagements with larger vessels ended in failure. Disgusted by such lack of enterprise, twenty-five of his men stole away in a forty-ton prize vessel and made for the East Indies, taking half the *St George*'s provisions, much of the ammunition, and Dampier's Letter of Marque from Queen Anne. Despite his paltry record, Dampier convinced the remaining crew that they could capture the legendary Manila galleon, which annually brought the wealth of the Philippines to the Mexican port of Acapulco, whence the treasure was taken overland to Veracruz before going to Spain. Not since Thomas Cavendish's success in 1587 had the Manila galleon fallen into enemy hands. On 6 December 1704 the great ship, with her four-storeyed deckhouse towering towards the sky, hove into view, gunports closed, unaware of danger – the captain had mistaken the *St George* for a supply ship sent to meet her. Now was the moment to discharge as many broadsides as possible before the huge cannons could be manned and primed. Instead, to the bewilderment of his men, Dampier ran up the English ensign and let off a single warning shot. This provoked uproar among his officers and complete inaction aboard the *St George*. During the hiatus the Spanish mounted their eighteen- and twenty-pounders and opened fire with such vehemence that Dampier gave the order to stand off. The vast galleon glided on towards Mexico. Thus, in only a few minutes, riches reputedly amounting to sixteen million pieces of eight had come and gone without being threatened. For half the crew of the *St George*, this fiasco was the final straw, and they departed. Among them was the purser, Morgan, who took with him the more valuable items of silver, which he later peddled in Amsterdam entirely for his own benefit.

After some further petty pirating off Colombia and Ecuador, Dampier himself abandoned ship, leaving the *St George* to founder in the Gulf of Panama; she was 'eaten like a honey-comb . . . in some places we could thrust our thumbs quite through with ease'. He and twenty-seven men crossed the Pacific in a small captured Spanish ship, were briefly detained by the Dutch in Jakarta, and reached England towards the close of 1707. At fifty-six, he had completed his second circumnavigation and had again returned minus, not only his own ship, but an assortment of sister ships, prize vessels, captains, lieutenants, crewmen, booty and his Letter of Marque. The failure of the four-year undertaking confirmed him as an incompetent commander. The backers, with substantial losses, instructed their solicitors to prepare a case of fraud against him.

By good fortune, another privateering expedition was being planned in Bristol, a highly professional and well funded venture. The syndicate boasted the Mayor of Bristol, an ex-mayor and a dozen prominent citizens, including some connected with Dampier's 'late disastrous voyage'. The commander was to be twenty-nine-year-old Woodes Rogers, a Poole man who had settled in Bristol and gave promise of developing into an exceptional leader and administrator (he eventually became Governor of the Bahamas). Rogers made clear to the syndicate there was only one choice as navigator: William Dampier, the man best qualified in the world to act as 'Pilot for the South Seas'. Since the investors agreed, the fraud case was dropped – in any case, Dampier could not recompense them. He must have been delighted, at such a comparatively advanced age, to be selected for this role, which carried officer status and the right to a percentage of the profits.

There were two ships, the *Duke* (320 tons, thirty guns) and *Dutchess* (260 tons, twenty-six guns). Rogers was a disciplinarian and insisted on double the usual complement of officers. The combined crews amounted to 330. Dampier sailed with Rogers in the *Duke*, whose second-in-command was one of the principal backers, Dr Thomas Dover. An immensely successful Bristol physician, he was the inventor of Dover's Powder, a palliative abracadabra consisting of ipecac and opium, the addictive properties of which secured him a healthy income. (The Italian army was still using it during the Second World War.) The *Dutchess* was captained by Stephen Courtney, a gentleman-adventurer, also an investor, but a proficient officer. The nature of the expedition was unlike anything Dampier had experienced, not least in the morning and evening prayers conducted for the ship's company.

The two frigates weighed from Bristol in August 1708. Their ultimate goal was to capture, in sixteen months' time, the same Manila–Acapulco treasure ship that had so easily eluded Dampier. Meanwhile they intended picking up anything that presented itself *en route*. This secondary aim was fruitfully realised, but the most memorable episode during the outward passage was the unplanned rescue on 2 February 1709 at Juan Fernández of Alexander Selkirk, who had marooned himself there four years and four months earlier. Learning that Dampier was on the *Duke*, he very nearly decided to remain 'out of humanity's reach' and had to be coaxed aboard.

Ten months later Dampier piloted the *Duke* to the precise point where he had met the Manila galleon five years before. In due time the great ship arrived and was engaged and overcome after ferocious fighting. This prize, the *Nuestra Señora de la Encarnación y Desengaño*, surpassed all expectation. Every barrel, bale and crate was crammed with riches: gold, silver, uncut diamonds, rubies, Chinese porcelain, beautiful painted fans, musk, cinnamon, satins, damasks, taffetas, chintz. Quantities were vast: the silk alone amounted to 45,000 lbs.

At fifty-eight, an age reached by few buccaneers, Dampier had finally achieved his dream, the getting of wealth. And there might have been more, for a second galleon appeared a few days later. But, being a new ship, she carried additional protective cladding and ordnance of sixty twelve-pounders. The *Duke* and *Dutchess* attacked for seven hours, withdrawing when English losses reached twenty.

Setting out for home, Dampier gave further evidence of his navigational skills by piloting the ships 6,000 miles across the Pacific direct to the tiny island of Guam, which he had not visited since 1686. They went on to the Philippines and Java, round the Cape of Good Hope, then revictualled at St Helena and Ascension before anchoring in the Thames on 14 October 1711.

Dampier had circumnavigated the world for a third time, and this time at a profit. At the age of sixty he allowed himself to retire on his share of the loot – a respectable £1,500. In a house in Coleman Street, just east of Moorgate in the City of London, he was looked after by his cousin Grace until his death three and a half years later in March 1715. It is not known where he was buried.

Returning to the picture of Dampier in the National

Portrait Gallery, one is struck by how guarded his look seems. He appears to know his worth, yet to be conscious that his recent, hard-won fame might be short-lived. In fact, his reputation has risen steadily over three centuries, with a growing recognition of the magnitude of his accomplishments. His three books have established him as the first outstanding British travel writer, still unequalled in range of interest, acuteness of observation or clarity of expression. And, because he was the first to write about so many faraway lands, his books have retained their immediacy and fascination. But they rank as more than superlative travel literature: they also have scientific importance. His object, he said, was 'to see all countries and observe the works of Nature'. He was insatiably curious about every facet of the physical world, and dozens of his descriptions – of avocado pears, breadfruit, cochineal, flamingos, typhoons, yams – passed straight into dictionaries and encyclopaedias. A high proportion of these proved so accurate that scientists continue to quote them in scholarly journals. The insects, fishes and plants named after him testify to the regard in which he is held. He is acknowledged as a pioneer of scientific exploration, commemorated in the Dampier Archipelago in the Indian Ocean, Dampier Strait in Papua New Guinea and the port of Dampier in Western Australia. In hydrography his influence has been enormous. *A Discourse of Winds*, in *Voyages and Descriptions*, was praised by Cook and Nelson and is now viewed as a classic exposition of the system of winds, tides and currents in the Southern Hemisphere. A hundred years elapsed before it needed modifications. 'As a continual investigator of hydrography and of the variation of the compass, of winds and the many minutiae of navigation, he is fundamental to all future discovery,' wrote J. C. Beaglehole. In 1948 the Royal Navy commissioned the 1,600-ton survey vessel HMS *Dampier* to mark his contribution to hydrography.

In literature his writings influenced Defoe and Swift. Defoe relied heavily on Dampier not just for *Robinson Crusoe*, but in *A General History of the Pirates* and *A New Voyage Round the World, by a Course Never Sailed Before*. Swift, in the introduction to *Gulliver's Travels,* has Lemuel Gulliver refer to 'my cousin Dampier'. Coleridge called him a 'man of exquisite mind' and drew on him for *The Ancient Mariner.*

Dampier has been fortunate in his recent editors and biographers – John Masefield, Clennell Wilkinson, Joseph C. Shipman, Christopher Lloyd – who have greatly increased our knowledge of him. Yet they were perhaps too generous towards his personality, inclined to doubt contemporary accusations against him and to prefer his own version of himself. In the 1927 Argonaut Press edition of *A New Voyage Round the World* Sir Albert Gray even called him 'a modest and courteous gentleman . . . He was with them [the buccaneers], but hardly one of them. As he was less of a buccaneer, so, as I believe, he was more of a gentleman.'

However, William Whaley, manager of the Jamaican sugar plantation where Dampier worked when he was twenty-three, told Squire Helyar that he 'bin nothing but a plage to me . . . he is a selfe conceated young man and one that understands leightle or nothing'. At his court martial in June 1702 Dampier was described as a vicious, violent commander, whose language sometimes encompassed obscenities beyond the comprehension of hardened seamen. Five years later, after the calamitous *St George* privateering voyage, Dampier's midshipman John Welbe published a pamphlet painting a lamentable picture of his captain as a hollow, lying coward, whose frequent forms of address to his men were 'son-of-a-bitch and other such vulgar expressions'. Despite his dreadful irresolution, 'he was always a man so much self-conceited that he would never hear any reason'. He was often stupefied with alcohol ('I did ever abhor drunkeness,' Dampier had written in *A New Voyage Round the World*).

Had he indeed been 'a modest and courteous gentleman', he would hardly have survived as a buccaneer for eight years. He did so through an innate instinct for self-preservation and other ungentlemanly traits, such as cowardice, which ensured he was more likely to be back at base guarding the camp than in the thick of the fighting.

But as an observer of people and nature, he was the complete opposite: scrupulously honest, modest, unflagging and uncompromising in his pursuit of enlightenment. 'The farther we went, the more knowledge and experience I should get, which was the main thing that I regarded.' His curiosity took him into real and uncharacteristic peril with alligators. It led him to lash a sloth to see if the creature could be 'provoked to move faster', and to clutch a mating male giant tortoise to find whether danger would diminish its ardour. When he squeezed two worms out of a large crippling boil on his leg, he neither squashed them nor flicked them away, but 'took them both up in my hand, and perceived each of them to be invested with three rows of black, short, stiff hair, running clear round them, one row near each end, the other in the middle, each row distinct from other, and all very regular and uniform'.

This need for exactness embraced anything and everything. In Mindanao, 'I had forgot to tell you that they have none but vocal music here, by what I could learn, except only a row of a kind of bells without clappers, 16 in number, and their weight increasing gradually from about 3 to 10 pound weight'. Such precision at times approached mania: 'Some [Crotalaria?] had fruit like peascods; in each of which there were just ten small peas: I opened many of them, and found no more or less.' An enduring memento of his infinite capacity for taking pains is the valuable collection of twenty-five plants that he picked in Western Australia in August 1699 and handed over to Dr John Woodward of the Royal Society after his return to England in June 1701. These specimens, the earliest documented collection of Australian flora, are today preserved in the Sherardian Herbarium of the Department of Plant Sciences at Oxford University. The condition of the plants three centuries later seems amazingly fine. How he managed to keep them so perfect over twenty months of shipboard life, the sinking of the *Roebuck* and six weeks as a castaway on Ascension Island is a mystery.

Dampier relates in *A New Voyage Round the World* that during his travels he protected his 'journal and other writings' by keeping them in a length of bamboo sealed at either end with wax. These documents, consisting presumably of loose pages, have not survived. His so-called 'journal' in the

British Library is a sturdy, ledger-size notebook in which he wrote a terse and somewhat bland outline of his first circumnavigation, without any nature notes. The style, literate yet almost devoid of punctuation, is the same as in his letters to the Admiralty held in the Public Record Office at Kew. These all lead one to believe that his three books were produced in conjunction with an experienced author like George Ridpath, who helped Woodes Rogers with *A Cruising Voyage Round the World*. Dampier says in the preface to *A Voyage to New Holland* that the text has been 'revised and corrected by friends', which is probably as much of an admission as his publisher James Knapton would countenance. None of this detracts from Dampier's greatness. 'It is not easy', wrote the historian Admiral James Burney, 'to name another voyager or traveller who has given more useful information to the world.'

GERALD NORRIS

CHAPTER
ONE

OUTWARD BOUND

My friends [family] did not originally design me for the sea, but bred me at school till I came to years fit for a trade. But upon the death of my father and mother, they who had the disposal of me, took other measures; and having removed me from the Latin school to learn writing and arithmetic, they soon after placed me with a master of a ship at Weymouth, complying with the inclinations I had very early of seeing the world. With him I made a short voyage to France; and returning thence, went to Newfoundland, being then about eighteen years of age. In this voyage I spent one summer; but so pinched with the rigour of that cold climate, that upon my return I was absolutely against going to those parts of the world, but went home again to my friends. Yet going up a while after to London, the offer of a warm voyage and a long one, both which I always desired, soon carried me to sea again. For hearing of an outward-bound East-Indiaman, the *John and Martha* of London, Captain Earning commander, I entered myself aboard, and was employed before the mast, for which my two former voyages had some way qualified me.

We went directly for Banten in the isle of Java, and staying there about two months, came home again in little more than a year; touching at St Jago [São Tiago] of the Cape Verde Islands at our going out, and at Ascension in our return. In this voyage I gained more experience in navigation, but kept no journal. We arrived at Plymouth about two months before Sir Robert Holmes went out to fall upon the Dutch Smyrna fleet;* and the second Dutch Wars breaking out upon this,

* During the middle of March 1672, the English attacked Dutch ship-

I forbore going to sea that summer, retiring to my brother in Somersetshire. But growing weary of staying ashore, I lifted myself on board the *Royal Prince*, commanded by Sir Edward Spragge, and served under him in the year 1673, being the last of the Dutch War. We had three engagements that summer; I was in two of them, but falling very sick, I was put aboard an hospital ship a day or two before the third engagement, seeing it at a distance only; and in this Sir Edward Spragge was killed.* Soon after I was sent to Harwich with the rest of the sick and wounded: and having languished a great while, I went home to my brother to recover my health.

By this time the war with the Dutch was concluded; and with my health, I recovered my old inclination for the sea. A neighbouring gentleman, Colonel Helyar of East Coker in Somersetshire, my native parish, made me a seasonable offer to go and manage a plantation of his in Jamaica, under one Mr Whaley: for which place I set out with Captain Kent in the *Content* of London . . . I went to Spanish Town, called St Jago [Santiago] de la Vega; where meeting with Mr Whaley, we went together to Colonel Helyar's plantation in Sixteen Mile Walk. In our way thither we passed through Sir Thomas Modyford's plantation, at the Angels, where at that time were annatto and cacao trees growing; and fording a pretty large river, we passed by the side of it two or three miles up the stream, there being high mountains on each side. The way to Sixteen Mile Walk was formerly a great deal about, round a large mountain; till Mr Cary Helyar, the colonel's brother, found out this way. For being desirous of making out a shorter cut, he and some others coasted along the river, till they found it run between a rock that stood up perpendicularly steep on each side, and with much difficulty they climbed over it. But a dog that belonged to them, finding a hole to creep through the rock, suggested to them that there

---

ping in the Atlantic and the Channel, where Sir Robert Holmes harried the Smyrna convoy. Smyrna is now Izmir.

* Sir Edward Spragge was drowned on 11 August 1673 during the Battle of the Texel when a shot sank the boat in which he was being rowed between ships.

was a hollow passage; and he cleared it by blowing up the rock with gunpowder, till he had made a way through it broad enough for a horse with a pack, and high enough for a man to ride through. This is called the Hollow Rock. Some other places he levelled, and made it an indifferent good passage.

He was a very ingenious gentleman, and doubtless had he lived, he might have propagated some advantageous arts on that island. He was once endeavouring to make saltpetre at the Angels, but did not bring it to perfection. Whether the earth there was not right, I know not; but probably there may be saltpetre earth in other places, especially about Passage Fort,* where, as I have been informed, the canes will not make good sugar, by reason of the saltness of the soil.

I lived with Mr Whaley at Sixteen Mile Walk for almost six months, and then entered myself into the service of one Captain Hemings, to manage his plantation at St Ann's, on the north side of the island, and accordingly rode from St Jago de la Vega toward St Ann's.

This road has but sorry accommodations for travellers. The first night I lay at a poor hunter's hut, at the foot of Mount Diablo on the south side of it, where for want of clothes to cover me in the night I was very cold when the land wind sprang up.

This mountain is part of the great ridge that runs the length of the island from east to west; to the east 'tis called the Blue Mountain, which is higher than this. The next day crossing Mount Diablo, I got a hard lodging at the foot of it on the north side; and the third day after arrived at Captain Hemings' plantation.

I was clearly out of my element there, and therefore as soon as Captain Hemings came thither I disengaged myself from him, and took my passage on board a sloop to Port Royal, with one Mr Statham, who used to trade round the island, and touched there at that time.

From Port Royal I sailed with one Mr Fishook, who traded to the north side of the island, and sometimes round it; and by these coasting voyages I came acquainted with all

* At the western end of Kingston harbour.

the ports and bays about Jamaica, and with all their manu-
factures; as also with the benefit of the land and sea winds.
For our business was to bring goods to, or carry them from
planters to Port Royal; and we were always entertained civilly
by them, both in their houses and plantations, having liberty
to walk about and view them. They gave us also plantains,
yams, potatoes, etc. to carry aboard with us; on which we
fed commonly all our voyage.

But after six or seven months, I left that employ also, and
shipped myself aboard one Captain Hudsel, who was bound
to the Bay of Campeachy [Campeche] to load logwood.

BOOBIES, CRABS, ALLIGATORS AND CROCODILES

*Owing to Captain Hudsel's happy-go-lucky seamanship, the return
journey from Campeche took thirteen weeks instead of six and in-
cluded grounding on Alacran Reef, north of Yucatán, and foraging
for food on the deserted Isle of Pines, off the south coast of Cuba.
Dampier used these stoppages to make his first nature notes, identi-
fying three species of birds on the reef and studying crabs, alligators
and crocodiles on Pines. (He also records that he and four comrades
came across footprints on a sandy beach at Pines, which 'troubled us
a little', since these were perhaps made by Spaniards. The episode
may have influenced Defoe in* Robinson Crusoe.)

All three sorts [of birds] are very tame, especially the boobies,
and so thick settled, that a man cannot pass through their
quarters, without coming within reach of their bills, with
which they continually pecked at us. I took notice that they
sat in pairs; and therefore at first thought them to be cock
and hen; but upon striking at them, one flew away from each
place, and that which was left behind seemed as malicious as
the other that was gone. I admired the boldness of those that
did not fly away, and used some sort of violence to force
them, but in vain; for indeed these were young ones, and
had not yet learned the use of their wings, though they were
as big and as well feathered as their dams, only their feathers
were something whiter and fresher. I took notice that an old
one, either the cock or hen, always sat with the young to

secure them; for otherwise these fowls would prey on each other, the strong on the weak, or at least those of a different kind would make bold with their neighbours: the men-of-war birds as well as the boobies left guardians to the young, when they went off to sea, lest they should be starved by their neighbours; for there were a great many old and lame men-of-war birds that could not fly off to sea to seek their own food. These did not inhabit among their consorts, but were either expelled from the community, or else chose to lie out at some distance from the rest, and that not altogether; but scattering here and there, where they could rob securest: I saw near twenty of them on one of the islands, which sometimes would sally into the camp to seek for booty, but presently retreated again, whether they got anything or nothing. If one of these lame birds found a young booby not guarded, it presently gave him a good poult on the back with his bill to make him disgorge, which they will do with one stroke, and it may be cast up a fish or two as big as a man's wrist; this they swallow in a trice, and march off, and look out for another prize. The sound men-of-war will sometimes serve the old boobies so off at sea. I have seen a man-of-war fly directly at a booby, and give it one blow, which has caused it to cast up a large fish, and the man-of-war flying directly down after it, has taken it in the air, before it reached the water . . .

The land animals are bullocks, hogs, deer, etc. Here are . . . land-crabs of two sorts, white and black: both of them make holes in the ground like conies, where they shelter themselves all day, and in the night come out to feed. They will eat grass, herbs, or such fruit as they find under the trees: the manchineel fruit, which neither bird nor beast will taste, is greedily devoured by them, without doing them any harm. Yet these very crabs that feed on manchineel, are venomous both to man and beast that feeds on them, though the others are very good meat. The white crabs are the largest sort; some of them are as big as a man's two fists joined together; they are shaped like sea-crabs, having one large claw, wherewith they will pinch very hard, neither will they let go their hold, though you bruise them in pieces, unless you break the claw too; but if they chance to catch your fingers, the way is to lay your hand, crab and all, flat on the ground, and he will immediately loose his hold and scamper away. These white ones build in wet swampy dirty ground near the sea, so that the tide washes into their holes; but the black crab is more cleanly, delighting to live in dry places, and makes its house in sandy earth: black crabs are commonly fat and full of eggs; they are also accounted the better meat, though both sorts are very good.

Here are also a great many alligators and crocodiles that haunt about this island, and are said to be the most daring in all the West Indies. I have heard of many of their tricks; as that they have followed a canoe, and put their noses in over the gunwale, with their jaws wide open, as if ready to devour the men in it: and that when they have been ashore in the night near the sea, the crocodiles have boldly come in among them, and made them run from their fire, and taken away their meat from them. Therefore when privateers are hunting on this island, they always keep sentinels out to watch for these ravenous creatures, as duly as they do in other places for fear of enemies, especially in the night, for fear of being devoured in their sleep.

AT ONE DRAUGHT

The protracted voyage from Campeche to Jamaica might have ended unhappily. Victuals ran so low that nothing remained except a tub of rotting meat to be eked out during the final days. Young Dampier gave his captain and shipmates navigational advice in an effort to speed their progress. When this was rejected, 'I was so much dissatisfied that I turned into my cabin and told them we should all be starved.' But Negril Point was at last sighted, with no casualties.

I think never any vessel before nor since, made such traverses in coming out of Campeachy Bay as we did, having first blundered over the Alacran Reef, and then visited those islands; from thence fell in among the Colorado shoals, afterward made a trip to Grand Cayman; and lastly, visited Pines, though to no purpose. In all these rambles we got as much experience as if we had been sent out on a design.

As soon as we came to anchor, we sent our boat ashore to buy provisions to regale ourselves, after our long fatigue and fasting, and were very busy going to drink a bowl of punch, when unexpectedly Captain Rawlins, commander of a small New England vessel, that we left at Carmen, and one Mr John Hooker, who had been in the bay a twelvemonth cutting logwood, and was now coming up to Jamaica to sell it, came aboard, and were invited into the cabin to drink with us. The bowl had not yet been touched (I think there might be six quarts in it) but Mr Hooker being drunk to by Captain Rawlins, who pledged Captain Hudsel, and having the bowl in his hand, said that he was under an oath to drink but three draughts of strong liquor a day, and putting the bowl to his head, turned it off at one draught, and so making himself drunk, disappointed us of our expectations, till we made another bowl.

CUTTING LOGWOOD ON CARMEN

His recent trip persuaded Dampier to join the logwoodmen on the island of Carmen in Campeche Bay, where good money could be earned. Though he does not say so, Carmen had been a pirate stronghold since 1558; across the bay stood Veracruz, the chief port from which Spanish treasure left for Europe. A logwoodman would often down tools and go buccaneering when extra crews were needed. The pirates were expelled from Carmen in 1717, two years after Dampier's death.

The logwood-cutters inhabit the creeks of the east and west lagoons, in small companies, building their huts close by the creeks' sides for the benefit of the sea-breezes, as near the logwood groves as they can, removing often to be near their business; yet when they are settled in a good open place, they choose rather to go half a mile in their canoes to work, than lose that convenience. Though they build their huts but slightly, yet they take care to thatch them very well with palm or palmetto leaves, to prevent the rains, which are there very violent, from soaking in.

For their bedding they raise a barbecue, or wooden frame three foot and a half above ground on one side of the house; and stick up four stakes, one at each corner, to fasten their pavilions; out of which here is no sleeping for mosquitoes.

Another frame they raise covered with earth for a hearth to dress their victuals; and a third to sit at when they eat it.

During the wet season, the land where the logwood grows is so overflowed, that they step from their beds into the water perhaps two foot deep, and continue standing in the wet all day, till they go to bed again; but nevertheless account it the best season in the year for doing a good day's labour in.

Some fell the trees, others saw and cut them into convenient logs, and one chips off the sap, and he is commonly a principal man; and when a tree is so thick, that after it is logged, it remains still too great a burthen for one man, we blow it up with gunpowder.

The logwood-cutters are generally sturdy strong fellows, and will carry burthens of three or four hundredweight; but every man is left to his choice to carry what he pleases, and commonly they agree very well about it: for they are contented to labour very hard.

But when ships come from Jamaica with rum and sugar, they are too apt to misspend both their time and money. If the commanders of these ships are free, and treat all that come the first day with punch, they will be much respected, and every man will pay honestly for what he drinks afterwards; but if he be niggardly, they will pay him with their worst wood, and commonly they have a stock of such laid by for that purpose; nay, they will cheat them with hollow wood filled with dirt in the middle and both ends plugged up with a piece of the same drove in hard, and then sawed off so neatly, that it's hard to find out the deceit; but if any man come to purchase with bills payable at Jamaica, they will be sure to give him the best wood.

In some places, especially in the west creek of the west lagoon, they go a hunting every Saturday to provide themselves with beef for the week following.

The cattle in this country are large and fat in February, March and April: at other times of the year they are fleshy, but not fat, yet sweet enough. When they have killed a beef, they cut it into four quarters, and taking out all the bones, each man makes a hole in the middle of his quarter, just big enough for his head to go through, then puts it on like a frock, and trudges home; and if he chances to tire, he cuts off some of it, and flings it away.

It is a diversion pleasant enough, though not without some danger, to hunt in a canoe; for then the cattle having no other feeding places than the sides of the savannahs, which are somewhat higher ground than the middle, they are forced sometimes to swim; so that we may easily come to shoot them, when they are thus in the water.

The beast, when she is so hard pursued that she cannot escape, turns about and comes full tilt at the canoe, and striking her head against the prow, drives her back twenty or thirty paces; then she scampers away again; but if she has received a wound, she commonly pursues us till she is knocked down. Our chiefest care is to keep the head of the canoe towards her; for if she should strike against the broadside, it would endanger oversetting it, and consequently wetting our arms and ammunition. Besides, the savannahs at this time swarm with alligators, and therefore are the more dangerous on that account.

These creatures in the wet season forsake the rivers, and inhabit the drowned savannahs to meet with purchase, and no flesh comes amiss to them, whether alive or dead. Their chief subsistence then is on young cattle, or such carcasses as we leave behind us, which in the dry season feed the carrion-crows, but now are a prey to the alligators. They remain here till the water drains off from the land; and then confine themselves to the stagnant ponds; and when they are dry, they ramble away to some creek or river.

The alligators in this bay are not so fierce as they are reported to be in other places; for I never knew them pursue any man, although we do frequently meet them, nay, they will flee from us: and I have drank out of a pond in the dry time that has been full of them, and the water not deep enough to cover their backs, and the compass of the pond so small, that I could get no water but by coming within two yards of the alligator's nose; they lying with their heads towards mine as I was drinking, and looking on me all the while. Neither did I ever hear of any bit in the water by them, though probably should a man happen in their way, they would seize upon him.

Having thus given some description of the country, I shall next give an account of my living with the logwood men, and of several occurrences that happened during my stay here.

Though I was a stranger to their employment and manner of living, as being known but to those few only of whom we bought our wood, in my former voyage hither; yet that little acquaintance I then got, encouraged me to visit them after my second arrival here; being in hopes to strike in to work with them. There were six in company, who had a hundred tons ready cut, logged and chipped, but not brought to the creekside, and they expected a ship from New England in a month or two, to fetch it away.

When I came hither, they were beginning to bring it to the creek: and because the carriage is the hardest work, they hired me to help them at the rate of a ton of wood per month; promising me that after this carriage was over, I should strike in to work with them, for they were all obliged in bonds to procure this hundred tons jointly together, but for no more.

This wood lay all in the circumference of five or six hundred yards, and about three hundred from the creekside in the middle of a very thick wood, unpassable with burthens. The first thing we did was to bring it all to one place in the middle, and from thence we cut a very large path to carry it to the creekside. We laboured at this work five days in the week; and on Saturdays went to the savannahs and killed beefs.

When we killed a beef, if there were more than four of us, the overplus went to seek fresh game, whilst the rest dressed it.

HOCKSING BULLOCKS

I went out the first Sunday and complied very well with my master's orders, which was only to help drive the cattle out of the savannahs into the woods, where two or three men lay to shoot them: and having killed our game, we marched home with our burthens. The next Saturday after I went with a design to kill a beef myself, thinking it more honour to try my own skill in shooting, than only to drive the game for others to shoot at. We went now to a place called the upper savannah, going four miles in our canoes, and then landing, walked one mile through the woods, before we came into the savannah, and marched about two miles in it, before we came up with any game. Here I gave my companions the slip, and wandered so far into the woods that I lost myself; neither could I find the way into the open savannah, but instead of that ran directly from it, through small spots of savannahs and skirts of woods. This was sometime in May, and it was between ten o'clock and one when I began to find that I was (as we called it, I suppose from the Spaniards) marooned, or lost, and quite out of the hearing of my comrades' guns. I was somewhat surprised at this; but however, I knew I should find my way out, as soon as the sun was a little lower. So I sat down to rest myself; resolving however to run no farther out of my way; for the sun being so near the zenith, I could not distinguish how to direct my course. Being weary and almost faint for want of water, I was forced to have recourse to the wild pines, and was by them supplied, or else I must have perished with thirst. About three o'clock I went due north, as near as I could judge, for the savannah lay east and west, and I was on the south side of it.

At sunset I got into the clear open savannah, being about two leagues wide in most places, but how long I know not. It is well stored with bullocks, but by frequent hunting they grow shy, and remove farther up into the country. Here I found myself four or five miles to the west of the place where I straggled from my companions. I made homewards with all the speed I could, but being overtaken by the night, I lay down on the grass a good distance from the woods, for the benefit of the wind, to keep the mosquitoes from me, but in vain: for in less than an hour's time I was so persecuted, that though I endeavoured to keep them off by fanning myself with boughs and shifting my quarters three or four times, yet still they haunted me so that I could get no sleep. At daybreak I got up and directed my course to the creek where we landed, from which I was then about two leagues. I did not see one beast of any sort whatever in all the way; though the day before I saw several young calves that could not follow their dams, but even these were now gone away, to my great vexation and disappointment, for I was very hungry. But about a mile farther, I spied ten or twelve guans* perching upon the boughs of a cotton tree. These were not shy, therefore I got well enough under them; and having a single bullet (but no shot) about me, fired at one of them, but missed it, though I had before often killed them so. Then I came up with, and fired at five or six turkeys, but with no better success. So that I was forced to march forward still in the savannah, toward the creek; and when I came to the path that led to it through the woods, I found (to my great joy) a hat stuck upon a pole: and when I came to the creek I found another. These were set up by my comrades, who were gone home in the evening, as signals that they would come and fetch me. Therefore I sat down and waited for them; for although I had not then above three leagues home by water, yet it would have been very difficult, if not impossible for me to have got thither over land, by reason of those vast unpassable thickets abounding everywhere along the creek side; wherein I have known some puzzled for two or three days, and have not advanced half a mile, though they laboured extremely every day. Neither was I disappointed of my hopes; for within half an hour after my arrival at the creek, my comrades came, bringing every man his bottle of water, and his gun, both to hunt for game, and to give me notice by firing, that I might hear them; for I have known several men lost in the like manner, and never heard of afterwards.

I kept to my work by myself, till I was hindered by a hard, red, and angry swelling like a boil, in my right leg, so painful that I was scarce able to stand on it; but I was directed to roast and apply the roots of white lilies (of which here is great plenty growing by the creek sides) to draw it to a head.

* A guan looks like a large hen-pheasant.

This I did three or four days, without any benefit. At last I perceived two white specks in the middle of the boil, and squeezing it, two small white worms spurted out: I took them both up in my hand, and perceived each of them to be invested with three rows of black, short, stiff hair, running clear round them; one row near each end; the other in the middle; each row distinct from other; and all very regular and uniform. The worms were about the bigness of a hen's quill, and about three quarters of an inch long.

I never saw worms of this sort breed in any man's flesh. Indeed Guinea worms are very frequent in some places of the West Indies, especially at Curaçao; they breed as well in whites as Negroes: and because that island was formerly a repository of Negroes, while the Dutch drove that trade with the Spaniards, and the Negroes were most subject to them; 'twas therefore believed that other people took them by infection from them. I rather judge that they are generated by drinking bad water; and 'tis as likely that the water of the other islands of Aruba and Bonaire* may produce the same effects; for many of those that went with me from thence to Virginia were troubled with them after our arrival there: particularly I myself had one broke out in my ankle, after I had been there five or six months.

These worms are no bigger than a large brown thread, but (as I have heard) five or six yards long, and if it breaks in drawing out, that part which remains in the flesh will putrefy, and be very painful, and endanger the patient's life; or at least the use of that limb: and I have known some that have been scarified and cut strangely, to take out the worm. I was in great torment before it came out: my leg and ankle swelled and looked very red and angry; and I kept a plaster to it to bring it to a head. At last drawing off my plaster out came about three inches of the worm; and my pain abated presently. Till then I was ignorant of my malady; and the gentlewomen, at whose house I was, took it for a nerve; but I knew well enough what it was, and presently rolled it up on a small stick. After that I opened it every morning and evening, and strained it out gently, about two inches at a time, not without

* Curaçao, Aruba and Bonaire are in the Lesser Antilles.

some pain, till at length I had got out about two foot.

Riding with one Mr Richardson, who was going to a Negro to have his horse cured of a galled back, I asked the Negro if he could undertake my leg: which he did very readily; and in the meantime I observed his method in curing the horse; which was this. First he stroked the sore place, then applying to it a little rough powder, which looked like tobacco leaves dried and crumbled small, and mumbling some words to himself, he blew upon the part three times, and waving his hands as often over it, said, it would be well speedily. His fee for the cure was a white cock.

Then coming to me, and looking on the worm in my ankle, he promised to cure it in three days, demanding also a white cock for his pains, and using exactly the same method with me, as he did with the horse. He bad me not open it in three days, but I did not stay so long; for the next morning the cloth being rubbed off, I unbound it, and found the worm broken off, and the whole quite healed up. I was afraid the remaining part would have given some trouble, but have not felt any pain there from that day to this.

This way of hocksing bullocks seems peculiar to the Spaniards; especially to those that live hereabouts, who are very dextrous at it. For this reason some of them are constantly employed in it all the year; and so become very expert. The hockser is mounted on a good horse, bred up to the sport; who knows so well when to advance or retreat upon occasion, that the rider has no trouble to manage him. His arms is a hocksing iron, which is made in the shape of a half-moon, and from one corner to the other is about six or seven inches; with a very sharp edge.

This iron is fastened by a socket to a pole about fourteen or fifteen foot long. When the hockser is mounted, he lays the pole over the head of his horse, with the iron forward, and then rides after his game, and having overtaken it, strikes his iron just above the hock, and hamstrings it. The horse presently wheels off to the left; for the wounded beast makes at him presently with all his force; but he scampers away a good distance before he comes about again. If the hamstring is not quite cut asunder with the stroke, yet the bullock by continual springing out his leg, certainly breaks it: and then can go but on three legs, yet still limps forward to be revenged on his enemy. Then the hockser rides up softly to him and strikes his iron into the knee of one of his forelegs; and then he immediately tumbles down. He gets off his horse, and taking a sharp-pointed strong knife, strikes it into his poll, a little behind the horns, so dextrously that at one blow he cuts the string of his neck; and down falls his head. This they call polling. Then the hockser immediately mounts, and rides after more game, leaving the other to the skinners, who are at hand, and ready to take off his hide.

The right ear of the hocksing-horse by the weight of the pole laid constantly over it when on duty, hangs down always, by which you may know it from other horses.

The Spaniards pick and choose only the bulls and old cows, and leave the young cattle to breed; by which means they always preserve their stock entire. On the contrary, the English and French kill without distinction; yea, the young rather than the old; without regard of keeping up their stock. Jamaica is a remarkable instance of this our folly in this particular. For when it was first taken by the English, the savannahs were well stocked with cattle; but were soon all destroyed by our soldiers, who suffered great hardships afterwards for it: and it was never stocked again till Sir Thomas Lynch was governor [in 1671]. He sent to Cuba for a supply of cattle, which are now grown very plentiful, because every man knows his own proper goods. Whereas before, when there was no property, each man destroyed as fast as he could. The French (I think) are greater destroyers than the English.

Had it not been for the great care of the Spaniards in stocking the West Indies with hogs and bullocks, the privateers must have starved. But now the main, as well as the island, is plentifully provided; particularly the Bay of Campeachy, the islands of Cuba, Pines, Hispaniola, Puerto Rico, etc. where, besides wild hogs, there are abundance of corrals or hog-farms; in some of which, I have heard, there are no less than 1,500. This was the main subsistence of the privateers.

But to return again to Beef Island [Punta Xicalango].

Our English hunters have much lessened the numbers of the cattle there. And those that are left, by constant shooting now are grown so wild and desperate, that it is dangerous for a single man to fire at them, or to venture through the savannahs. For the old bulls that have been formerly shot, will make at him: and they will all draw up in battle formation to defend themselves upon our approach; the old bulls in the front; behind them the cows, in the same manner; and behind them the young cattle. And if we strive to wheel about to get in the rear, the bulls will certainly face about that way, and still present a front to us. Therefore we seldom strive to shoot any out of a great herd, but walk about in the woods, close by the savannah, and there we light of our game. The beast makes directly at the hunter, if it be desperately wounded (as I have experienced myself) but if but slightly, they commonly run away. The old hunters tell us, that a cow is more dangerous of the two; because they say, she runs at her enemy with her eyes open; but the bull shuts his, so that you may easily avoid him. But this I cannot affirm upon my own knowledge, and rather doubt the truth of it . . .

We went ashore to kill a beef for supper; where I was surprised with an odd accident. Passing through a small savannah, about two or three foot deep, we smelt a strong scent of an alligator, and presently after I stumbled over one, and fell down immediately. I cried out for help; but my consorts, instead of assisting me, ran away towards the wood. I had no sooner got up to follow them, but I stumbled on him a second time; and a third time also; expecting still when I fell down to be devoured. Yet at last I got out safe; but so frightened that I never cared for going through the water again as long as I was in the bay.

THE GREAT STORM OF JUNE 1676

Dampier's principal account of the storm is in A Discourse of Winds, *but* The Campeachy Voyages *presents another picturesque detail: 'So away we went for Beef Island and, coming within a league of it, we saw a flag in the woods made fast to a pole and placed on the top of a high tree. And coming still nearer, we at last saw a ship in the woods, about two hundred yards from the sea. We rowed directly towards her; and when we came to the woods' side, found a pretty clear passage made by the ship through the woods, the trees being all broken down, and about three foot of water home to the ship.'*

Two days before this storm began, the wind whiffled about to the south, and back again to the east, and blew very faintly. The weather also was very fair, and the men-of-war birds came hovering over the land in great numbers, which is very unusual for them to do. This made some of our logwood-cutters say that we should have some ships come hither in a short time; for they believed it was a certain token of the arrival of ships when these birds came thus hovering over the land. And some of them said they had lived at Barbados, where it was generally taken notice of: and that as many of these birds as they saw hovering over the town, so many ships there were coming thither. And according to that rule they foolishly guessed that here were a great many ships coming hither at that time; though 'tis impossible that they could imagine there could be the hundredth part of the ships arrive, that they saw birds fly over their heads. But that which I did most admire was to see the water keep ebbing for two days together, without any flood, till the creek where we lived was almost dry. There was commonly at low water seven or eight foot water; but now not above three, even in the middle of the creek.

About four o'clock the second day after this unusual ebb, the sky looked very black, and the wind sprung up fresh at south-east and increasing. In less than two hours' time it blew down all our huts but one; and that with much labour we propped up with posts, and with ropes cast over the ridge, and fastening both ends to stumps of trees, we secured the roof from flying away. In it we huddled all together till the storm ceased. It rained very hard the greatest part of the storm, and about two hours after the wind first sprang up, the waters flowed very fast in. The next morning it was as high as the banks of the creek: which was higher than I had ever seen it before.

The flood still increased, and ran faster up the creek than ever I saw it do in the greatest spring tide; which was somewhat strange, because the wind was at south, which is right off the shore on this coast. Neither did the rain anything abate, and by ten o'clock in the morning the banks of the creek were all overflown. About twelve noon we brought our canoe to the side of our hut, and fastened it to the stump of a tree that stood by it; that being the only refuge that we could now expect; for the land a little way within the banks of the creek is much lower than where we were, so that there was no walking through the woods because of the water. Besides, the trees were torn up by the roots, and tumbled down so strangely across each other, that it was almost impossible to pass through them.

The storm continued all this day and the night following till ten o'clock: then it began to abate, and by two in the morning it was quite calm.

This storm made very strange work in the woods by tearing up the trees by the roots: the ships also riding at Carmen and at One-Bush-Key, felt the fury of it to their sorrow; for of four that were riding at One-Bush-Key, three were driven away from their anchors, one of which was blown into the woods of Beef Island. And of the four ships that were at Carmen, three also were driven from their anchors, one of which was cast up about twenty paces beyond high-water-mark on the island of Carmen. The other two were driven off to sea; and one of them was never heard of since.

The poor fish also suffered extremely by this storm, for we saw multitudes of them either cast on the shore, or floating dead on the lagoons. Yet this storm did not reach thirty leagues to windward of Carmen, for Captain Vally of Jamaica went hence but three days before the storm began, and was not past thirty leagues off when we had it so fierce, yet he felt none of it; but only saw very black dismal clouds to the westward, as he reported at his return from Jamaica to Carmen four months after.

'They were a great company dancing from tree to tree,
over my head, chattering and making a great noise'

ILL-MANNERED MONKEYS AND OTHER ANIMALS

The terrible storm and ensuing floods put an end to Dampier's thriving logwood work, and 'I, with many more in my circumstances, was forced to range about to seek a subsistence in company of some privateers then in the Bay. In which rambles we visited all the rivers between Carmen and Alvarado and made many descents into the country among the villages there.' In other words, he became a pirate. However, he has little to say about these small-scale raids down Tabasco's rivers. After a year he went back to cutting logwood on Carmen and ten months later embarked for England.

His 'rambles' are memorable for descriptions of the region's animals and the native communities in the area around Villahermosa.

The monkeys that are in these parts are the ugliest I ever saw. They are much bigger than a hare, and have great tails about two foot and a half long. The underside of their tails is all bare, with a black hard skin; but the upper side, and all the body is covered with coarse, long, black, staring hair. These creatures keep together twenty or thirty in a company, and ramble over the woods, leaping from tree to tree. If they meet with a single person they will threaten to devour him. When I have been alone I have been afraid to shoot them, especially the first time I met them. They were a great company dancing from tree to tree, over my head, chattering and making a terrible noise, and a great many grim faces, and showing antic gestures. Some broke down dry sticks and threw at me; others scattered their urine and dung about my ears;* at last one, bigger than the rest, came to a small limb just over my head; and leaping directly at me, made me start back; but the monkey caught hold of the bough with the tip of his tail, and there continued swinging to and fro, and making mouths at me. At last I passed on, they still keeping me company, with the like menacing postures, till I came to

* Swift's *Gulliver's Travels: A Voyage to the Houyhnhnms*, Chapter One: 'Several of this cursed brood [the Yahoos] getting hold of the branches behind, leaped up into the tree, from whence they began to discharge their excrements on my head. However, I escaped pretty well, by sticking close to the stem of the tree, but was almost stifled with the filth, which fell about me from every side.'

our huts. The tails of these monkeys are as good to them as one of their hands, and they will hold as fast by them. If two or more of us were together they would hasten from us. The females with their young ones are much troubled to leap after the males; for they have commonly two: one she carries under one of her arms; the other sits on her back, and clasps her two forepaws about her neck. These monkeys are the most sullen I ever met with; for all the art we could use would never tame them. It is a hard matter to shoot one of them, so as to take it; for if it gets hold with its claws or tail, it will not fall as long as one breath of life remains. After I have shot at one and broke a leg or an arm, I have pitied the poor creatures to see it look and handle the wounded limb, and turn it about from side to side. These monkeys are very rarely, or (as some say) never on the ground.

The ant-bear is a four-footed beast, as big as a pretty large dog; with rough black-brown hair. It has short legs; a long nose and little eyes, a very little mouth, and a slender tongue like an earthworm about five or six inches long. This creature feeds on ants; therefore you always find them near an ants' nest or path. It takes its food thus. It lays its nose down flat on the ground, close by the path that the ants travel in (whereof here are many in this country), and then puts out its tongue athwart the path: the ants passing forwards and backwards continually, when they come to the tongue make a stop, and in two or three minutes' time it will be covered all over with ants; which she perceiving draws in her tongue, and then eats them; and after puts it out again to trepan more. They smell very strong of ants, and taste much stronger; for I have eaten of them. I have met with these creatures in several places of America, as well as here; i.e. in the San Blas Islands, and in the South Seas, on the Mexican continent.

The sloth is a four-footed, hairy, sad-coloured animal; somewhat less than the ant-bear, and not so rough. Its head is round, its eyes small; it has a short nose, and very sharp teeth, short legs, but extraordinary long sharp claws. This creature feeds on leaves; whether indifferently of all sorts, or only on some particular kinds, I know not. They are very mischievous to the trees where they come, and are so slow in motion that when they have eaten all the leaves on one tree, before they can get down from that and climb another, and settle themselves to their fresh banquet (which takes them up five or six days, though the trees stand near), they are nothing but skin and bones, although they came down plump and fat from the last tree. They never descend till they have stripped every limb and bough, and made them as bare as winter. It takes them up eight or nine minutes to move one of their feet three inches forward, and they move all their four feet one after another, at the same slow rate; neither will stripes make them mend their pace; which I have tried to do, by whipping them; but they seem insensible, and can neither be frighted, or provoked to move faster.

The armadillo (so called from its suit of armour) is as big as a small sucking pig: the body of it pretty long. This creature is enclosed in a thick shell, which guards all its back, and comes down on both sides, and meets under the belly, leaving room for the four legs; the head is small, with a nose like a pig, a pretty long neck, and can put out its head before its body when it walks; but on any danger it puts it in under the shell; and drawing in its feet, it lies stock still like a land-turtle: and though you toss it about it will not move itself. The shell is jointed in the middle of the back; so that it can turn the forepart of its body about which way it pleases. The feet are like those of a land-turtle, and it has strong claws wherewith it digs holes in the ground like a coney; the flesh is very sweet, and tastes much like a land-turtle . . .

Here are a great many poisonous creatures in this country; more particularly snakes of divers sorts, some yellow, some green, and others of a dun colour, with black and yellowish spots. The yellow snake is commonly as big as the small of a man's leg, and six or seven foot long. These are a lazy sort of creature, for they lie still and prey on lizards, guanoes, or other small animals that come in their way.

It is reported that sometimes they lurk in trees: and that they are so mighty in strength, as to hold a bullock fast by one of his horns, when they happen to come so near that it can twist itself about the limb of the tree, and the horn at once. These are accounted very good meat by some, and are eaten frequently: I myself have tried it for curiosity, but cannot commend it. I have heard some bay-men report, that they have seen some of this kind here as big as an ordinary man's waist; but I never saw any such.

The green snakes are no bigger about than a man's thumb, yet four or five foot long: the backs are of a very lively green colour, but their bellies inclining to yellow. These are commonly in bushes among the green leaves, and prey upon small birds. This I have often seen, and was once in danger to be bit by one before I saw it: for I was going to take hold of a bird that fluttered and cried out just by me, yet did not fly away, neither could I imagine the reason, till reaching out my hand, I perceived the head of a snake close by it; and looking more narrowly, I saw the upper part of the snake, about two or three inches from his head, twisted about the poor bird . . .

Here are also a sort of spiders of a prodigious size, some near as big as a man's fist, with long small legs like the spiders in England: they have two teeth, or rather horns an inch and a half, or two inches long, and of a proportionable bigness, which are black as jet, smooth as glass, and their small end sharp as a thorn; they are not straight but bending. These teeth we often preserve. Some wear them in their tobacco pouches to pick their pipes. Others preserve them for toothpickers, especially such as were troubled with the toothache; for by report they will expel that pain, though I cannot justify it of my own knowledge. The backs of these spiders are covered with a dark yellowish down, as soft as velvet. Some say these spiders are venomous, others not; whether it is true I cannot determine.

Though this country be so often overflowed with water, yet it swarms with ants, of several sorts, viz. great, small, black, yellow, etc. The great black ant stings or bites almost as bad as a scorpion; and next to this the small yellow ant's bite is most painful, for their sting is like a spark of fire, and they are so thick among the boughs in some places, that one shall be covered with them before he is aware. These creatures have nests on great trees, placed on the body between the limbs: some of their nests are as big as a hogshead: this is their winter habitation, for in the wet season they all repair to these their cities: here they preserve their eggs. Ants' eggs are as much esteemed by the planters in the West Indies for feeding their chickens, as great oatmeal with us in England. In the dry season when they leave their nests, they swarm over all the woodland; for they never trouble the savannahs. You may then see great paths made by them in the woods of three or four inches broad beaten as plain as the roads in England. They go out light, but bring home heavy loads on their backs, all of the same substance, and equal in bigness: I never observed anything besides pieces of green leaves, so big that I could scarce see the insect for his burthen, yet they would march stoutly, and so many still pressing after, that it was a very pretty sight, for the path looked perfectly green with them. There was one sort of ant of a black colour, pretty large, with long legs; these would march in troops, as if they were busy in seeking somewhat; they were always in haste, and followed their leaders exactly, let them go whither they would; these had no beaten paths to walk in, but rambled about like hunters. Sometimes a band of these ants would happen to march through our huts, over our beds, or into our pavilions, nay sometimes into our chests, and there ransack every part; and wherever the foremost went, the rest all came after. We never disturbed them, but gave them free liberty to search where they pleased; and they would all march off before night. These companies were so great, that they would be two or three hours in passing by, though they went very fast . . .

The humming-bird is a pretty little feathered creature, no bigger than a great overgrown wasp, with a black bill no bigger than a small needle, and his legs and feet in proportion to his body. This creature does not wave his wings like other birds when it flies, but keeps them in a continued quick motion like bees or other insects, and like them makes a continual humming noise as it flies. It is very quick in motion, and haunts about flowers and fruit, like a bee gathering honey, making many near addresses to its delightful*

* favoured.

objects, by visiting them on all sides, and yet still keeps in motion, sometimes on one side, sometimes on the other; as often rebounding a foot or two back on a sudden, and as quickly returns again, keeping thus about one flower five or six minutes, or more. There are two or three sorts of them, some bigger than others, but all very small, neither are they coloured alike; the largest are of a blackish colour . . .

Alligators are also in great numbers in all the creeks, rivers and lagoons in the Bay of Campeachy, and I think that no part of the universe is better stocked with them.*

The alligator is a creature so well known everywhere, that I should not describe it, were it not to give an account of the difference between it and the crocodile; for they resemble each other so nearly in their shape and bulk, as also in their natures, that they are generally mistaken for the same species; only the one supposed to be the male, the other the female. Whether they are so or not, the world may judge by the following observations. As to their bulk and length, I never saw any so large as some I have heard and read of; but according to my best judgment, though I have seen thousands, I never met with any above sixteen or seventeen foot long, and as thick as a large colt. He is shaped like a lizard, of a dark brown colour, with a large head and very long jaws, with great strong teeth, especially two of a remarkable length, that grow out of, and at the very end of the under jaw in the smallest part, on each side one; there are two holes in the upper jaw to receive these, otherwise he could not shut his mouth. He has four short legs and broad claws, with a long tail. The head, back and tail is fenced with pretty hard scales, joined together with a very thick tough skin: over its eyes there are two hard scaly knobs, as big as a man's fist, and from the head to the tail, along the ridge of his back 'tis full of such knotty hard scales, not like fish-scales, which are loose, but so united to the skin, that it is all one with it, and can't be taken asunder, but with a sharp knife. From the ridge of the back down on the ribs towards the belly (which is of a dusky yellow colour like a frog) there are many of these scales, but not so substantial nor so thick placed as the

* There is now an alligator hatchery, the El Finex Ranch, on Carmen.

other. These scales are no hindrance to him in turning; for he will turn very quick, considering his length. When he goes on land his tail drags on the ground.

The flesh smells very strong of musk, especially four kernels or cods that are always found about them, two of which grow in the groin, near each thigh; the other two at the breast, one under each foreleg, and about the bigness of a pullet's egg; therefore when we kill an alligator, we take out these, and having dried them wear them on our hats for a perfume. The flesh is seldom eaten but in case of necessity, because of its strong scent.

Now the crocodile has none of these kernels, neither does his flesh taste at all musky, therefore esteemed better food. He is of a yellow colour, neither has he such long teeth in his under jaw. The crocodile's legs also are longer, and when it runs on land, it bears its tail above the ground, and turns up the tip of it in a round bow, and the knots on the back are much thicker, higher and firmer than those of the alligator, and differ also as to the places where they are found. For in some parts, as here in the Bay of Campeachy, are abundance of alligators, where yet I never saw nor heard of any crocodiles. At the isle Grand Cayman, there are crocodiles, but no alligators. At Pines by Cuba, there are abundance of crocodiles, but I cannot say there are no alligators, though I never saw any there. Both kinds are called Caymans by the Spaniards; therefore probably they may reckon them for the same. And I know of no other difference, for they both lay eggs alike, which are not distinguishable to the eye: they are as big as a goose-egg, but much longer, and good meat; yet the alligators' eggs taste very musky. They prey both alike in either element, for they love flesh as well as fish, and will live in either fresh or salt water. Beside these creatures, I know none that can live anywhere, or upon any sort of food, like them. 'Tis reported, that they love dog's flesh better than any other flesh whatsoever. This I have seen with my own eyes, that our dogs were so much afraid of them, that they would not very willingly drink at any great river or creek where those creatures might lurk and hide themselves, unless they were (through necessity) constrained to it; and then they would stand five or six foot from the brink of the creek or river, and bark a considerable time before they would adventure nearer; and then even at the sight of their own shadows in the water, they would again retire to the place from whence they came, and bark vehemently a long time; so that in the dry season, when there was no fresh water but in ponds and creeks, we used to fetch it ourselves and give it our dogs; and many times in our hunting, when we came to a large creek that we were to pass through, our dogs would not follow us; so that we often took them in our arms, and carried them over.

Besides the afore-mentioned difference between the alligator and crocodile, the latter is accounted more fierce and daring than the alligator: therefore when we go to the Isles of Pines or Grand Cayman to hunt, we are often molested by them, especially in the night. But in the Bay of Campeachy, where there are only alligators, I did never know any mischief done by them, except by accident men run themselves into their jaws. I remember one instance of this nature, which is as follows.

In the very height of the dry time seven or eight men (English and Irish) went to a place called Pies Pond, on Beef Island, to hunt. This pond was never dry, so that the cattle drew hither in swarms, but after two or three days' hunting they were shy, and would not come to the pond till night, and then if an army of men had lain to oppose them, they would not have been debarred of water. The hunters, knowing their custom, lay still all day, and in the night visited this pond, and killed as many beef as they could. This trade they had driven a week, and made great profit. At length an Irishman going to the pond in the night, stumbled over an alligator that lay in the path: the alligator seized him by the knee, at which the man cries out, 'Help! help!' His comrades, not knowing what the matter was, ran all away from their huts, supposing that he was fallen into the clutches of some Spaniards, of whom they were afraid every dry season. But poor Daniel, not finding any assistance, waited till the beast opened his jaw to take better hold, because it is usual for the alligator to do so; and then snatched away his knee, and slipped the butt end of his gun in the room of it, which the alligator gripped so hard, that he pulled it out of his hand and so went away. The man being near a small tree climbed up out of his reach, and then cried out to his comrades to come and assist him; who being still within call, and watching to hear the issue of the alarm, made haste to him with firebrands in their hands, and brought him away in their arms to his hut; for he was in a deplorable condition, and not able to stand on his feet, his knee was so torn with the alligator's teeth.

His gun was found the next day ten or twelve paces from the place where he was seized, with two large holes made in the butt-end of it, one on each side, near an inch deep; for I saw the gun afterwards. This spoiled their sport for a time, they being forced to carry the man to the island Carmen, where their ships were, which was six or seven leagues distant.

NATIVES OF THE VILLAHERMOSA REGION

The men are obliged by the padres (as I have been informed) to marry when they are fourteen years old, and the women when twelve: and if at that age they are not provided, the priest will choose a virgin for the man (or a man for the virgin) of equal birth and fortune; and join them together.

The Spaniards give several reasons for this imposition, viz. that it preserves them from debauchery, and makes them industrious. That it brings them to pay taxes both to the king and church; for as soon as they are married they pay to both. And that it keeps them from rambling out of their own parish, and settling in another, which would by so much lessen the padre's profit. They love each other very well; and live comfortably by the sweat of their brows; they build good large houses, and inhabit altogether in towns. The side walls are mud or wattling, plastered on the inside, and thatched with palm or palmetto leaves.

The churches are large, built much higher than the common houses, and covered with pantile; and within adorned with coarse pictures and images of saints, which are all

painted tawny like the Indians themselves. Besides these
ornaments, there are kept in the churches pipes, hautboys,
drums, visors and perukes* for their recreation at solemn
times; for they have little or no sport or pastime but in common, and that only upon Saints' Days, and the nights
ensuing . . .

They are generally well-shaped, of a middle size; straight
and clean-limbed. The men more spare, the women plump
and fat, their faces are round and flat, their foreheads low,
their eyes little, their noses of a middle size, somewhat flattish; full lips; pretty full but little mouths; white teeth, and
their colour of a dark tawny, like other Indians. They sleep
in hammocks made with small cords like a net, fastened at
each end to a post. Their furniture is but mean, viz. earthen
pots to boil their maize in, and abundance of calabashes. They
are a very harmless sort of people; kind to any strangers;
and even to the Spaniards, by whom they are so much kept
under, that they are worse than slaves: nay, the very Negroes
will domineer over them; and are countenanced to do so
by the Spaniards. This makes them very melancholy and
thoughtful: however they are very quiet, and seem contented with their condition, if they can tolerably subsist: but
sometimes when they are imposed on beyond their ability,
they will march off whole towns, men, women and children
together.

* Masks and wigs.

CHAPTER
TWO

Dampier returned home in August 1678, on the eve of his twenty-seventh birthday, 'and at the beginning of the following year I set out again for Jamaica, in order to have gone thence to Campeachy, but it proved to be a voyage round the world'. This took twelve and a half years – longer than Odysseus' epic journey – during which time James II came to the throne and fled from it.

Before the reader proceed any further in the perusal of this work, I must bespeak a little of his patience here to take along with him this short account of it. It is composed of a mixed relation of places and actions, in the same order of time in which they occurred; for which end I kept a journal of every day's observations.

In the description of places, their product, etc., I have endeavoured to give what satisfaction I could to my country-men; though possibly to the describing several things that may have been much better accounted for by others – choosing to be more particular than might be needful with respect to the intelligent reader, rather than to omit what I thought might tend to the information of persons no less sensible and inquisitive, though not so learned or experi-enced. For which reason, my chief care has been to be as particular as was consistent with my intended brevity, in setting down such observables as I met with. Nor have I given myself any great trouble since my return, to compare my discoveries with those of others: the rather, because, should it so happen that I have described some places, or things which others have done before me, yet in different accounts, even of the same things, it can hardly be but there will be some new light afforded by each of them. But after all, considering that the main of this voyage has its scene laid in long tracts of the remoter parts, both of the East and West Indies, some of which very seldom visited by Englishmen, and others are rarely by any Europeans, I may without vanity encourage the reader to expect many things wholly new to him, and many others more fully described than he may have seen elsewhere; for which not only in this voyage, though itself of many years' continuance, but also several former long and distant voyages have qualified me.

As for the actions of the company among whom I made the greatest part of this voyage, a thread of which I have carried on through it, 'tis not to divert the reader with them that I mention them, much less that I take any pleasure in relating them: but for method's sake, and for the reader's satisfaction; who could not so well acquiesce in my description of places, etc. without knowing the particular traverses I made among them; nor in these, without an account of the concomitant circumstances: besides, that I would not prejudice the truth and sincerity of my relation, though by omissions only. And as for the traverses themselves, they make for the reader's advantage, how little soever for mine; since thereby I have been the better enabled to gratify his curiosity; as one who rambles about a country can give usually a better account of it, than a carrier who jogs on to his inn, without ever going out of his road.

As to my style, it cannot be expected, that a seaman should affect politeness; for were I able to do it, yet I think I should be little solicitous about it, in a work of this nature. I have frequently indeed, divested my self of sea-phrases, to gratify the land reader; for which the seamen will hardly forgive me: and yet, possibly, I shall not seem complaisant enough to the other; because I still retain the use of so many sea-terms. I confess I have not been at all scrupulous in this matter, either as to the one or the other of these; for I am persuaded, that if what I say be intelligible, it matters not greatly in what words it is expressed . . .

I first set out of England on this voyage at the beginning

of the year 1679, in the *Loyal Merchant of London*, bound for Jamaica, Captain Knapman commander. I went a passenger, designing when I came thither, to go from thence to the Bay of Campeachy, in the Gulf of Mexico, to cut logwood: where in a former voyage I had spent about three years in that employ; and so was well acquainted with the place and the work.

We sailed with a prosperous gale without any impediment or remarkable passage in our voyage: unless that when we came in sight of the island Hispaniola, and were coasting along on the south side of it by the little Île-à-vache, I observed Captain Knapman was more vigilant than ordinary, keeping at a good distance off-shore, for fear of coming too near those small low islands; as he did once, in a voyage from England, about the year 1673, losing his ship there, by the carelessness of his mates. But we succeeded better; and arrived safe at Port Royal in Jamaica some time in April 1679, and went immediately ashore.

I had brought some goods with me from England, which I intended to sell here, and stock myself with rum and sugar, saws, axes, hats, stockings, shoes and such other commodities, as I knew would sell among the Campeachy logwood-cutters. Accordingly I sold my English cargo at Port Royal; but upon some maturer considerations of my intended voyage to Campeachy, I changed my thoughts of that design, and continued at Jamaica all that year, in expectation of some other business.

I shall not trouble the reader with my observations at that isle, so well known to Englishmen; nor with the particulars of my own affairs during my stay there. But in short, having there made a purchase of a small estate in Dorsetshire, near my native country of Somerset, of one whose title to it I was well assured of, I was just embarking myself for England, about Christmas 1679, when one Mr Hobby invited me to go first a short trading voyage to the country of the Mosquitoes.* I was willing to get up some money before my return, having laid out what I had at Jamaica; so I sent the writing of my new purchase along with the same friends

* On the east coast of Nicaragua.

whom I should have accompanied to England, and went on board Mr Hobby.

Soon after our setting out we came to an anchor again in Negril [Long] Bay, at the west end of Jamaica; but finding there Captain Coxon, Sawkins, Sharp, and other privateers, Mr Hobby's men all left him to go with them, upon an expedition they had contrived, leaving not one with him, beside myself; and being thus left alone, after three or four days' stay with Mr Hobby, I was the more easily persuaded to go with them too.

It was shortly after Christmas 1679 when we set out. The first expedition was to Portobelo; which being accomplished, it was resolved to march by land over the Isthmus of Darien, upon some new adventures in the South Seas. Accordingly on 5 April 1680, we went ashore on the isthmus, near Golden Island [Isla de Oro], one of the San Blas Islands, to the number of between three and four hundred men, carrying with us such provisions as were necessary, and toys wherewith to gratify the wild Indians, through whose country we were to pass. In about nine days' march we arrived at El Real de Santa Maria, and took it, and after a stay there of about three days, we went on to the South Sea coast, and there embarked ourselves in such canoes and pirogues,* as our Indian friends furnished us withal. We were in sight of Panama by 23 April, and having in vain attempted Pueblo Nuevo,† before which Sawkins, then commander-in-chief, and others, were killed, we made some stay at the neighbouring isles of Coiba.

Here we resolved to change our course, and stand away to the southward for the coast of Peru. Accordingly we left the keys or isles of Coiba on 6 June, and spent the rest of the year in that southern course; for touching at the isles of Gorgona and Plata, we came to Ilo, a small town on the coast of Peru, and took it. This was in October, and in November we went thence to Coquimbo on the same coast, and about Christmas were got as far as the isle of Juan Fernandez, which was the farthest of our course to the southward.

---

* Canoes produced by hollowing out the trunks of two trees and binding them together.
† Pueblo Nuevo is now a ruin.

After Christmas we went back again to the northward, having a design upon Arica, a strong town advantageously situated in the hollow of the elbow, or bending of the Peruvian coast. But being there repulsed with great loss, we continued our course northward, till by the middle of April we were come in sight of the isle of Plata, a little to the southward of the Equinoctial Line.

I have related this part of my voyage thus summarily and concisely, as well because the world has accounts of it already, in the relations that Mr Ringrose and others have given of Captain Sharp's expedition, who was made chief commander, upon Sawkins' being killed; as also, because in the prosecution of this voyage I shall come to speak of these parts again, upon occasion of my going the second time into the South Seas: and shall there describe at large the places both of the North and South America, as they occurred to me.

All therefore that I have to add to the introduction, is this; that while we lay at the isle of Juan Fernandez, Captain Sharp was, by general consent, displaced from being commander; the company being not satisfied either with his courage or behaviour. In his stead, Captain Watling was advanced: but he being killed shortly after before Arica, we were without a commander during all the rest of our return towards Plata. Now Watling being killed, a great number of the meaner sort began to be as earnest for choosing Captain Sharp again into the vacancy, as before they had been as forward as any to turn him out: and on the other side, the abler and more experienced men, being altogether dissatisfied with Sharp's former conduct, would by no means consent to have him chosen. In short, by that time we were come in sight of the island Plata, the difference between the contending parties was grown so high, that they resolved to part companies; having first made an agreement, that which party soever should upon polling, appear to have the majority, they should keep the ship: and the other should content themselves with the launch or longboat, and canoes, and return back over the isthmus, or go to seek their fortune otherways, as they would.

Accordingly we put it to the vote; and upon dividing,

Captain Sharp's party carried it. I, who had never been
pleased with his management, though I had hitherto kept
my mind to myself, now declared myself on the side of those
that were out-voted; and according to our agreement, we
took our shares of such necessaries, as were fit to carry overland with us (for that was our resolution), and so prepared
for our departure.

CROSSING THE ISTHMUS OF DARIEN

*Parting from Captain Sharp, the smaller band of buccaneers
returned to Panama and travelled by foot over the Isthmus of Darien,
which they had first crossed a year earlier. The following two extracts
cover the fourth to eighth days' march and the conclusion of their
journey. Among Dampier's comrades was the surgeon Lionel Wafer,
whose* A New Voyage and Description of the Isthmus of
America *appeared in 1699, two years after* A New Voyage
Round the World.

The fourth day we began our march betimes, for the fore-
noons were commonly fair, but much rain afternoon –
though whether it rained or shined it was much at one with
us, for I verily believe we crossed the rivers thirty times this
day, the Indians having no paths to travel from one part of
the country to another; and therefore guided themselves by
the rivers. We marched this day twelve miles, and then built
our hut, and lay down to sleep; but we always kept two men
on the watch, otherwise our own slaves might have knocked
us on the head while we slept. It rained violently all the afternoon, and most part of the night. We had much ado to kindle
a fire this evening: our huts were but very mean or ordinary,
and our fire small, so that we could not dry our clothes,
scarce warm ourselves, and no sort of food for the belly; all
which made it very hard with us. I confess these hardships
quite expelled the thoughts of an enemy, for now having
been four days in the country, we began to have but few
other cares than how to get guides and food, the Spaniards
were seldom in our thoughts.

The fifth day we set out in the morning betimes, and having travelled seven miles in those wild pathless woods, by

ten o'clock in the morning we arrived at a young Spanish Indian's house, who had formerly lived with the Bishop of Panama. The young Indian was very brisk, spoke very good Spanish, and received us very kindly. This plantation afforded us store of provisions, yams, and potatoes, but nothing of any flesh, besides two fat monkeys we shot, part whereof we distributed to some of our company, who were weak and sickly; for others we got eggs, and such refreshment as the Indians had, for we still provided for the sick and weak. We had a Spanish Indian in our company, who first took up arms with Captain Sawkins, and had been with us ever since his death. He was persuaded to live here by the master of the house, who promised him his sister in marriage, and to be assistant to him in clearing a plantation: but we would not consent to part from him here, for fear of some treachery, but promised to release him in two or three days, when we were certainly out of danger of our enemies. We stayed here all the afternoon, and dried our clothes and ammunition, cleared our guns, and provided ourselves for a march the next morning.

Our surgeon, Mr Wafer, came to a sad disaster here: being drying his powder, a careless fellow passed by with his pipe lighted, and set fire to his powder, which blew up and scorched his knee,* and reduced him to that condition, that he was not able to march; wherefore we allowed him a slave to carry his things, being all of us the more concerned at the accident, because liable ourselves every moment to misfortune, and none to look after us but him. This Indian plantation was seated on the bank of the River Congo, in a very fat soil, and thus far we might have come in our canoe, if I could have persuaded them to it.

The sixth day we set out again, having hired another guide. Here we first crossed the River Congo in a canoe, having been from our first landing on the west side of the river, and being over, we marched to the eastward two miles, and came

---

* Wafer writes: 'I was sitting on the ground near one of our men, who was drying off gunpowder in a silver plate, but, not managing it as he should, it blew up and scorched my knee to that degree that the bone was left bare, the flesh being torn away and my thigh burnt for a great way above it.'

to another river, which we forded several times, though it was very deep. Two of our men were not able to keep company with us, but came after us as they were able. The last time we forded the river, it was so deep, that our tallest men stood in the deepest place, and handed the sick, weak and short men; by which means we all got over safe, except those two who were behind. Foreseeing a necessity of wading through rivers frequently in our land march, I took care before I left the ship to provide myself a large joint of bamboo, which I stopped at both ends, closing it with wax, so as to keep out any water. In this I preserved my journal and other writings from being wet, though I was often forced to swim. When we were over this river, we sat down to wait the coming of our comrades who were left behind, and in half an hour they came. But the river by that time was so high, that they could not get over it, neither could we help them over, but bid them be of good comfort, and stay till the river did fall: but we marched two miles farther by the side of the river, and there built our huts, having gone this day six miles. We had scarce finished our huts, before the river rose much higher, and overflowing the banks, obliged us to remove into higher ground: but the night came on before we could build more huts, so we lay straggling in the woods, some under one tree, some under another, as we could find conveniency, which might have been indifferent comfortable if the weather had been fair; but the greatest part of the night we had extraordinary hard rain, with much lightning, and terrible claps of thunder. These hardships and inconveniencies made us all careless, and there was no watch kept (though I believe nobody did sleep); so our slaves taking the opportunity, went away in the night; all but one, who was hid in some hole and knew nothing of their design, or else fell asleep. Those that went away carried with them our surgeon's gun and all his money.

The next morning being the eighth day, we went to the river's side, and found it much fallen; and here our guide would have us ford it again, which being deep, and the current running swift, we could not. Then we contrived to swim over; those that could not swim, we were resolved to help over as well as we could: but this was not so feasible; for we should not be able to get all our things over. At length we concluded to send one man over with a line, who should haul over all our things first, and then get the men over. This being agreed on, one George Gayny took the end of a line and made it fast about his neck, and left the other end ashore, and one man stood by the line, to clear it away to him. But when Gayny was in the midst of the water, the line in drawing after him chanced to kink or grow entangled; and he that stood by to clear it away, stopped the line which turned Gayny on his back, and he that had the line in his hand threw it all into the river after him, thinking he might recover himself; but the stream running very swift, and the man having three hundred dollars* at his back, was carried down, and never seen more by us. Those two men whom we left behind the day before, told us afterwards that they found him lying dead in a creek, where the eddy had driven him ashore, and the money on his back; but they meddled not with any of it, being only in care how to work their way through a wild unknown country . . .

Thus we finished our journey from the South Sea to the North in twenty-three days; in which time by my account we travelled 110 miles, crossing some very high mountains; but our common march was in the valleys among deep and dangerous rivers. At our first landing in this country, we were told that the Indians were our enemies; we knew the rivers to be deep, the wet season to be coming in; yet, excepting those we left behind, we lost but one man, who was drowned, as I said. Our first landing place on the south coast was very disadvantageous, for we travelled at least fifty miles more than we need to have done, could we have gone up Chepo River, or Tuira River; for at either of these places a man may pass from sea to sea in three days' time with ease. The Indians can do it in a day and a half, by which you may see how easy it is for a party of men to travel over. I must confess the Indians did assist us very much, and I question whether ever we had got over without their assistance, because they brought us from time to time to their plantations,

* Silver dollars, or pieces of eight.

where we always got provision, which else we should have
wanted. But if a party of 500 or 600 men, or more, were
minded to travel from the North to the South Seas, they may
do it without asking leave of the Indians; though it be much
better to be friends with them.

On 24 May (having lain one night at the river's mouth), we
all went aboard the privateer, who lay at La Sound's Key.*
It was a French vessel, Captain Tristian commander. The
first thing we did was to get such things as we could to gratify
our Indian guides, for we were resolved to reward them to
their hearts' content. This we did by giving them beads,
knives, scissors, and looking-glasses, which we bought off
the privateer's crew: and half a dollar a man from each of us;
which we would have bestowed in goods also, but could not
get any, the privateer having no more toys. They were so
well satisfied with these, that they returned with joy to their
friends; and were very kind to our comrades whom we left
behind; as Mr Wafer our surgeon and the rest of them told
us, when they came to us some months afterwards, as shall
be said hereafter.

I might have given a further account of several things
relating to this country; the inland parts of which are so
little known to the Europeans. But I shall leave this province
to Mr Wafer, who made a longer abode in it than I, and is
better able to do it than any man that I know, and is now
preparing a particular description of this country for the
press.

MOSQUITO INDIANS

*Dampier served for a few months with Captain Tristian and with
another filibuster, Captain Archambaut, before transferring to an
English buccaneer vessel commanded by Captain Wright. The
French thought well enough of him to invite him to go to France. He
liked their captains, but found the ordinary French seamen 'the
saddest creatures that ever I was among; for though we had bad
weather that required many hands aloft, yet the biggest part of them
never stirred out of their hammocks but to eat or ease themselves'.*

* Near Ticantiqui, among the San Blas Islands.

On the other hand, he much admired the Mosquito [Meskito]
Indians, who were invaluable members of any crew.

They are tall, well-made, raw-boned, lusty, strong, and
nimble of foot, long-visaged, lank black hair, look stern,
hard favoured, and of a dark copper-colour complexion.
They are but a small nation or family, and not a hundred men
of them in number, inhabiting on the main on the north side,
near Cape Gracias a Dios; between Cape Honduras [Camarón]
and Nicaragua. They are very ingenious at throwing the
lance, fizgig,* harpoon, or any manner of dart, being bred to
it from their infancy; for the children imitating their parents,
never go abroad without a lance in their hands, which they
throw at any object, till use has made them masters of the art.
Then they learn to put by a lance, arrow, or dart. The manner
is thus: two boys stand at a small distance, and dart a blunt
stick at one another; each of them holding a small stick in
his right hand, with which he strikes away that which was
darted at him. As they grow in years they become more
dexterous and courageous, and then they will stand a fair
mark, to anyone that will shoot arrows at them, which they
will put by with a very small stick, no bigger than the rod of
a fowling-piece; and when they are grown to be men, they
will guard themselves from arrows, though they come very
thick at them, provided two do not happen to come at once.
They have extraordinary good eyes, and will descry a sail at
sea farther, and see anything better than we. Their chiefest
employment in their own country is to strike fish, turtle, or
manatee. For this they are esteemed and coveted by all
privateers; for one or two of them in a ship, will maintain a
hundred men: so that when we careen our ships,† we choose
commonly such places where there is plenty of turtle or
manatee for these Mosquito men to strike: and it is very rare
to find privateers destitute of one or more of them, when the
commander, or most of the men are English; but they do
not love the French, and the Spaniards they hate mortally.

* A kind of harpoon or spear, with barbed prongs and a line attached.
† Careening a vessel involves heaving it over on one side in order to
clean or repair the bottom.

When they come among privateers, they get the use of guns, and prove very good marksmen. They behave themselves very bold in fight, and never seem to flinch nor hang back; for they think that the white men with whom they are, know better than they do when it is best to fight, and let the disadvantage of their party be never so great, they will never yield nor give back while any of their party stand. I could never perceive any religion nor any ceremonies, or superstitious observances among them, being ready to imitate us in whatsoever they saw us do at any time. Only they seem to fear the Devil, whom they call Willesaw; and they say he often appears to some among them, whom our men commonly call their priests, when they desire to speak with him on urgent business; but the rest know not anything of him, nor how he appears, otherwise than as these priests tell them. Yet they all say they must not anger him, for then he will beat them, and that sometimes he carries away these their priests. Thus much I have heard from some of them who speak good English.

They marry but one wife, with whom they live till death separates them. At their first coming together, the man makes a very small plantation, for there is land enough, and they may choose what spot they please. They delight to settle near the sea, or by some river, for the sake of striking fish, their beloved employment.

For within land there are other Indians, with whom they are always at war. After the man has cleared a spot of land, and has planted it, he seldom minds it afterward, but leaves the managing of it to his wife, and he goes out a-striking. Sometimes he seeks only for fish, at other times for turtle, or manatee, and whatever he gets he brings home to his wife, and never stirs out to seek for more till it is all eaten. When hunger begins to bite, he either takes his canoe and seeks for more game at sea, or walks out into the woods and hunts about for peccary, warree – each a sort of wild hog or deer – and seldom returns empty-handed, nor seeks for any more so long as any of it lasts. Their plantations are so small, that they cannot subsist with what they produce: for their largest plantations have not above twenty or thirty plantain-trees, a bed of yams and potatoes, a bush of Indian pepper, and a small spot of pineapples; which last fruit is a main thing they delight in; for with these they make a sort of drink which our men call pine-drink, much esteemed by these Mosquitoes, and to which they invite each other to be merry, providing fish and flesh also. Whoever of them makes of this liquor treats his neighbours, making a little canoe full at a time, and so enough to make them all drunk; and it is seldom that such feasts are made, but the party that makes them has some design, either to be revenged for some injury done him, or to debate of such differences as have happened between him and his neighbours, and to examine into the truth of such matters. Yet before they are warmed with drink, they never speak one word of their grievances: and the women, who commonly know their husbands' designs, prevent them from doing any injury to each other, by hiding their lances, harpoons, bows and arrows, or any other weapon that they have.

The Mosquitoes are in general very civil and kind to the English, of whom they receive a great deal of respect, both when they are aboard their ships, and also ashore, either in Jamaica, or elsewhere, whither they often come with the seamen. We always humour them, letting them go any whither as they will, and return to their country in any vessel bound that way, if they please. They will have the management of themselves in their striking, and will go in their own little canoe, which our men could not go in without danger of oversetting: nor will they then let any white man come in their canoe, but will go a-striking in it just as they please: all which we allow them. For should we cross them, though they should see shoals of fish, or turtle, or the like, they will purposely strike their harpoons and turtle-irons aside, or so glance them as to kill nothing. They have no form of government among them, but acknowledge the King of England for their sovereign. They learn our language, and take the Governor of Jamaica to be one of the greatest princes in the world.

While they are among the English they wear good clothes, and take delight to go neat and tight; but when they return again to their own country they put by all their clothes, and go after their own country fashion, wearing only a small piece of linen tied about their waists, hanging down to their knees.

POOR NAKED INDIANS

Captain Wright and his crew cruised around the Caribbean with sporadic success, capturing a few prizes of moderate value and calling at a number of small islands, among which were the Islas del Maiz, off the coast of Nicaragua.

Here we arrived the next day, and went ashore on one of them, but found none of the inhabitants; for here are but a few poor naked Indians that live here; who have been so often plundered by the privateers that they have but little provision; and when they see a sail they hide themselves; otherwise ships that come here would take them, and make slaves of them; and I have seen some of them that have been slaves. They are people of a mean stature, yet strong limbs; they are of a dark copper-colour, black hair, full round faces, small black eyes, their eyebrows hanging over their eyes, low foreheads, short thick noses, not high, but flattish; full lips, and short chins. They have a fashion to cut holes in the lips of the boys when they are young, close to their chin, which they keep open with little pegs till they are fourteen or fifteen years old: then they wear beards in them, made of turtle or tortoiseshell. The little notch at the upper end they put in through the lip, where it remains between the teeth and the lip; the underpart hangs down over their chin. This they commonly wear all day, and when they sleep they take it out. They have likewise holes bored in their ears, both men and women when young; and by continual stretching them with great pegs, they grow to be as big as a milled five-shilling piece. Herein they wear pieces of wood cut very round and smooth, so that their ear seems to be all wood, with a little skin about it. Another ornament the women use is about their legs, which they are very curious in; for from the infancy of the girls, their mothers make fast a piece of cotton

'Both men and women go naked,
only a clout about their waists'

cloth about the small of their leg, from the ankle to the calf, very hard; which makes them have a very full calf: this the women wear to their dying day. Both men and women go naked, only a clout about their waists; yet they have but little feet, though they go barefoot.

JOLLY FRENCH TARS

Captain Wright sailed down to the coast of Venezuela, visiting several islands, including Curaçao, Bonaire and the Islas las Aves. Dampier's description of the island here closely accords with that in Robinson Crusoe; *in Defoe's novel also a foreign vessel is wrecked on a shelf of rocks extending from the island, and its contents are washed ashore.*

This island Aves lies about eight or nine leagues to the eastward of the island Bonaire, about fourteen or fifteen leagues from the main, and about latitude 11° 45′ N. It is but small, not above four mile in length, and towards the east end not half a mile broad. On the north side it is low land, commonly overflown with the tide; but on the south side there is a great rocky bank of coral thrown up by the sea. The west end is, for near a mile space, plain even savannah land, without any trees. There are two or three wells dug by privateers, who often frequent this island, because there is a good harbour about the middle of it on the north side where they may conveniently careen. The reef or bank of rocks on which the French fleet was lost runs along from the east end to the northward about three mile, then trends away to the westward making as it were a half-moon. This reef breaks off all the sea, and there is good riding in even sandy ground to the westward of it. There are two or three small low sandy keys or islands within this reef, about three miles from the main island. The Count d'Estrées lost his fleet here in this manner.* Coming from the eastward, he fell in on the back of the reef, and fired guns to give warning to the rest of his fleet: but they, supposing their admiral was engaged with enemies, hoisted up their topsails, and crowded all the sails

* In 1677. Four years later he was created a marshal of France.

they could make, and ran full sail ashore after him; all within half a mile of each other. For his light being in the maintop was an unhappy beacon for them to follow; and there escaped but one king's ship and one privateer. The ships continued whole all day, and the men had time enough, most of them, to get ashore, yet many perished in the wreck; and many of those that got safe on the island, for want of being accustomed to such hardships, died like rotten sheep. But the privateers who had been used to such accidents lived merrily, from whom I had this relation: and they told me, that if they had gone to Jamaica with £30 a man in their pockets, they could not have enjoyed themselves more. For they kept in a gang by themselves, and watched when the ships broke, to get the goods that came from them, and though much was staved against the rocks, yet abundance of wine and brandy floated over the reef, where the privateers waited to take it up. They lived here about three weeks, waiting an opportunity to transport themselves back again to Hispaniola; in all which time they were never without two or three hogsheads of wine and brandy in their tents, and barrels of beef and pork; which they could live on without bread well enough, though the newcomers out of France could not. There were about forty Frenchmen on board in one of the ships where there was good store of liquor, till the afterpart of her broke away and floated over the reef, and was carried away to sea, with all the men drinking and singing, who being in drink, did not mind the danger, but were never heard of afterwards.

A COCOA PLANTATION AT CARACAS

The buccaneers prowled along the coast of Venezuela 'and went ashore in some of the bays and took seven or eight tons of cocoa; and after that three barques, one laden with hides, the second with European commodities, the third with earthenware and brandy'. When they put in at Caracas, Dampier left his companions, who were 'drunk and quarrelling', and went sightseeing. His remarkably accurate description of the cultivation and harvesting of cocoa will have provided most of his readers with details entirely new to them.

The cocoa tree has a body about a foot and an half thick (the largest sort) and seven or eight foot high, to the branches, which are large, and spreading like an oak, with a pretty thick, smooth, dark-green leaf, shaped like that of a plum tree, but larger. The nuts are enclosed in cods as big as both a man's fists put together, at the broad end of which there is a small, tough, limber stalk, by which they hang pendulous from the body of the tree, in all parts of it from top to bottom, scattered at irregular distances; and from the greater branches a little way up; especially at the joints of them or partings, where they hang thickest; but never on the smaller boughs. There may be ordinarily about twenty or thirty of these cods upon a well-bearing tree; and they have two crops of them in a year, one in December, but the best in June. The cod itself or shell is almost half an inch thick; neither spongy nor woody, but of a substance between both, brittle, yet harder than the rind of a lemon; like which its surface is grained or knobbed, but more coarse and unequal. The cods at first are of a dark green, but the side of them next the sun of a muddy red. As they grow ripe, the green turns to a fine bright yellow, and the muddy to a more lively, beautiful red, very pleasant to the eye. They neither ripen, nor are gathered at once, but for three weeks or a month when the season is, the overseers of the plantations go every day about to see which are turned yellow; cutting at once, it may be, not above one from a tree. The cods thus gathered, they lay in several heaps to sweat, and then bursting the shell with their hands, they pull out the nuts, which are the only substance they contain, having no stalk or pith among them, and (excepting that these nuts lie in regular rows) are placed like the grains of maize, but sticking together, and so closely stowed, that after they have been once separated, it would be hard to place them again in so narrow a compass. There are generally near a hundred nuts in a cod; in proportion to the greatness of which, for it varies, the nuts are bigger or less. When taken out they dry them in the sun upon mats spread on the ground; after which they need no more care, having a thin hard skin of their own, and much oil, which preserves them. Salt water will not hurt them; for we had our bags rotten, lying in the bottom of our ship, and yet the nuts never the worse. They raise the young trees of nuts, set with the great end downward, in fine black mould, and in the same places where they are to bear; which they do in four or five years' time, without the trouble of transplanting. There are ordinarily of these trees, from 500 to 2,000 and upward in a plantation or cocoa-walk, as they call them; and they shelter the young trees from the weather with plantains set about them for two or three years; destroying all the plantains by such time the cocoa trees are of a pretty good body, and able to endure the heat; which I take to be the most pernicious to them of anything; for though these valleys lie open to the north winds, unless a little sheltered here and there, by some groves of plantain trees which are purposely set near the shores of the several bays, yet by all that I could either observe or learn, the cocoas in this country are never blighted, as I have often known them to be in other places. Cocoa nuts are used as money in the Bay of Campeachy.

DAMPIER TO THE RESCUE

After a year in the Caribbean with Captain Wright, 'twenty of us (for we were about sixty) took one of the [captured] vessels and our share of the goods and went directly for Virginia.' Dampier remained in the colony from July 1682 to August 1683, but 'that country is so well known to our nation that I shall say nothing of it, nor shall I detain the reader with the story of my own affairs and the trouble that befell me during about thirteen months of my stay there'. What trouble befell him we do not know. On 23 August 1683 he embarked from Accomac County under the command of Captain John Cook in a buccaneer ship bound for the Pacific. Before the voyage was many days old, they encountered 'one of the worst storms I was ever in'. The novel way in which he and a comrade came to the ship's rescue can be enjoyed without seafaring knowledge.

We scudded before the wind and sea some time, with only our bare poles; and the ship, by the mistake of him that conned [steered], broached to, and lay in the trough of the sea; which then went so high that every wave threatened to overwhelm us. And indeed if any one of them had broke in upon our deck, it might have foundered us. The master, whose fault this was, raved like a madman, and called for an axe to cut the mizzen shrouds, and turn the mizzenmast overboard; which indeed might have been an expedient to bring her to her course again. Captain Davis was then quartermaster, and a more experienced seaman than the master. He bid him hold his hand a little, in hopes to bring her some other way to her course: the captain also was of his mind. Now our mainyard and foreyard were lowered down a portlast, as we call it, that is, down pretty nigh the deck, and the wind blew so fierce that we did not dare to loose any headsail, for they must have blown away if we had, neither could all the men in the ship have furled them again; therefore we had no hopes of doing it that way. I was at this time on the deck with some others of our men; and among the rest one Mr John Smallbone, who was the main instrument at that time of saving us all. Come! said he to me, let us go a little way up the foreshrouds, it may be that may make the ship wear [shift course]; for I have been doing it before now. He never tarried for an answer, but run forward presently, and I followed him. We went up the shrouds half-mast up, and there we spread abroad the flaps of our coats, and presently the ship wore. I think we did not stay there above three minutes before we gained our point* and came down again.

THE MAROONED MOSQUITO INDIAN

On course for Cape Horn, the buccaneers captured a splendid Danish slave ship laden with sixty black girls. Here was flagrant piracy, since England and Denmark were not enemies. Dampier draws a veil over this and other incidents: 'I shall not trouble the reader with an account of every day's run, but hasten to the less known parts of the world to give a description of them, only relating such memorable accidents as happened to us and such places as we touched at by the way.'

Preferring the Danish ship to their own and rechristening her

* Of the compass.

Batchelor's Delight, *they shaped for the Horn and rounded it in*
such cold that a man could down three quarts of burnt brandy a day
and keep his legs. They fell in with another dubious English vessel
and made for Más-a-Tierra, largest of the Juan Fernández islands,
400 miles west of Chile.

On 22 March 1684 we came in sight of the island, and the
next day got in and anchored in a bay at the south end of the
island, in twenty-five fathom water, not two cables' length
from the shore. We presently got out our canoe, and went
ashore to seek for a Mosquito Indian, whom we left here
when we were chased hence by three Spanish ships in the
year 1681, a little before we went to Arica; Captain Watling
being then our commander, after Captain Sharp was turned
out.

This Indian lived here alone above three years, and although he was several times sought after by the Spaniards,
who knew he was left on the island, yet they could never find
him. He was in the woods, hunting for goats, when Captain
Watling drew off his men, and the ship was under sail before
he came back to shore. He had with him his gun and a knife,
with a small horn of powder, and a few shot; which being
spent, he contrived a way of notching his knife, to saw the
barrel of his gun into small pieces, wherewith he made
harpoons, lances, hooks and a long knife, heating the pieces
first in the fire, which he struck with his gunflint, and a piece
of the barrel of his gun, which he hardened; having learnt to
do that among the English. The hot pieces of iron he would
hammer out and bend as he pleased with stones, and saw
them with his jagged knife; or grind them to an edge by long
labour, and harden them to a good temper as there was occasion. All this may seem strange to those that are not acquainted with the sagacity of the Indians; but it is no more
than these Mosquito men are accustomed to in their own
country, where they make their own fishing and striking
instruments, without either forge or anvil; though they
spend a great deal of time about them.

Other wild Indians who have not the use of iron, which
the Mosquito men have from the English, make hatchets of

a very hard stone, with which they will cut down trees (the cotton tree especially, which is a soft tender wood), to build their houses or make canoes; and though in working their canoes hollow, they cannot dig them so neat and thin, yet they will make them fit for their service. This their digging or hatchet-work they help out by fire; whether for the felling of trees, or for the making the inside of their canoe hollow. These contrivances are used particularly by the savage Indians of Bluefield's Bay,* whose canoes and stone hatchets I have seen. These stone hatchets are about ten inches long, four broad, and three inches thick in the middle. They are ground away flat and sharp at both ends. Right in the midst, and clear round it, they make a notch, so wide and deep that a man might place his finger along it, and taking a stick or withy about four foot long, they bind it round the hatchet-head, in that notch, and so twisting it hard, use it as an handle or helve; the head being held by it very fast. Nor are other wild Indians less ingenious. Those of Patagonia, particularly, head their arrows with flint, cut or ground; which I have seen and admired. But to return to our Mosquito man on the isle of Juan Fernandez. With such instruments as he made in that manner, he got such provision as the island afforded; either goats or fish. He told us that at first he was forced to eat seal, which is very ordinary meat, before he had made hooks: but afterwards he never killed any seals but to make lines, cutting their skins into thongs. He had a little house or hut half a mile from the sea, which was lined with goatskin; his couch or barbecue of sticks lying along about two foot distant from the ground, was spread with the same, and was all his bedding. He had no clothes left, having worn out those he brought from Watling's ship, but only a skin about his waist. He saw our ship the day before we came to an anchor, and did believe we were English, and therefore killed three goats in the morning, before we came to an anchor, and dressed them with cabbage, to treat us when we came ashore. He came then to the seaside to congratulate our safe arrival. And when we landed, a Mosquito Indian, named Robin, first leaped ashore, and running to his brother

* On the east coast of Nicaragua.

Mosquito man, threw himself flat on his face at his feet, who helping him up, and embracing him, fell flat with his face on the ground at Robin's feet, and was by him taken up also. We stood with pleasure to behold the surprise, and tenderness, and solemnity of this interview, which was exceedingly affectionate on both sides; and when their ceremonies of civility were over, we also that stood gazing at them drew near, each of us embracing him we had found here, who was overjoyed to see so many of his old friends come hither, as he thought purposely to fetch him. He was named Will, as the other was Robin. These were names given them by the English, for they had no names among themselves; and they take it as a great favour to be named by any of us; and will complain for want of it, if we do not appoint them some name when they are with us: saying of themselves they are poor men, and have no name.

THE GALÁPAGOS ISLANDS

The buccaneers' visit to the Galápagos Islands, 600 miles west of Ecuador, prompted one of Dampier's finest descriptive passages, running to three times the length of the following extract. His account can stand comparison with that of Charles Darwin 150 years later, whose stay here in 1835 put him on the path towards the theory of evolution. It is worth remembering that while Darwin, educated at the universities of Edinburgh and Cambridge, arrived at these islands during a scientific voyage backed by the full resources of the Admiralty, Dampier came as a deckhand on a stolen frigate. Most of his time was spent on Isla San Salvador, where the Batchelor's Delight *is thought to have anchored in Caleta Bucanero (Buccaneer Cove).*

The Galapagos Islands are a great number of uninhabited islands, lying under, and on both sides of the Equator . . . The Spaniards who first discovered them, and in whose draughts alone they are laid down, report them to be a great number stretching north-west from the line, as far as 5° N. but we saw not above fourteen or fifteen. They are some of them seven or eight leagues long, and three or four broad.

They are of a good height, most of them flat and even on the top; four or five of the eastermost are rocky, barren and hilly, producing neither tree, herb, nor grass, but a few dildo trees, except by the seaside. The dildo tree is a green prickly shrub, that grows about ten or twelve foot high, without either leaf or fruit. It is as big as a man's leg, from the root to the top, and it is full of sharp prickles, growing in thick rows from top to bottom; this shrub is fit for no use, not so much as to burn. Close by the sea there grows in some places bushes of buttonwood, which is very good firing. This sort of wood grows in many places in the West Indies, especially in the Bay of Campeachy, and the San Blas Islands. I did never see any in these seas but here. There is water on these barren islands, in ponds and holes among the rocks. Some other of these islands are mostly plain and low, and the land more fertile, producing trees of divers sorts, unknown to us. Some of the westermost of these islands, are nine or ten leagues long, and six or seven broad; the mould deep and black. These produce trees of great and tall bodies, especially mamey trees,* which grow here in great groves. In these large islands, there are brooks of good water. The Spaniards when they first discovered these islands, found multitudes of iguanas, and land-turtle or tortoise, and named them the Galapagos Islands.† I do believe there is no place in the world that is so plentifully stored with those animals. The iguanas here are fat and large as any that I ever saw; they are so tame, that a man may knock down twenty in an hour's time with a club. The land-turtle are here so numerous, that five or six hundred men might subsist on them alone for several months, without any other sort of provision: they are extraordinary large and fat; and so sweet, that no pullet eats more pleasantly. One of the largest of these creatures will weigh 150 or 200 weight, and some of them are two foot, or two foot six inches over the calipee‡ or belly. I did never see any but at this place, that will weigh above thirty pound weight. I have heard that at the Isle of St Lawrence or

---

* Also known as marmalade trees, bearing a delicious fruit.
† Galápago originally meant a saddle, later a turtle.
‡ The glutinous part of the turtle, next to the upper shell.

Madagascar, and at the English Forest, an island near it, called also Don Mascarin [Réunion], and now possessed by the French; there are very large ones, but whether so big, fat, and sweet as these, I know not.* There are three or four sorts of these creatures in the West Indies.† One is called by the Spaniards, hecatee; these live most in freshwater ponds, and seldom come on land. They weigh about ten or fifteen pounds; they have small legs and flat feet, and small long necks. Another sort is called terrapin; these are a great deal less than the hecatee; the shell on their backs is all carved naturally, finely wrought, and well clouded: the backs of these are rounder than those before-mentioned; they are otherwise much of the same form. These delight to live in wet swampy places, or on the land near such places. Both these sorts are very good meat. They are in great plenty on the Isle of Pines near Cuba: there the Spanish hunters when they meet them in the woods bring them home to their huts, and mark them by notching their shells, then let them go; this they do to have them at hand, for they never ramble far from there. When these hunters return to Cuba, after about a month or six weeks' stay, they carry with them three or four hundred or more of these creatures to sell; for they are very good meat, and every man knows his own by their marks. These tortoise in the Galapagos are more like the hecatee, except that, as I said before, they are much bigger; and they have very long small necks and little heads. There are some green snakes on these islands, but no other land animal that I did ever see. There are great plenty of turtle-doves so tame, that a man may kill five or six dozen in a forenoon with a stick. They are somewhat less than a pigeon, and are very good meat, and commonly fat . . .

There is another sort of green turtle in the South Seas

---

* Rodriguez, also in the Mascarenes, may have had even better specimens of the *testudo rasmaeri* than those on Réunion.
† Daniel Defoe's *A General History of the Pirates* (1724), Chapter XI: 'There are three or four sorts of these creatures in the West Indies, the largest of which will weigh 150 or 200 pound weight or more; but those that were found upon this island were of the smallest kind, weighing ten or twelve pounds each, with a fine natural wrought shell and beautifully clouded.'

which are but small, yet pretty sweet: these lie westward on the coast of Mexico. One thing is very strange and remarkable in these creatures; that at the breeding time they leave for two or three months their common haunts, where they feed most of the year, and resort to other places, only to lay their eggs: and 'tis not thought that they eat anything during this season: so that both he's and she's grow very lean; but the he's to that degree that none will eat them. The most remarkable places that I did ever hear of for their breeding, is at an island in the West Indies called Grand Cayman, and the isle Ascension in the Western Ocean: and when the breeding time is past, there are none remaining. Doubtless they swim some hundreds of leagues to come to those two places: for it has been often observed, that at Grand Cayman, at the breeding time, there are found all those sorts of turtle before described. The South Keys of Cuba are above forty leagues from there, which is the nearest place that these creatures can come from; and it is most certain, that there could not live so many there as come here in one season.

Those that go to lay at Ascension, must needs travel much farther; for there is no land nearer it than 300 leagues: and it is certain, that these creatures live always near the shore. In the South Sea likewise, the Galapagos is the place where they live the biggest part of the year; yet they go from thence at their season over to the main, to lay their eggs; which is a hundred leagues, the nearest place. Although multitudes of these turtles go from their common places of feeding and abode, to those laying places, yet they do not all go: and at the time when the turtle resort to these places to lay their eggs, they are accompanied with abundance of fish, especially sharks; the places which the turtle then leave being at that time destitute of fish, which follow the turtle.

When the she's go thus to their places to lay, the males accompany them, and never leave them till they return. Both male and female are fat at the beginning of the season; but before they return, the males, as I said, are so lean, that they are not fit to eat, but the females are good to the very last; yet not so fat as at the beginning of the season. It is reported of these creatures, that they are nine days engendering, and in the water; the male on the female's back. It is observable, that the males, while engendering, do not easily forsake their female: for I have gone and taken hold of the male when engendering; and a very bad striker may strike them then, for the male is not shy at all: but the female seeing a boat, when they rise to blow, would make her escape, but that the male grasps her with his two fore-fins, and holds her fast. When they are thus coupled, it is best to strike the female first, then you are sure of the male also. These creatures are thought to live to a great age; and it is observed by the Jamaica turtlers, that they are many years before they come to their full growth.

DEATH AND BURIAL OF CAPTAIN COOK

The buccaneer voyage in the Pacific had not been too successful. They seized a merchantman with seven tons of quince marmalade, a mule for the President of Panama and a carving of the Virgin Mary, then learnt from the Spanish crew that they had missed a sister ship carrying 800,000 pieces of eight. To make matters worse, Captain Cook became very ill.

They steered north from the Galápagos, skirting Coco, an un-inhabited island two hundred miles south-west of Costa Rica which is now famous for legends of vast pirate treasure and boasts a Cabo Dampier. Next they made for Costa Rica's Cabo Blanco.

Captain Cook, who was taken sick at Juan Fernandez, continued so till we came within two or three leagues of Cape Blanco, and then died of a sudden; though he seemed that morning to be as likely to live, as he had been some weeks before; but it is usual with sick men coming from the sea, where they have nothing but the sea-air, to die off as soon as ever they come within the view of the land. About four hours after we all came to an anchor, a league within the cape, right against the brook of fresh-water, in fourteen fathom clean hard sand. Presently after we came to an anchor Captain Cook was carried ashore to be buried, twelve men carried their arms to guard those that were ordered to dig the grave: for although we saw no appearance of inhabitants, yet we did not know but the country might be thick inhabited.

CHAPTER
THREE

FAILURE AT AMAPALA

Edward Davis, who succeeded John Cook as captain of the
Batchelor's Delight, *continued the voyage northwards and sailed
into the Golfo de Fonseca, south-east of San Salvador. Having
captured a friar on the tiny island of Meanguera, the buccaneers went
to the more important island of El Tigre and climbed the path to
its chief town, Amapala.*

The town, as is before noted, is about a mile from the landing-
place, standing in a plain on the top of a hill, having a very
steep ascent to go to it. All the Indians stood on the top of
the hill waiting Captain Davis's coming.

The Secretary* had no great kindness for the Spaniards.
It was he that persuaded the Indians to await Captain Davis's
coming; for they were all running into the woods; but he
told them, that if any of the Spaniards' enemies came thither,
it was not to hurt them, but the Spaniards whose slaves they
were; and that their poverty would protect them. This man
with the Casica stood more forward than the rest, at the bank
of the hill, when Captain Davis with his company appeared
beneath. They called out therefore in Spanish, demanding of
our men, what they were, and from where they came? To
whom Captain Davis and his men replied, they were Biscayers, and that they were sent there by the King of Spain
to clear those seas from enemies; that their ships were coming into the gulf to careen, and that they came there before
the ships, to seek a convenient place for it, as also to desire
the Indians' assistance. The Secretary, who was the only man

* The Secretary and the Casica were local Indian officials.

that could speak Spanish, told them that they were welcome, for he had a great respect for any Old Spain men, especially for the Biscayers, of whom he had heard a very honourable report; therefore he desired them to come up to their town. Captain Davis and his men immediately ascended the hill, the friar going before; and they were received with a great deal of affection by the Indians. The Casica and Secretary embraced Captain Davis, and the other Indians received his men with the like ceremony. These salutations being ended, they all marched towards the church, for that is the place of all public meetings, and all plays and pastimes are acted there also; therefore in the churches belonging to Indian towns they have all sorts of visors, and strange antic dresses both for men and women, and abundance of musical hautboys and strumstrums. The strumstrum is made somewhat like a cittern; most of those that the Indians use are made of a large gourd cut in the midst, and a thin board laid over the hollow, and which is fastened to the sides; this serves for the belly, over which the strings are placed. The nights before any holidays, or the nights ensuing, are the times when they all meet to make merry. Their mirth consists in singing, dancing and sporting in those antic habits, and using as many antic gestures. If the moon shine they use but few torches, if not, the church is full of light. There meet at these times all sorts of both sexes. All the Indians that I have been acquainted with who are under the Spaniards, seem to be more melancholy than other Indians that are free; and at these public meetings, when they are in the greatest of their jollity, their mirth seems to be rather forced than real. Their songs are very melancholy and doleful; so is their music: but whether it be natural to the Indians to be thus melancholy, or the effect of their slavery, I am not certain. But I have always been prone to believe, that they are then only condoling their misfortunes, the loss of their country and liberties; which, although these that are now living do not know, nor remember what it was to be free, yet there seems to be a deep impression of the thoughts of the slavery which the Spaniards have brought them under, increased probably by some traditions of their ancient freedom.

Captain Davis intended when they were all in the church to shut the doors, and then make a bargain with them, letting them know what he was, and so draw them afterwards by fair means to our assistance, the friar being with him, who had also promised to engage them to it: but before they were all in the church, one of Captain Davis's men pushed one of the Indians to hasten him into the church. The Indian immediately ran away, and all the rest taking the alarm, sprang out of the church like deer; it was hard to say which was first: and Captain Davis, who knew nothing of what happened, was left in the church only with the friar. When they were all fled, Captain Davis's men fired and killed the Secretary.

THE RAFTS OF THE PERUVIAN INDIANS

Captain Davis joined forces with other buccaneers and cruised down the coast of South America, capturing the town of Paita in northern Peru, but 'the inhabitants ran away as fast as they could', leaving it 'emptied both of money and goods; there was not so much as a meal of victuals left'. The buccaneers demanded a ransom for the town, waited five days in vain, then set it on fire. Dampier used the time to inspect the neighbourhood, taking special interest in the Indian rafts. These were possibly of balsawood, like the raft in which Thor Heyerdahl embarked on the Kon-Tiki Expedition from Peru in 1947.

Bark-logs are made of many round legs of wood, in manner of a raft, and very different according to the use that they are designed for, or the humour of the people that make them, or the matter that they are made of. If they are made for fishing, then they are only three or four logs of light wood, of seven or eight foot long, placed by the side of each other, pinned fast together with wooden pins, and bound hard with withy. The logs are so placed, that the middlemost are longer than those by the sides, especially at the head or forepart, which grows narrower gradually into an angle or point, the better to cut through the water. Others are made to carry goods: the bottom of these is made of twenty or thirty great trees of about twenty, thirty or forty foot long, fastened like

the other, side to side, and so shaped; on the top of these they
place another shorter row of trees across them, pinned fast
to each other, and then pinned to the undermost row – this
double row of planks makes the bottom of the float, and of a
considerable breadth. From this bottom the raft is raised to
about ten foot higher, with rows of posts sometimes set upright, and supporting a floor or two; but those I observed
were raised by thick trees laid across each other, as in wood-
piles; only not close together, as in the bottom of the float,
but at the ends and sides only, so as to leave the middle all
hollow like a chamber; except that here and there a beam
goes across it, to keep the float more compact. In this hollow,
at about four foot height from the beams at the bottom, they
lay small poles along, and close together, to make a floor for
another room, on the top of which also they lay another such
floor made of poles; and the entrances into both these rooms
is only by creeping between the great traverse trees which
make the walls of this sea-house. The lowest of these stories
serves as a cellar: there they lay great stones for ballast, and
their jars of fresh water closed up, and whatever may bear
being wet; for by the weight of the ballast and cargo, the
bottom of this room, and of the whole vessel, is sunk so deep,
as to lie two or three feet within the surface of the water. The
second story is for the seamen, and their necessaries. Above
this second story the goods are stowed, to what height they
please, usually about eight or ten feet, and kept together by
poles set upright quite round: only there is a little space abaft
for the steersmen (for they have a large rudder), and afore for
the fire-hearth, to dress their victuals, especially when they
make long voyages, as from Lima to Trujillo, or Guayaquil,
or Panama, which last voyage is five or six hundred leagues.
In the midst of all, among the goods rises a mast, to which is
fastened a large sail, as in our West Country barges in the
Thames. They always go before the wind, being unable to
ply against it; and therefore are fit only for these seas, where
the wind is always in a manner the same, not varying above
a point or two all the way from Lima, till such time as they
come into the Bay of Panama: and even there they meet with
no great sea; but sometimes northerly winds; and then they

lower their sails, and drive before it, waiting a change. All their care then is only to keep off from shore; for they are so made that they cannot sink at sea. These rafts carry sixty or seventy tons of goods and upwards; their cargo is chiefly wine, oil, flour, sugar, Quito-cloth,* soap, goatskins dressed, etc. The float is managed usually by three or four men, who being unable to return with it against the Trade Wind, when they come to Panama dispose of the goods and bottom together; getting a passage back again for themselves in some ship or boat bound to the port they came from; and there they make a new bark-log for their next cargo.

The smaller sort of bark-logs, described before, which lie flat on the water, and are used for fishing, or carrying water to ships, or the like (half a ton or a ton at a time) are more governable than the other, though they have masts and sails too. With these they go out at night by the help of the land-wind (which is seldom wanting on this coast) and return back in the daytime with the sea-wind.

These sorts of floats are used in many places both in the East and West Indies. On the coast of Coromandel in the East Indies they call them catamarans. These are but one log, or two sometimes of a sort of light wood, and are made without sail or rudder, and so small, that they carry but one man, whose legs and rump are always in the water, and he manages his log with a paddle, appearing at a distance like a man sitting on a fish's back.

CHOCK-FULL

Although a respected leader, Captain Davis seemed momentarily indecisive and turned north again – 'we jogged on,' says Dampier. They captured a ship off the coast of Colombia and brought it to a nearby island. 'At this island, Gorgona, we rummaged our prize and found a few boxes of marmalade and three or four jars of brandy.' To add further to the gloom, Dampier wrote, 'It rains abundantly here all the year long . . . it pours as out of a sieve.'

---

* Quito, capital of Ecuador, stands 9,300 ft above sea-level, and is still important for the manufacture of textiles.

I have been at this isle three times, and always found it very rainy, and the rains very violent. I remember when we touched there on our return from Captain Sharp, we boiled a kettle of chocolate before we cleaned our bark, and having every man his calabash full, we began to sup it off, standing all the time in the rain; but I am confident not a man among us all did clear his dish, for it rained so fast and such great drops into our calabashes, that after we had supped off as much chocolate and rainwater together as sufficed us, our calabashes were still above half full; and I heard some of the men swear that they could not sup it up so fast as it rained in; at last I grew tired with what I had left, and threw it away: and most of the rest did so likewise.

THE BATTLE OF PANAMA BAY

Captain Davis took the Batchelor's Delight *up to the Bay of Panama, hoping to meet other pirate vessels in sufficient quantity to attack the Spanish treasure fleet expected soon from Lima. His ambition was realised, for he encountered several like-minded commanders, including the Frenchman François Grogniet. The English ships carried so many men that their galleys could not feed them. To rectify this, the boiling house of a Panamanian sugar factory was robbed of its huge copper kettles, which were used for cooking the buccaneers' meals. On 22 May 1685 Captain Davis anchored at Pacheca Island, forty miles south-east of Panama City.*

The island is the northermost of the King's Islands.* It is a small low island about a league round. On the south side of it there are two or three small islands, neither of them half a mile round. Between Pacheca and these islands is a small channel not above six or seven paces wide, and about a mile long. Through this Captain Townley made a bold run, being pressed hard by the Spaniards in the fight I am going to speak of, though he was ignorant whether there was a sufficient depth of water or not. On the east side of this channel all our fleet lay waiting for the Lima fleet, which we were in hopes would come this way.

* Archipiélago de las Perlas.

'There is another sort of green turtle in the South Seas
which are but small, yet pretty sweet' (*page 53*)

Dampier's battle with the Spanish fleet:
'Being all under sail, we bore down
right afore the wind on our enemies'

The 28th day we had a very wet morning, for the rains were come in, as they do usually in May, or June, sooner or later; so that May is here a very uncertain month. Hitherto, till within a few days, we had good fair weather, and the wind at NNE but now the weather was altered, and the wind at SSW.

However about eleven o'clock it cleared up, and we saw the Spanish fleet about three leagues WNW from the island Pacheca, standing close on a wind to the eastward; but they could not fetch the island by a league. We were riding a league south-east from the island between it and the main; only Captain Grogniet was about a mile to the northward of us near the island: he weighed so soon as they came in sight, and stood over for the main; and we lay still, expecting when he would tack and come to us: but he took care to keep himself out of harm's way.

Captain Swan and Townley came aboard of Captain Davis to order how to engage the enemy, who we saw came purposely to fight us, they being in all fourteen sail, besides pirogues, rowing with twelve and fourteen oars apiece. Six sail of them were ships of good force: first the Admiral forty-eight guns, 450 men; the Vice-Admiral forty guns, 400 men; the Rear-Admiral thirty-six guns, 360 men; a ship of twenty-four guns, 300 men; one of eighteen guns, 250 men; and one of eight guns, 200 men; two great fireships, six ships only with small arms, having 800 men on board them all; besides two or three hundred men in pirogues. This account of their strength we had afterwards from Captain Knight, who being to the windward on the coast of Peru, took prisoners, of whom he had this information, being what they brought from Lima. Besides these men, they had also some hundreds of Old Spain men that came from Portobelo, and met them at Los Santos, from whence they now came: and their strength of men from Lima was 3,000 men, being all the strength they could make in that Kingdom; and for greater security, they had first landed their treasure at Los Santos.

Our fleet consisted of ten sail: first Captain Davis thirty-six guns, 156 men, most English; Captain Swan sixteen guns, 140 men, all English: these were the only ships of force that

we had; the rest having none but small arms. Captain
Townley had 110 men, all English. Captain Grogniet 308
men, all French. Captain Harris 100 men, most English.
Captain Branly thirty-six men, some English, some French;
Davis's tender eight men; Swan's tender eight men; Townley's bark eighty men; and a small bark of thirty tons made a
fireship, with a canoe crew in her. We had in all 960 men.
But Captain Grogniet came not to us till all was over, yet we
were not discouraged at it, but resolved to fight them, for
being to windward of the enemy, we had it at our choice,
whether we would fight or not. It was three o'clock in the
afternoon when we weighed, and being all under sail, we
bore down right afore the wind on our enemies, who kept
close on a wind to come to us; but night came on without
anything beside the exchanging of a few shot on each side.
When it grew dark, the Spanish admiral put out a light, as a
signal for his fleet to come to an anchor. We saw the light in
the admiral's top, which continued about half an hour, and
then it was taken down. In a short time after we saw the light
again, and being to windward we kept under sail, supposing
the light had been in the admiral's top; but as it proved this
was only a stratagem of theirs; for this light was put out the
second time at one of their bark's topmast-head, and then she
was sent to leeward; which deceived us: for we thought still
the light was in the admiral's top, and by that means thought
ourselves to windward of them.

In the morning therefore, contrary to our expectation, we
found they had got the weather-gauge* of us, and were coming upon us with full sail; so we ran for it, and after a running fight all day, and having taken a turn almost round the
Bay of Panama, we came to an anchor again at the Isle of
Pacheca, in the very same place from whence we set out in
the morning.

Thus ended this day's work, and with it all that we had
been projecting for five or six months; when instead of making ourselves masters of the Spanish fleet and treasure, we
were glad to escape them; and owed that too, in a great
measure, to their want of courage to pursue their advantage.

* They lay advantageously to windward.

The 30th day in the morning when we looked out we saw the Spanish fleet all together three leagues to leeward of us at an anchor. It was but little wind till ten o'clock, and then sprung up a small breeze at south, and the Spanish fleet went away to Panama. What loss they had, I know not; we lost but one man. And having held a consult, we resolved to go to the keys of Coiba, to seek Captain Harris, who was forced away from us in the fight; that being the place appointed for our rendezvous upon any such accident. As for Grogniet, he said his men would not suffer him to join us in the fight; but we were not satisfied with that excuse; so we suffered him to go with us to the isles of Coiba, and there cashiered our cowardly companion. Some were for taking from him the ship which we had given him; but at length he was suffered to keep it with his men, and we sent them away in it to some other place.

THE CAPTURE OF LEÓN

After the debacle in Panama Bay, the buccaneers decided to attack León, chief town of Nicaragua, ten miles from the Pacific coast. León, where the poet Rubén Dario spent his childhood, is today the country's second largest city, after the new capital, Managua, yet it manages to retain the charm it possessed three hundred years ago.

Our countryman Mr Gage,* who travelled in these parts, recommends it to the world as the pleasantest place in all America, and calls it the paradise of the Indies. Indeed if we consider the advantage of its situation, we may find it surpassing most places for health and pleasure in America, for the country about it is of a sandy soil, which soon drinks up all the rain that falls, to which these parts are much subject. It is encompassed with savannahs, so that they have the benefit of the breezes coming from any quarter; all which makes it a very healthy place. It is a place of no great trade, and therefore not rich in money. Their wealth lies in their pastures, and cattle, and plantations of sugar. It is said that they make cordage here of hemp, but if they have any such manu-

* Thomas Gage, author of *The English-American, His Travail by Sea and Land; or a New Survey of the West Indies* (1648).

factory, it is at some distance from the town, for here is no sign of any such thing.

Thither our men were now marching; they went from the canoes about eight o'clock. Captain Townley, with eighty of the briskest men, marched before, Captain Swan with a hundred men marched next, and Captain Davis with 170 men marched next, and Captain Knight brought up the rear. Captain Townley, who was near two miles ahead of the rest, met about seventy horsemen four miles before he came to the city, but they never stood him. About three o'clock Captain Townley, only with his eighty men, entered the town, and was briskly charged in a broad street, with 170 or 200 Spanish horsemen, but two or three of their leaders being knocked down, the rest fled. Their foot consisted of about 500 men, which were drawn up in the parade; for the Spaniards in these parts make a large square in every town, though the town itself be small. The square is called the parade: commonly the church makes one side of it, and the gentlemens' houses, with their galleries about them, the other. But the foot also seeing their horse retire left an empty city to Captain Townley; beginning to save themselves by flight. Captain Swan came in about four o'clock, Captain Davis with his men about five, and Captain Knight with as many men as he could encourage to march, came in about six, but he left many men tired on the road; these, as is usual, came dropping in one or two at a time, as they were able. The next morning the Spaniards killed one of our tired men; he was a stout old grey-headed man, aged about eighty-four, who had served under Oliver* in the time of the Irish Rebellion; after which he was at Jamaica, and had followed privateering ever since. He would not accept of the offer our men made him to tarry ashore, but said he would venture as far as the best of them: and when surrounded by the Spaniards, he refused to take quarter, but discharged his gun amongst them, keeping a pistol still charged, so they shot him dead at a distance. His name was Swan;† he was a very merry hearty old man,

---

* Cromwell.
† John Swan, in the original manuscript. Captain Swan's Christian name was Charles.

and always used to declare he would never take quarter. But they took Mr Smith who was tired also: he was a merchant belonging to Captain Swan, and being carried before the Governor of Leon, was known by a Mulatta woman that waited on him. Mr Smith had lived many years in the Canaries, and could speak and write very good Spanish, and it was there this Mulatta woman remembered him. He, being examined how many men we were, said 1,000 at the city, and 500 at the canoes, which made well for us at the canoes, who straggling about every day, might easily have been destroyed. But this so daunted the governor, that he did never offer to molest our men, although he had with him above 1,000 men, as Mr Smith guessed. He sent in a flag of truce about noon, pretending to ransom the town, rather than let it be burnt, but our captains demanded 300,000 pieces of eight for its ransom, and as much provision as would victual 1,000 men four months, and Mr Smith to be ransomed for some of their prisoners; but the Spaniards did not intend to ransom the town, but only capitulated day after day to prolong time, till they had got more men. Our captains therefore, considering the distance that they were from the canoes, resolved to be marching down. The 14th day in the morning, they ordered the city to be set on fire, which was presently done, and then they came away.

AVOCADO, GUAVA, PRICKLY PEAR, COCHINEAL

Throughout the buccaneers' sporadic progress up the coast of Central America during the summer of 1685 Dampier continued to compile his nature notes, examining the avocado in Panama, the guava and prickly pear in Nicaragua, and cochineal in Guatemala. All of these were fascinating, exotic rarities practically unknown in Britain. At that time cochineal dye was thought to be made from plant seeds, but Dampier correctly identified its basis as an insect: this was confirmed by the Dutch microscopist, Antoni van Leeuwenhoek, in 1703, five years after A New Voyage Round the World *was published in translation at The Hague.*

The avocado pear tree is as big as most pear trees, and is

commonly pretty high; the skin or bark black, and pretty smooth; the leaves large, of an oval shape, and the fruit as big as a large lemon. It is of a green colour till it is ripe, and then it is a little yellowish. They are seldom fit to eat till they have been gathered two or three days; then they become soft, and the skin or rind will peel off. The substance in the inside is green, or a little yellowish, and as soft as butter. Within the substance there is a stone as big as a horse-plum. This fruit has no taste of itself, and therefore 'tis usually mixed with sugar and lime-juice, and beaten together in a plate; and this is an excellent dish. The ordinary way is to eat it with a little salt and a roasted plantain; and thus a man that's hungry may make a good meal of it. It is very wholesome eaten any way. It is reported that this fruit provokes lust,* and therefore is said to be much esteemed by the Spaniards: and I do believe they are much esteemed by them, for I have met with plenty of them in many places in the North Seas, where the Spaniards are settled, as in the Bay of Campeachy, on the coast of Cartagena,† and the coast of Caracas; and there are some in Jamaica, which were planted by the Spaniards when they possessed that island . . .

The guava fruit grows on a hard scrubbed shrub, whose bark is smooth and whitish, the branches pretty long and small, the leaf somewhat like the leaf of a hazel, the fruit much like a pear, with a thin rind. It is full of small hard seeds, and it may be eaten while it is green, which is a thing very rare in the Indies: for most fruit, both in the East or West Indies, is full of clammy, white, unsavoury juice, before it is ripe, though pleasant enough afterwards. When this fruit is ripe it is yellow, soft, and very pleasant. It bakes as well as a pear, and it may be coddled, and it makes good pies. There are of divers sorts, different in shape, taste, and colour. The inside of some is yellow, of others red. When this fruit is eaten green, it is binding, when ripe, it is loosening.

The prickly pear bush or shrub, of about four or five foot high, grows in many places of the West Indies, as at Jamaica,

---

* The word avocado derives from the Spanish, *aguacate*, which in turn derives from the Náhuatl word, *ahuacatl*, meaning testicle.
† In Colombia.

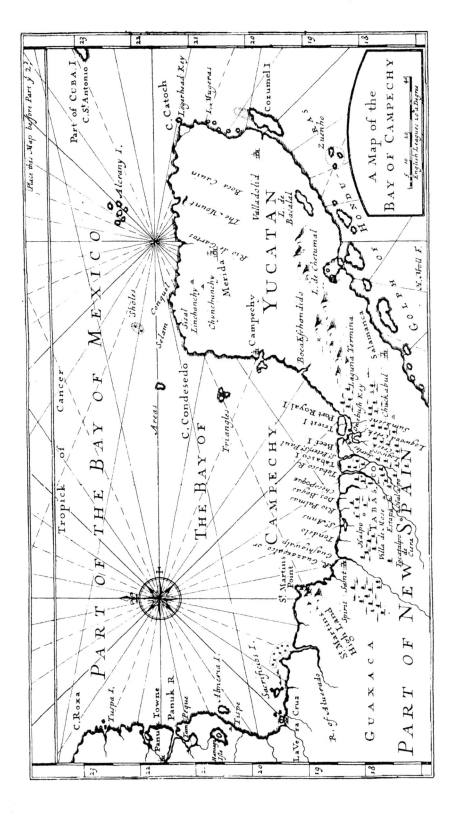

A Map of the
BAY of CAMPECHY

English Leagues 20 à Degree

Place this Map before Part 2?

Part of CUBA I.
C. S.t Antonio

PART OF THE BAY OF MEXICO

Tropick of Cancer

C. Roxa
Tuspa I.
Towne
Panuk R.
S.t Iuan Pique
Almeria I.
Tuspe
Sacrificios I.
St Martins Point

THE BAY OF CAMPECHY

Areas
C. Condesedo
Triangles

Sholts
Conquel
Selam
Sisal
Limchonchy
Chunchunchu
Merida
Rio de Garros
The Mount
Boca Cauin
Campechy
Valladolid
L. de Bacalal
YUCATAN

C. Catoch
Logerhead Kay
I. Mugeras
Cozumel I

Zumho

HONDURO

GOLPH OF

Boca Escondido
L. de Cechumal
Laguna Termina
Conlogh Kay
Salamanca
Chinkabul
Summtrolio
Laambel

Beef I
Triest I Port Royal I
Tabasco I
S.t Peter S.t Paul
Rio Palma
Dos Bogas
Chiropoque
S.t Anne
Tenidolo
Guazaqualp or Guazacualco
High Land
S.t Martins
H.t Holy Spirit Salut Is.t

Halpo
Villa de Mose
Estapa
Ixcatlapo
Xdalapro
Cura

La Vera Cruz
R. of Aluerado
GUAXACA

PART OF NEW SPAIN

K. Neil I.

and most other islands there; and on the main in several places. This prickly shrub delights most in barren sandy grounds; and they thrive best in places that are near the sea: especially where the sand is saltish. The tree, or shrub, is three or four foot high, spreading forth several branches; and on each branch two or three leaves. These leaves (if I may call them so) are round, as broad every way as the palm of a man's hand, and as thick; their substance like house-leek. These leaves are fenced round with strong prickles above an inch long. The fruit grows at the farther edge of the leaf: it is as big as a large plum, growing small near the leaf, and big towards the top, where it opens like a medlar. This fruit at first is green like the leaf, from whence it springs with small prickles about it; but when ripe it is of a deep red colour. The inside is full of small black seeds, mixed with a certain red pulp, like thick syrup. It is very pleasant in taste, cooling and refreshing;* but if a man eats fifteen or twenty of them they will colour his water, making it look like blood. This I have often experienced, yet found no harm by it . . .

The cochineal is an insect, bred in a sort of fruit much like the prickly pear. The tree or shrub that bears it is like the prickly pear tree, about five foot high, and so prickly; only the leaves are not quite so big, but the fruit is bigger. On the top of the fruit there grows a red flower. This flower, when the fruit is ripe, falls down on the top of the fruit, which then begins to open, and covers it so, that no rain nor dew can wet the inside. The next day, or two days after its falling down, the flower being then scorched away by the heat of the sun, the fruit opens as broad as the mouth of a pint-pot, and the inside of the fruit is by this time full of small red insects, with curious thin wings. As they were bred here, so here they would die for want of food, and rot in their husks (having by this time eaten up their mother-fruit), did not the Indians, who plant large fields of these trees, when once they perceive the fruit open, take care to drive them out: for they spread under the branches of the tree a large linen cloth, and then with sticks they shake the branches, and so disturb the poor

* In T. S. Eliot's *The Hollow Men* (1925) the prickly pear is perhaps an inappropriate symbol for sterility.

insects, that they take wing to be gone, yet hovering still over the head of their native tree, but the heat of the sun so disorders them, that they presently fall down dead on the cloth spread for that purpose, where the Indians let them remain two or three days longer, till they are thoroughly dry. When they fly up they are red, when they fall down they are black; and when first they are quite dry they are white as the sheet wherein they lie, though the colour change a little after. These yield the much esteemed scarlet.

EL BUFFADORE

Continuing up the Pacific coast, the buccaneers reached Mexico and put into Santa Cruz Huatulco. Three hundred years later El Buffadore, now called El Bufadero, is still blowing. 'It makes a especial snort sound,' wrote the Department of Tourism's Alvaro A. Hernandez Altamirano, in response to an enquiry for this edition.

We coasted a league farther and came to Huatulco. This port is in latitude 15° 30′; it is one of the best in all this kingdom of Mexico. Near a mile from the mouth of the harbour, on the east side, there is a little island close by the shore; and on the west side of the mouth of the harbour there is a great hollow rock, which by the continual working of the sea in and out makes a great noise, which may be heard a great way off. Every surge that comes in forces the water out of a little hole on its top, as out of a pipe, from whence it flies out just like the blowing of a whale; to which the Spaniards also liken it. They call this rock and spout the Buffadore; upon what account I know not. Even in the calmest seasons the sea beats in there, making the water spout from the hole; so that this is always a good mark to find the harbour by.

THE TREASURE SHIPS

By now Dampier had left Captain Davis, who intended going back to Peru. He joined Captain Swan's ship, the Cygnet, *'to get some knowledge of the northern parts of this continent of Mexico; and I knew that Captain Swan determined to coast it as far north as he thought convenient and then pass over for the East Indies, which was a way very agreeable to my inclination' – 'more to indulge my curiosity than to get wealth', he wrote in his journal. Captain Swan formed an alliance with Captain Townley, and they sailed along to Acapulco.*

Acapulco is a pretty large town, 17° north of the Equator. It is the seaport for the City of Mexico, on the west side of the continent; as Veracruz, or St John de Ulúa in the Bay of Nova Hispania, is on the north side. This town is the only place of trade on all this coast; for there is little or no traffic by sea on all the north-west part of this vast kingdom, here being, as I have said, neither boats, barks nor ships (that I could ever see), unless only what come hither from other parts, and some boats near the south-east end of California; as I guess, by the intercourse between that and the main, for pearl-fishing.

The ships that trade hither are only three, two that constantly go once a year between this and Manila in Luzon, one of the Philippine Islands, and one ship more every year to and from Lima. This from Lima commonly arrives a little before Christmas; she brings them quicksilver, cocoa, and pieces of eight. Here she stays till the Manila ships arrive, and then takes in a cargo of spices, silks, calicoes, and muslins, and other East India commodities, for the use of Peru, and then returns to Lima. This is but a small vessel of twenty guns, but the two Manila ships are each said to be above a thousand tons. These make their voyages alternately, so that one or other of them is always at the Manilas. When either of them sets out from Acapulco, it is at the latter end of March, or the beginning of April; she always touches to refresh at Guam, one of the Ladrone [Mariana] Islands, in about sixty days' space after she sets out. There she stays but two or three days, and then prosecutes her voyage to Manila, where she commonly arrives some time in June. By that time the other is ready to sail from thence, laden with East India commodities. She stretches away to the north as far as 36°, or sometimes into 40° of north latitude before she gets a wind to stand over to the American shore. She falls in first with the coast of California, and then coasts along the shore

to the south again, and never misses a wind to bring her away
from thence quite to Acapulco. When she gets the length of
Cape St Lucas, which is the southermost point of California,
she stretches over to Cape Corrientes, which is in about 20°
of north latitude. From thence she coasts along till she comes
to Tzalahua,* and there she sets ashore passengers that are
bound to the city of Mexico. From thence she makes her best
way, coasting still along shore, till she arrives at Acapulco,
which is commonly about Christmas, never more than eight
or ten days before or after. Upon the return of this ship to
Manila, the other which stays there till her arrival, takes her
turn back to Acapulco.

THE DEATH OF BASIL RINGROSE

*Captain Townley, with 140 men in twelve canoes, paddled silently
by night into Acapulco Bay, aiming to steal the Lima ship, which
had recently docked; but the port proved so well fortified that he
abandoned the attempt. He now determined to capture the Manila
ship expected imminently off Cape Corrientes; so Swan and he
sailed up the cape, patrolling for three weeks until, short of provisions,
they went into Banderas Bay and landed men to hunt for beef, at
which time the galleon cruised safely past. Townley broke off the
partnership and followed Davis towards Peru. Swan travelled north,
capturing the town of Santa Pecaque, near Santiago Ixcuintla.*

Captain Swan, and his other men at the town, caught a
prisoner, who said, that there were near a thousand men of
all colours, Spaniards and Indians, Negroes and Mulattos,
in arms, at a place called St Jago [Santiago], but three leagues
off, the chief town on this river; that the Spaniards were
armed with guns and pistols, and the copper-coloured with
swords and lances. Captain Swan, fearing the ill consequence
of separating his small company, was resolved the next day
to march away with the whole party; and therefore he
ordered his men to catch as many horses as they could, that
they might carry the more provision with them. Accordingly,
the next day, being 19 February 1686, Captain Swan called

* On the outskirts of Manzanillo.

out his men betimes to be gone; but they refused to go, and
said, that they would not leave the town till all the provision
was in the canoes: therefore he was forced to yield to them,
and suffered half the company to go as before. They had now
fifty-four horses laden, which Captain Swan ordered to be
tied one to another, and the men to go in two bodies, twenty-
five before, and as many behind; but the men would go at
their own rate, every man leading his horse. The Spaniards,
observing their manner of marching, had laid an ambush
about a mile from the town, which they managed with such
success, that falling on our body of men, who were guarding
the corn to the canoes, they killed them every one. Captain
Swan, hearing the report of their guns, ordered his men, who
were then in the town with him, to march out to their
assistance; but some opposed him, despising their enemies,
till two of the Spaniards' horses that had lost their riders,
came galloping into the town in a great fright, both bridled
and saddled, with each a pair of holsters by their sides, and
one had a carbine newly discharged; which was an apparent
token that our men had been engaged, and that by men better
armed than they imagined they should meet with. Therefore
Captain Swan immediately marched out of the town, and his
men all followed him; and when he came to the place where
the engagement had been, he saw all his men that went out
in the morning lying dead. They were stripped, and so cut
and mangled, that he scarce knew one man. Captain Swan
had not more men then with him, than those were who lay
dead before him, yet the Spaniards never came to oppose
him, but kept at a great distance; for 'tis probable, the
Spaniards had not cut off so many men of ours, but with the
loss of a great many of their own. So he marched down to
the canoes, and came aboard the ship with the maize that was
already in the canoes. We had about fifty men killed, and
among the rest, my ingenious friend Mr Ringrose was one,
who wrote that part of the *History of the Buccaneers*, which
relates to Captain Sharp. He was at this time Cape Merchant,
or Supercargo* of Captain Swan's ship. He had no mind to
this voyage; but was necessitated to engage in it or starve.

* Officer responsible for commercial matters and in charge of the cargo.

DESPERATE DISEASES . . .

*After the catastrophe in Santa Pecaque, the survivors put to sea,
anchoring next at María Magdalena, the middle one of the three
Islas Marías, sixty miles from the Mexican coast. 'Here Captain
Swan proposed to go into the East Indies. Many were well pleased
with the voyage; but some thought, such was their ignorance, that he
would carry them out of the world.' In the original manuscript
Dampier wrote, 'It was ever a design between Captain Swan and
myself to promote it and use our utmost endeavour to persuade the
unthinking rabble to it' – a rare self-revealing flourish that he later
censored. But of more immediate concern at that moment was his
deteriorating health.*

I was taken sick of a fever and ague that afterwards turned to
a dropsy, which I laboured under a long time after; and many
of our men died of this distemper, though our surgeons used
their greatest skill to preserve their lives. The dropsy is a
general distemper on this coast, and the natives say, that the
best remedy they can find for it, is the stone or cod of an
alligator (of which they have four, one near each leg, within
the flesh) pulverised and drunk in water. This receipt we also
found mentioned in an almanack made at Mexico: I would
have tried it, but we found no alligators here, though there
are several . . . [Instead] I was laid and covered all but my
head in the hot sand: I endured it near half an hour, and then
was taken out and laid to sweat in a tent. I did sweat exceedingly while I was in the sand, and I do believe it did me much
good, for I grew well soon after.*

ACROSS THE PACIFIC

*Having convinced his crew that riches lay ahead, Captain Swan
embarked for the East Indies, with Dampier apparently as navi-*

* Dampier's ailment was presumably not epidemic dropsy, first identified in 1877, but may have been beri-beri, caused by a deficiency of
thiamine (Vitamin B1) and also producing dangerous accumulations of
serous fluid. Dampier's desperate remedy, used also to counter scurvy,
sometimes proved fatal: Vitus Bering, of Strait and Sea, died similarly
immersed in 1741.

gator. The voyage, according to Dampier's calculations, covered 7,323 miles and took fifty-two days, which was sixteen days shorter than Drake's Pacific crossing in 1579.

I have given an account of the resolutions we took of going over to the East Indies. But having more calmly considered on the length of our voyage, from hence to Guam, which is the first place that we could touch at, and there also being not certain to find provisions, most of our men were almost daunted at the thoughts of it; for we had not sixty days' provision, at a little more than half a pint of maize a day for each man, and no other provision, except three meals of salted jewfish;* and we had a great many rats aboard, which we could not hinder from eating part of our maize. Beside, the great distance between Cape Corrientes and Guam, which is variously set down. The Spaniards, who have the greatest reason to know best, make it to be between 2,300 and 2,400 leagues; our books also reckon it differently, between 90° and 100°, which all comes short indeed of 2,000 leagues; but even that was a voyage enough to frighten us, considering our scanty provisions. Captain Swan, to encourage his men to go with him, persuaded them that the English books did give the best account of the distance; his reasons were many, although but weak. He urged among the rest, that Cavendish and Sir Francis Drake did run it in less than fifty days,† and that he did not question but that our ships were better sailers, than those which were built in that age, and that he did not doubt to get there in little more than forty days; this being the best time in the year for breezes, which undoubtedly is the reason that the Spaniards set out from Acapulco about this time; and that although they are sixty days in their voyage, it is because they are great ships deep laden, and very heavy sailers; besides, they, wanting nothing, are in no great haste in their way, but sail with a great deal of their usual

---

* Dampier writes earlier: 'The jewfish is a very good fish and I judge so called by the English because it has scales and fins, therefore a clean fish according to the Levitical law, and the Jews at Jamaica buy them and eat them very freely. It is a very large fish, shaped much like a cod.'
† Cavendish took forty-five days; Drake, sixty-eight.

caution. And when they come near the island Guam, they lie by in the night for a week, before they make land. In prudence we also should have contrived to lie by in the night when we came near land, for otherwise we might have run ashore, or have out-sailed the islands, and lost sight of them before morning. But our bold adventurers seldom proceed with such wariness when in any straits.

But of all Captain Swan's arguments, that which prevailed most with them was, his promising them, as I have said, to cruize off Manila. So he and his men being now agreed, and they encouraged with the hope of gain, which works its way through all difficulties, we set out from Cape Corrientes, 31 March 1686. We were two ships in company, Captain Swan's ship and a bark commanded under Captain Swan, by Captain Teat, and we were 150 men, a hundred aboard the ship, and fifty aboard the bark, besides slaves, as I said.

We had a small land-wind at ENE which carried us three or four leagues, then the sea-wind came at WNW a fresh gale, so we steered away south-west. By six o'clock in the evening we were about nine leagues south-west from the cape, then we met a land-wind which blew fresh all night; and the next morning about ten o'clock we had the sea-breeze at NNE so that at noon we were thirty leagues from the cape. It blew a fresh gale of wind which carried us off into the true Trade Wind, for although the constant sea-breeze near the shore is at WNW yet the true Trade off at sea, when you are clear of the land-winds, is at ENE. At first we had it at NNE so it came about northerly, and then to the east as we run off. At 250 leagues' distance from the shore we had it at ENE and there it stood till we came within forty leagues of Guam. When we had eaten up our three meals of salted jewfish, in so many days' time we had nothing but our small allowance of maize.

After 31 March we made great runs every day, having very fair clear weather, and a fresh Trade Wind, which we made use of with all our sails, and we made many good observations of the sun. At our first setting out, we steered into the latitude 13°, which is near the latitude of Guam; then we steered west, keeping in that latitude. By that time we had sailed twenty days, our men, seeing we had made such great runs, and the wind like to continue, repined because they were kept at such short allowance.* Captain Swan endeavoured to persuade them to have a little patience; yet nothing but an augmentation of their daily allowance would appease them. Captain Swan, though with much reluctance, gave way to a small enlargement of our commons, for now we had about ten spoonfuls of boiled maize a man, once a day, whereas before we had but eight: I do believe that this short allowance did me a great deal of good, though others were weakened by it; for I found that my strength increased, and my dropsy wore off. Yet I drank three times every twenty-four hours; but many of our men did not drink in nine or ten days' time, and some not in twelve days; one of our men did not drink in seventeen days' time, and said he was not dry when he did drink; yet he made water every day more or less. One of our men in the midst of these hardships was found guilty of theft, and condemned for the same to have three blows from each man in the ship, with a two-inch-and-a-half rope on his bare back. Captain Swan began first, and struck with a good will; whose example was followed by all of us.

It was very strange, that in all this voyage we did not see one fish, not so much as a flying-fish, nor any sort of fowl, but at one time, when we were by my account 4,975 miles west from Cape Corrientes, then we saw a great number of boobies, which we supposed came from some rocks not far from us, which were mentioned in some of our sea-charts, but we did not see them.

After we had run the 1,900 leagues by our reckoning, which made the English account to Guam, the men began to murmur against Captain Swan, for persuading them to come this voyage; but he gave them fair words, and told them that the Spanish account might probably be the truest,

* 'The kettle was boiled but once a day,' says the original manuscript, 'and there was no occasion to call the men to victuals. All hands came up to see the quartermaster share it, and he had need to be exact. We had two dogs and two cats on board, and they likewise had a small allowance given them, and they waited with as much eagerness to see it shared as we did.'

and seeing the gale was likely to continue, a short time longer would end our troubles.

As we drew nigh the island, we met with some small rain, and the clouds settling in the west were an apparent token that we were not far from land; for in these climates, between or near the tropics, where the Trade Wind blows constantly, the clouds which fly swift over head, yet seem near the limb* of the horizon to hang without much motion or alteration, where the land is near. I have often taken notice of it, especially if it is high land, for you shall then have the clouds hang about it without any visible motion.

The 20 May, our bark being about three leagues ahead of our ship, sailed over a rocky shoal, on which there was but four fathom water, and abundance of fish swimming about the rocks. They imagined by this that the land was not far off; so they clapped on a wind with the bark's head to the north, and, being past the shoal, lay by for us. When we came up with them, Captain Teat came aboard us, and related what he had seen. We were then in latitude 12° 55', steering west. The island Guam is laid down in latitude 13° N. by the Spaniards, who are masters of it, keeping it as a baiting-place† as they go to the Philippine Islands. Therefore we clapped on a wind and stood to northward, being somewhat troubled and doubtful whether we were right, because there is no shoal laid down in the Spanish drafts about the island Guam. At four o'clock, to our great joy, we saw the island Guam, at about eight leagues' distance.

It was well for Captain Swan that we got sight of it before our provision was spent, of which we had but enough for three days more; for, as I was afterwards informed, the men had contrived,‡ first to kill Captain Swan and eat him when the victuals was gone, and after him all of us who were accessory in promoting the undertaking this voyage. This made Captain Swan say to me after our arrival at Guam, 'Ah! Dampier, you would have made them but a poor meal'; for I was as lean as the captain was lusty and fleshy. The wind

---

* Limb: the utmost edge. A term used in astronomy.
† Baiting-place: provisioning place.
‡ plotted.

was at ENE and the land bore at NNE, therefore we stood
to the northward, till we brought the island to bear east, and
then we turned to get in to an anchor.

CHAPTER
FOUR

COCONUT AND BREADFRUIT

Dampier's accounts of the coconut and breadfruit on the island of Guam have become justly well known and remain models of their kind. In A Voyage to the South Sea Undertaken by Command of His Majesty, for the Purpose of Conveying the Bread-Fruit Tree to the West Indies in His Majesty's Ship The Bounty *(1792), William Bligh quotes Dampier's breadfruit passage in full to help explain the origins of his ill-starred mission: some prominent West Indian planters and Sir Joseph Banks, President of the Royal Society, had deduced that breadfruit was the ideal food for slaves. But on the page preceding his description Dampier writes of the coconut, 'Yet this tree, that is of such great use, and esteemed so much in the East Indies, is scarce regarded in the West Indies, for want of the knowledge of the benefit which it may produce. And 'tis partly for the sake of my countrymen in our American plantations that I have spoken so largely of it.' So the coconut was already growing in the West Indies! After Bligh eventually delivered the breadfruit to Jamaica in February 1793, the natives sampled it and found it unappetising. A closer reading of Dampier might have spared them the ordeal, opened their eyes to the coconut's potential – and avoided a mutiny.*

The coconut trees grow by the sea, on the western side in great groves, three or four miles in length, and a mile or two broad. This tree is in shape like the cabbage tree, and at a distance they are not to be known each from other, only the coconut tree is fuller of branches; but the cabbage tree generally is much higher, though the coconut trees in some places are very high.

The nut or fruit grows at the head of the tree, among the branches and in clusters, ten or twelve in a cluster. The branch to which they grow is about the bigness of a man's arm, and as long, running small towards the end. It is of a yellow colour, full of knots, and very tough. The nut is generally bigger than a man's head. The outer rind is near two inches thick, before you come to the shell; the shell itself is black, thick, and very hard. The kernel in some nuts is near an inch thick, sticking to the inside of the shell clear round, leaving a hollow in the middle of it, which contains about a pint, more or less, according to the bigness of the nut, for some are much bigger than others.

This cavity is full of sweet, delicate, wholesome and refreshing water. While the nut is growing, all the inside is full of this water, without any kernel at all; but as the nut grows towards its maturity, the kernel begins to gather and settle round on the inside of the shell, and is soft like cream; and as the nut ripens, it increases in substance and becomes hard. The ripe kernel is sweet enough, but very hard to digest, therefore seldom eaten, unless by strangers, who know not the effects of it; but while it is young and soft like pap, some men will eat it, scraping it out with a spoon, after they have drunk the water that was within it. I like the water best when the nut is almost ripe, for it is then sweetest and briskest.

When these nuts are ripe and gathered, the outside rind becomes of a brown rusty colour; so that one would think that they were dead and dry; yet they will sprout out like onions, after they have been hanging in the sun three or four months, or thrown about in a house or ship, and if planted afterward in the earth, they will grow up to a tree. Before they thus sprout out, there is a small spongy round knob grows in the inside, which we call an apple. This at first is no bigger than the top of one's finger, but increases daily, sucking up the water till it is grown so big as to fill up the cavity of the coconut, and then it begins to sprout forth. By this time the nut that was hard, begins to grow oily and soft, thereby giving passage to the sprout that springs from the apple, which nature has so contrived, that it points to the hole in the shell (of which there are three, till it grows ripe, just where it's fastened by its stalk to the tree; but one of these holes remain open, even when it is ripe), through which it creeps and spreads forth its branches. You may let these teeming nuts sprout out a foot and half, or two foot high before you plant them, for they will grow a great while like an onion out of their own substance.

Beside the liquor or water in the fruit, there is also a sort of wine drawn from the tree called toddy, which looks like whey. It is sweet and very pleasant, but it is to be drunk within twenty-four hours after it is drawn, for afterwards it grows sour. Those that have a great many trees, draw a spirit from the sour wine, called arrack. Arrack is distilled also from rice, and other things in the East Indies; but none is so much esteemed for making punch as this sort, made of toddy, or the sap of the coconut tree, for it makes most delicate punch; but it must have a dash of brandy to hearten it, because this arrack is not strong enough to make good punch of itself.* This sort of liquor is chiefly used about Goa; and therefore it has the name of Goa arrack. The way of drawing the toddy from the tree is by cutting the top of a branch that would bear nuts; but before it has any fruit; and from thence the liquor which was to feed its fruit, distils into the hole of a calabash that is hung upon it.

This branch continues running almost as long as the fruit would have been growing, and then it dries away. The tree has usually three fruitful branches, which if they be all tapped thus, then the tree bears no fruit that year; but if one or two only be tapped, the other will bear fruit all the while. The liquor which is thus drawn is emptied out of the calabash duly morning and evening, so long as it continues running, and is sold every morning and evening in most towns in the East Indies, and great gain is produced from it even this way; but those that distil it and make arrack, reap the greatest profit. There is also great profit made of the fruit, both of the nut and the shell.

* Nevertheless, Lionel Wafer records that some of his mates who drank about twenty gallons of coconut liquid 'could neither go nor stand. Nor could they return on board the ship without the help of those who had not been partakers in the frolic; nor did they recover in under four or five days' time.'

The kernel is much used in making broth. When the nut is dry, they take off the husk, and giving two good blows on the middle of the nut, it breaks in two equal parts, letting the water fall on the ground; then with a small iron rasp made for the purpose, the kernel or nut is rasped out clean, which being put into a little fresh water, makes it become white as milk. In this milky water, they boil a fowl, or any other sort of flesh, and it makes very savoury broth. English seamen put this water into boiled rice, which they eat instead of rice-milk, carrying nuts purposely to sea with them. This they learnt from the natives.

But the greatest use of the kernel is to make oil, both for burning and for frying. The way to make the oil is to grate or rasp the kernel, and steep it in fresh water; then boil it, and scum off the oil at top as it rises: but the nuts that make the oil ought to be a long time gathered, so as that the kernel may be turning soft and oily.

The shell of this nut is used in the East Indies for cups, dishes, ladles, spoons, and in a manner for all eating and drinking vessels. Well-shaped nuts are often brought home to Europe, and much esteemed. The husk of the shell is of great use to make cables; for the dry husk is full of small strings and threads, which, being beaten, become soft, and the other substance which was mixed among it falls away like saw-dust, leaving only the strings. These are afterwards spun into long yarns, and twisted up into balls for convenience: and many of these rope-yarns joined together make good cables. This manufactory is chiefly used at the Maldive Islands, and the threads sent in balls into all places that trade thither, purposely for to make cables. I made a cable at Achin [Banda Aceh] with some of it. These are called coir cables; they will last very well. But there is another sort of coir cables (as they are called) that are black, and more strong and lasting; and are made of strings that grow like horsehair, at the heads of certain trees, almost like the coconut tree. This sort comes most from the island Timor. In the South Seas the Spaniards do make oakum to caulk their ships, with the husk of the coconut, which is more serviceable than that made of hemp, and they say it will never rot. I have been told

by Captain Knox,* who wrote the *Relation of Ceylon*, that in
some places of India they make a sort of coarse cloth of the
husk of the coconut, which is used for sails. I myself have
seen a sort of coarse sailcloth made of such a kind of substance; but whether the same or no I know not.

I have been the longer on this subject, to give the reader a
particular account of the use and profit of a vegetable, which
is possibly of all others the most generally serviceable to the
conveniences, as well as the necessities of human life. Yet
this tree, that is of such great use, and esteemed so much in
the East Indies, is scarce regarded in the West Indies, for
want of the knowledge of the benefit which it may produce. And 'tis partly for the sake of my countrymen, in our
American plantations, that I have spoken so largely of it.
For the hot climates there are a very proper soil for it: and
indeed it is so hardy, both in the raising it, and when grown,
that it will thrive as well in dry sandy ground as in rich land.
I have found them growing very well in low sandy islands
(on the west of Sumatra) that are overflowed with the sea
every Spring tide; and though the nuts there are not very
big, yet this is no loss, for the kernel is thick and sweet; and
the milk, or water, in the inside, is more pleasant and sweet
than of the nuts that grow in rich ground, which are commonly large indeed, but not very sweet. These at Guam grow
in dry ground, are of a middle size, and I think the sweetest
that I did ever taste. Thus much for the coconut . . .

The breadfruit (as we call it) grows on a large tree, as big
and high as our largest apple trees. It has a spreading head
full of branches, and dark leaves. The fruit grows on the
boughs like apples: it is as big as a penny loaf, when wheat is
at five shillings the bushel. It is of a round shape, and has a
thick tough rind. When the fruit is ripe, it is yellow and soft,
and the taste is sweet and pleasant. The natives of this island
use it for bread: they gather it when full grown, while it is
green and hard; then they bake it in an oven, which scorches

* Robert Knox (1641–1720), author of *An Historical Relation of Ceylon*
(1681), was captive in Ceylon (now Sri Lanka) for nineteen years before
escaping. Like Dampier, with whom he was acquainted, he was the
source of several passages in *Robinson Crusoe* and other works by Daniel
Defoe.

the rind and makes it black: but they scrape off the outside black crust, and there remains a tender thin crust, and the inside is soft, tender and white, like the crumb of a penny loaf. There is neither seed nor stone in the inside, but all is of a pure substance like bread: it must be eaten new, for if it is kept above twenty-four hours, it becomes dry, and eats harsh and choky; but 'tis very pleasant before it is too stale. This fruit lasts in season eight months in the year; during which time the natives eat no other sort of food of bread-kind. I did never see of this fruit anywhere but here. The natives told us, that there is plenty of this fruit growing on the rest of the Ladrone [Mariana] Islands; and I did never hear of any of it anywhere else.

MINDANAO AND ITS PEOPLE

From Guam the buccaneers sailed to Cotabato on the island of Mindanao in the Philippines. 'The inhabitants of Mindanao being then, as we were told (though falsely), at war with the Spaniards, our men, who, it should seem, were very squeamish of plundering without licence, derived hopes from thence of getting a commission there from the prince of the island to plunder the Spanish ships about Manila.' They reached Cotabato on 18 July 1686, but, succumbing to its delights, could not wrench themselves away until 14 January 1687. Corpulent Captain Swan sank slowly into blissful torpor. The Sultan of Mindanao hoped the buccaneers would settle in his kingdom and protect him from the Dutch, so the captain was fêted with ceaseless feasts and dancing girls. Since Swan had acquired wealth, principally by defrauding his last employers, he began to essay a princely style himself and, says Dampier, 'his two trumpeters sounded all the time that he was at dinner'. The Sultan's brother, devious Rajah Laut, also patronised the buccaneers, the bulk of whom followed Swan's example and gave themselves up to pleasure. Dampier was an exception, learning Malayan and using the six months to research and prepare his first extended description of a country and its people.

The Mindanaoans properly so called, are men of mean statures; small limbs, straight bodies, and little heads. Their faces are oval, their foreheads flat, with black small eyes, short low noses, pretty large mouths; their lips thin and red, their teeth black, yet very sound, their hair black and straight, the colour of their skin tawny, but inclining to a brighter yellow than some other Indians, especially the women. They have a custom to wear their thumbnails very long, especially that on their left thumb, for they do never cut it but scrape it often. They are indued with good natural wits, are ingenious, nimble, and active when they are minded; but generally very lazy and thievish, and will not work except forced by hunger. This laziness is natural to most Indians; but these people's laziness seems rather to proceed not so much from their natural inclinations, as from the severity of their prince, of whom they stand in awe: for he dealing with them very arbitrarily, and taking from them what they get, this damps their industry, so they never strive to have anything but from hand to mouth. They are generally proud, and walk very stately. They are civil enough to strangers, and will easily be acquainted with them, and entertain them with great freedom; but they are implacable to their enemies, and very revengeful if they are injured, frequently poisoning secretly those that have affronted them.

They wear but few clothes; their heads are circled with a short turban, fringed or laced at both ends; it goes once about the head, and is tied in a knot, the laced ends hanging down. They wear frocks and breeches, but no stockings nor shoes.

The women are fairer than the men; and their hair is black and long, which they tie in a knot, that hangs behind their heads. They are more round-visaged than the men, and generally well featured; only their noses are very small, and so low between their eyes, that in some of the female children the rising that should be between the eyes is scarce discernible; neither is there any sensible rising in their foreheads. At a distance they appear very well; but, being nigh, these impediments are very obvious. They have very small limbs. They wear but two garments; a frock, and a sort of petticoat; the petticoat is only a piece of cloth, sewn both ends together: but it is made two foot too big for their waists, so that they may wear either end uppermost: that part that comes up to their waist, because it is so much too big, they gather it in their hands, and twist it till it fits close to their waists, tucking in the twisted part between their waist and the edge of the petticoat, which keeps it close. The frock fits loose about them, and reaches down a little below the waist. The sleeves are a great deal longer than their arms, and so small at the end that their hands will scarce go through. Being on, the sleeve sits in folds about the wrist, wherein they take great pride.

The better sort of people have their garments made of long cloth; but the ordinary sort wear cloth made of plantain-tree, which they call *saggen*, by which name they call the plantain. They have neither stocking or shoe, and the women have very small feet.

The women are very desirous of the company of strangers, especially of white men; and doubtless would be very familiar, if the custom of the country did not debar them from that freedom, which seems coveted by them. Yet from the highest to the lowest they are allowed liberty to converse with, or treat strangers in the sight of their husbands.

There is a kind of begging custom at Mindanao, that I have not met elsewhere with in all my travels; and which I believe is owing to the little trade they have; which is thus: when strangers arrive here, the Mindanao men will come aboard, and invite them to their houses, and enquire who has a comrade (which word I believe they have from the Spaniards), or a *pagally*, and who has not. A comrade is a familiar male friend; a *pagally* is an innocent platonic friend of the other sex. All strangers are in a manner obliged to accept of this acquaintance and familiarity, which must be first purchased with a small present, and afterwards confirmed with some gift or other to continue the acquaintance: and as often as the stranger goes ashore, he is welcome to his comrade or *pagally*'s house, where he may be entertained for his money, to eat, drink, or sleep; and complimented, as often as he comes ashore, with tobacco and betel-nut, which is all the entertainment he must expect gratis. The richest men's wives are allowed the freedom to converse with her *pagally* in public, and may give or receive presents from him. Even the Sultan's and the general's wives, who are always cooped up, will yet look out of their cages when a stranger passes by, and demand of him if he wants a *pagally*: and to invite him to their friendship, will send a present of tobacco and betel-nut to him by their servants.

The chiefest city on this island [Cotabato] is called by the same name of Mindanao. It is seated on the south side of the island, in latitude 7° 20' N. on the banks of a small river, about two mile from the sea. The manner of building is somewhat strange: yet generally used in this part of the East Indies. Their houses are all built on posts, about fourteen, sixteen, eighteen, or twenty foot high. These posts are bigger or less, according to the intended magnificence of the super-structure. They have but one floor, but many partitions or rooms, and a ladder or stairs to go up out of the streets. The roof is large, and covered with palmetto or palm-leaves. So there is a clear passage like a piazza (but a filthy one) under the house. Some of the poorer people that keep ducks or hens, have a fence made round the posts of their houses, with a door to go in and out; and this under-room serves for no other use. Some use this place for the common draught [closet] of their houses, but building mostly close by the river in all parts of the Indies, they make the river receive all the filth of their house; and at the time of the land-floods, all is washed very clean.

The Sultan's house is much bigger than any of the rest. It stands on about 180 great posts or trees, a great deal higher than the common building, with great broad stairs made to go up. In the first room he has about twenty iron guns, all Saker and Minion,* placed on field-carriages. The general and other great men have some guns also in their houses. About twenty paces from the Sultan's house there is a small low house, built purposely for the reception of ambassadors or merchant strangers. This also stands on posts, but the floor is not raised above three or four foot above the ground, and is neatly matted purposely for the Sultan and his council

* The Saker and the Minion were cannons of a little less than medium size.

to sit on; for they use no chairs, but sit cross-legged like tailors on the floor.

The common food at Mindanao is rice, or sago, and a small fish or two. The better sort eat buffalo, or fowls ill dressed, and abundance of rice with it. They use no spoons to eat their rice, but every man takes a handful out of the platter, and by wetting his hand in water, that it may not stick to his hand, squeezes it into a lump, as hard as possibly he can make it, and then crams it into his mouth. They all strive to make these lumps as big as their mouth can receive them; and seem to vie with each other, and glory in taking in the biggest lump; so that sometimes they almost choke themselves. They always wash after meals, or if they touch anything that is unclean; for which reason they spend abundance of water in their houses. This water, with the washing of their dishes, and what other filth they make, they pour down near their fireplace: for their chambers are not boarded, but floored with split bamboos, like lathe, so that the water presently falls underneath their dwelling rooms, where it breeds maggots, and makes a prodigious stink. Besides this filthiness, the sick people ease themselves, and make water in their chambers; there being a small hole made purposely in the floor, to let it drop through. But healthy sound people commonly ease themselves, and make water in the river. For that reason you shall always see abundance of people of both sexes in the river, from morning till night; some easing themselves, others washing their bodies or clothes. If they come into the river purposely to wash their clothes, they strip and stand naked till they have done; then put them on, and march out again: both men and women take great delight in swimming, and washing themselves, being bred to it from their infancy. I do believe it is very wholesome to wash mornings and evenings in these hot countries, at least three or four days in the week: for I did use myself to it when I lived afterwards at Bengkulu,* and found it very refreshing and comfortable. It is very good for those that have fluxes to wash and stand in the river mornings and evenings. I speak it experimentally; for I was brought very low with that

* On the south-west coast of Sumatera.

distemper at Achin; but by washing constantly mornings and evenings I found great benefit, and was quickly cured by it.

In the city of Mindanao they speak two languages indifferently; their own Mindanao language, and the Malay: but in other parts of the island they speak only their proper language, having little commerce abroad. They have schools, and instruct children to read and write, and bring them up in the Mahometan religion. Therefore many of the words, especially their prayers, are in Arabic; and many of the words of civility the same as in Turkey; and especially when they meet in the morning, or take leave of each other, they express themselves in that language.

Many of the old people, both men and women, can speak Spanish, for the Spaniards were formerly settled among them, and had several forts on this island; and then they sent two friars to the city, to convert the Sultan of Mindanao and his people. At that time these people began to learn Spanish, and the Spaniards encroached on them, and endeavoured to bring them into subjection; and probably before this time had brought them all under their yoke, if they themselves had not been drawn off from this island to Manila, to resist the Chinese, who threatened to invade them there. When the Spaniards were gone, the old Sultan of Mindanao, father to the present, in whose time it was, razed and demolished their forts, brought away their guns, and sent away the friars; and since that time will not suffer the Spaniards to settle on the islands.

They are now most afraid of the Dutch, being sensible how they have enslaved many of the neighbouring islands. For that reason they have a long time desired the English to settle among them, and have offered them any convenient place to build a fort in, as the general himself told us; giving this reason, that they do not find the English so encroaching as the Dutch or Spanish. The Dutch are no less jealous of their admitting the English, for they are sensible what detriment it would be to them if the English should settle here.

There are but few tradesmen at the city of Mindanao. The chiefest trades are goldsmiths, blacksmiths, and carpenters.

There are but two or three goldsmiths; these will work in gold or silver, and make anything that you desire: but they have no shop furnished with ware ready-made for sale. Here are several blacksmiths who work very well, considering the tools that they work with. Their bellows are much different from ours. They are made of a wooden cylinder, the trunk of a tree, about three foot long, bored hollow like a pump, and set upright on the ground, on which the fire itself is made. Near the lower end there is a small hole, in the side of the trunk next the fire, made to receive a pipe, through which the wind is driven to the fire by a great bunch of fine feathers fastened to one end of the stick, which closing up the inside of the cylinder, drives the air out of the cylinder through the pipe: two of these trunks or cylinders are placed so nigh together, that a man standing between them may work them both at once alternately, one with each hand. They have neither vice nor anvil, but a great hard stone or a piece of an old gun, to hammer upon: yet they will perform their work, making both common utensils and iron-works for ships to admiration. They work altogether with charcoal. Every man almost is a carpenter, for they can work with the axe and adze. Their axe is but small, and so made that they can take it out of the helve, and by turning it make an adze of it. They have no saws, but when they make plank, they split the tree in two, and make a plank of each part, planing it with the axe and adze. This requires much pains, and takes up a great deal of time; but they work cheap, and the goodness of the plank thus hewed, which has its grain preserved entire, makes amends for their cost and pains.

They build good and serviceable ships or barks for the sea, some for trade, others for pleasure; and some ships of war. Their trading vessels they send chiefly to Manila. Thither they transport beeswax, which I think is the only commodity, besides gold, that they vend there. The inhabitants of the city of Mindanao get a great deal of beeswax themselves: but the greatest quantity they purchase is of the Mountaneers,* from whom they also get the gold which

* Mountain people, known as Hilanoones, living in the middle of the island. Today these are the Tiruray and T'boli tribes.

they send to Manila; and with these they buy there calicoes, muslins, and China silk. They send sometimes their barks to Borneo and other islands; but what they transport thither, or import from thence, I know not. The Dutch come hither in sloops from Ternate and Tidore,* and buy rice, beeswax and tobacco: for here is a great deal of tobacco grows on this island, more than in any island or country in the East Indies that I know of, Manila only excepted. It is an excellent sort of tobacco; but these people have not the art of managing this trade to their best advantage, as the Spaniards have at Manila. I do believe the seeds were first brought hither from Manila by the Spaniards, and even thither, in all probability, from America: the difference between the Mindanao and Manila tobacco is, that the Mindanao tobacco is of a darker colour; and the leaf larger and grosser than the Manila tobacco, being propagated or planted in a fatter soil. The Manila tobacco is of a bright yellow colour, of an indifferent size, not strong, but pleasant to smoke. The Spaniards at Manila are very curious about this tobacco, having a peculiar way of making it up neatly in the leaf. For they take two little sticks, each about a foot long, and flat, and placing the stalks of the tobacco leaves in a row, forty or fifty of them between the two sticks, they bind them hard together, so that the leaves hang dangling down. One of these bundles is sold for a riyal at Fort St George:† but you may have ten or twelve pound of tobacco at Mindanao for a riyal; and the tobacco is as good, or rather better than the Manila tobacco, but they have not that vent for it as the Spaniards have.

The Mindanao people are much troubled with a sort of leprosy, the same as we observed at Guam. This distemper runs with a dry scurf all over their bodies, and causes great itching in those that have it, making them frequently scratch and scrub themselves, which raises the outer skin in small whitish flakes, like the scales of little fish when they are raised on end with a knife. This makes their skin extraordinary rough, and in some you shall see broad white spots in several

* Two small Maluku islands off the west coast of Halmahera.
† In Madras.

parts of their body.* I judge such have had it, but were cured; for their skins were smooth, and I did not perceive them to scrub themselves: yet I have learnt from their own mouths that these spots were from this distemper. Whether they use any means to cure themselves, or whether it goes away of itself, I know not: but I did not perceive that they made any great matter of it, for they did never refrain any company for it; none of our people caught it of them, for we were afraid of it, and kept off. They are sometimes troubled with the smallpox, but their ordinary distempers are fevers, agues, fluxes, with great pains, and gripings in their guts. The country affords a great many drugs and medicinal herbs, whose virtues are not unknown to some of them that pretend to cure the sick.

The Mindanao men have many wives: but what ceremonies are used when they marry I know not. There is commonly a great feast made by the bridegroom to entertain his friends, and the most part of the night is spent in mirth.

The Sultan is absolute in his power over all his subjects. He is but a poor prince; for as I mentioned before, they have but little trade, and therefore cannot be rich. If the Sultan understands that any man has money, if it be but twenty dollars, which is a great matter among them, he will send to borrow so much money, pretending urgent occasions for it; and they dare not deny him. Sometimes he will send to sell one thing or another that he has to dispose of, to such whom he knows to have money, and they must buy it, and give him his price; and if afterwards he has occasion for the same thing, he must have it if he sends for it. He is but a little man, between fifty or sixty years old, and by relation very good-natured, but overruled by those about him. He has a queen, and keeps about twenty-nine women, or wives more, in whose company he spends most of his time. He has one daughter by his Sultaness or queen, and a great many sons and daughters by the rest. These walk about the streets, and would be always begging things of us; but it is reported that the young princess is kept in a room, and never stirs out,

* John Masefield suggests this might have been 'a form of herpes due to excessive eating of certain kinds of shellfish'.

and that she did never see any man but her father and Rajah Laut her uncle, being then about fourteen years old.

When the Sultan visits his friends he is carried in a small couch on four men's shoulders, with eight or ten armed men to guard him; but he never goes far this way; for the country is very woody, and they have but little paths, which renders it the less commodious. When he takes his pleasure by water, he carries some of his wives along with him. The proas that are built for this purpose, are large enough to entertain fifty or sixty persons or more. The hull is neatly built, with a round head and stern, and over the hull there is a small slight house built with bamboo; the sides are made up with split bamboo, about four foot high, with little windows in them of the same, to open and shut at their pleasure. The roof is almost flat, neatly thatched with palmetto leaves. This house is divided into two or three small partitions or chambers, one particularly for himself. This is neatly matted underneath and round the sides; and there is a carpet and pillows for him to sleep on. The second room is for his women, much like the former. The third is for the servants, who tend them with tobacco and betel-nut; for they are always chewing or smoking. The fore and afterparts of the vessel are for the mariners to sit and row . . .

The Sultan has a brother called Rajah Laut, a brave man. He is the second man in the kingdom. All strangers that come hither to trade must make their address to him, for all sea-affairs belong to him. He licenses strangers to import or export any commodity, and 'tis by his permission that the natives themselves are suffered to trade: nay, the very fishermen must take a permit from him; so that there is no man can come into the river or go out but by his leave. He is two or three years younger than the Sultan, and a little man like him. He has eight women, by some of whom he has issue. He has only one son, about twelve or fourteen years old, who was circumcised while we were there. His eldest son died a little before we came hither, for whom he was still in great heaviness. If he had lived a little longer he should have married the young princess; but whether this second son must have her I know not, for I did never hear any discourse about it. Rajah Laut is a very sharp man; he speaks and writes Spanish, which he learned in his youth. He has by often conversing with strangers, got a great sight into the customs of other nations, and by Spanish books has some knowledge of Europe. He is general of the Mindanaoans, and is accounted an expert soldier, and a very stout man; and the women in their dances, sing many songs in his praise.

The Sultan of Mindanao sometimes makes war with his neighbours the Mountaneers or Alfoores.* Their weapons are swords, lances, and some krisses. The kris† is a small thing like a bayonet, which they always wear in war or peace, at work or play, from the greatest of them to the poorest, or the meanest persons. They do never meet each other so as to have a pitched battle, but they build small works or forts of timber, wherein they plant little guns, and lie in sight of each other two or three months, skirmishing every day in small parties, and sometimes surprising a breast-work; and whatever side is like to be worsted, if they have no probability to escape by flight, they sell their lives as dear as they can; for there is seldom any quarter given, but the conqueror cuts and hacks his enemies to pieces.

The religion of these people is Mahometanism; Friday is their Sabbath; but I did never see any difference that they make between this day and any other day; only the Sultan himself goes then to the mosque twice. Rajah Laut never goes to the mosque, but prays at certain hours, eight or ten times in a day; wherever he is, he is very punctual to his canonical hours, and if he be aboard will go ashore, on purpose to pray. For no business nor company hinders him from this duty. Whether he is at home or abroad, in a house or in the field, he leaves all his company, and goes about a hundred yards off, and there kneels down to his devotion. He first kisses the ground, then prays aloud, and divers time in his prayers he kisses the ground, and does the same when he leaves off. His servants and his wives and children talk and sing, or play how they please all the time, but himself is very

---

* The Alfoores were another tribe on the island.
† Kris: a Malay dagger with a scalloped blade and, occasionally, a poisoned point.

serious. The meaner sort of people have little devotion: I did never see any of them at their prayers, or go into a mosque.

In the Sultan's mosque there is a great drum with but one head called a gong; which is instead of a clock. This gong is beaten at twelve o'clock, at three, six, and nine; a man being appointed for that service. He has a stick as big as a man's arm, with a great knob at the end, bigger than a man's fist, made with cotton, bound fast with small cords: with this he strikes the gong as hard as he can, about twenty strokes; beginning to strike leisurely the first five or six strokes; then he strikes faster, and at last strikes as fast as he can; and then he strikes again slower and slower so many more strokes: thus he rises and falls three times, and then leaves off till three hours after. This is done night and day.

They circumcise the males at eleven or twelve years of age, or older; and many are circumcised at once. This ceremony is performed with a great deal of solemnity. There had been no circumcision for some years before our being here; and then there was one for Rajah Laut's son. They choose to have a general circumcision when the Sultan, or general, or some other great person has a son fit to be circumcised; for with him a great many more are circumcised. There is notice given about eight or ten days before for all men to appear in arms, and great preparation is made against the solemn day. In the morning before the boys are circumcised, presents are sent to the father of the child that keeps the feast; which, as I said before, is either the Sultan, or some great person: and about ten or eleven o'clock the Mahometan priest does his office. He takes hold of the foreskin with two sticks, and with a pair of scissors snips it off. After this most of the men, both in city and country, being in arms before the house, begin to act as if they were engaged with an enemy, having such arms as I described. Only one acts at a time, the rest make a great ring of two or three hundred yards round about him. He that is to exercise comes into the ring with a great shriek or two, and a horrid look; then he fetches two or three large stately strides, and falls to work. He holds his broad sword in one hand, and his lance in the other, and traverses his ground, leaping from one side of the ring to the other; and, in a menacing posture and look, bids defiance to the enemy, whom his fancy frames to him; for there is nothing but air to oppose him. Then he stamps and shakes his head, and grinning with his teeth makes many rueful faces. Then he throws his lance, and nimbly snatches out his kris, with which he hacks and hews the air like a madman, often shrieking. At last, being almost tired with motion, he flies to the middle of the ring, where he seems to have his enemy at his mercy, and with two or three blows cuts on the ground as if he was cutting off his enemy's head. By this time he is all of a sweat, and withdraws triumphantly out of the ring, and presently another enters with the like shrieks and gestures. Thus they continue combating their imaginary enemy all the rest of the day; towards the conclusion of which the richest men act, and at last the general, and then the Sultan concludes this ceremony: he and the general, with some other great men, are in armour, but the rest have none. After this the Sultan returns home, accompanied with abundance of people, who wait on him there till they are dismissed. But at the time when we were there, there was an after-game to be played; for the general's son being then circumcised, the Sultan intended to give him a second visit in the night, so they all waited to attend him thither. The general also provided to meet him in the best manner, and therefore desired Captain Swan with his men to attend him. Accordingly Captain Swan ordered us to get our guns, and wait at the general's house till further orders. So about forty of us waited till eight o'clock in the evening, when the general with Captain Swan, and about 1,000 men, went to meet the Sultan, with abundance of torches that made it as light as day. The manner of the march was thus: first of all there was a pageant,* and upon it two dancing women gorgeously apparelled, with coronets on their heads full of glittering spangles, and pendants of the same hanging down over their breast and shoulders. These are women bred up purposely for dancing: their feet and legs are but little employed, except sometimes to turn round very gently; but their hands, arms, head and body are in continual motion, especially their

* A decorated or triumphal float.

arms, which they turn and twist so strangely, that you would think them to be made without bones. Besides the two dancing women, there were two old women in the pageant holding each a lighted torch in their hands close by the two dancing women, by which light the glittering spangles appeared very gloriously. This pageant was carried by six lusty men. Then came six or seven torches, lighting the general and Captain Swan, who marched side by side next, and we that attended Captain Swan followed close after, marching in order six and six abreast, with each man his gun on his shoulder, and torches on each side. After us came twelve of the general's men with old Spanish matchlocks, marching four in a row. After them about forty lances, and behind them as many with great swords, marching all in order. After them came abundance only with krisses by their sides, who marched up close without any order. When we came near the Sultan's house, the Sultan and his men met us, and we wheeled off to let them pass. The Sultan had three pageants went before him: in the first pageant were four of his sons, who were about ten or eleven years old. They had gotten abundance of small stones, which they roguishly threw about on the people's heads. In the next were four young maidens, nieces to the Sultan, being his sister's daughters; and in the third, there was three of the Sultan's children, not above six years old. The Sultan himself followed next, being carried in his couch, which was not like your Indian palanquins,* but open, and very little and ordinary. A multitude of people came after, without any order: but as soon as he was passed by, the general, and Captain Swan, and all our men, closed in just behind the Sultan, and so all marched together to the general's house. We came thither between ten and eleven o'clock, where the biggest part of the company were immediately dismissed; but the Sultan and his children, and his nieces, and some other persons of quality, entered the general's house. They were met at the head of the stairs by the general's women, who with a great deal of respect conducted them into the house. Captain Swan, and we that were with him, followed after. It was not long before the general

* Covered litters.

caused his dancing women to enter the room and divert the company with that pastime. I had forgot to tell you that they have none but vocal music here, by what I could learn, except only a row of a kind of bells with clappers, sixteen in number, and their weight increasing gradually from about three to ten pound weight.* These are set in a row on a table in the general's house, where for seven or eight days together before the circumcision day, they were struck each with a little stick, for the biggest part of the day making a great noise, and they ceased that morning. So these dancing women sung themselves, and danced to their own music. After this the general's women, and the Sultan's sons, and his nieces danced. Two of the Sultan's nieces were about eighteen or nineteen years old, the other two were three or four years younger. These young ladies were very richly dressed, with loose garments of silk, and small coronets on their heads. They were much fairer than any women I did ever see there, and very well featured; and their noses, though but small, yet higher than the other women's, and very well proportioned. When the ladies had very well diverted themselves and the company with dancing, the general caused us to fire some sky-rockets, that were made by his and Captain Swan's order, purposely for this night's solemnity; and after that the Sultan and his retinue went away with a few attendants, and we all broke up, and thus ended this day's solemnity: but the boys, being sore with their amputation, went straddling for a fortnight after.

They are not, as I said before, very curious, or strict in observing any days, or times of particular devotions, except it be Ramadan time, as we call it. The Ramadan time was then in August, as I take it, for it was shortly after our arrival here. In this time they fast all day, and about seven o'clock in the evening they spend near an hour in prayer. Towards the latter end of their prayer they loudly invoke their prophet for about a quarter of an hour, both old and young bawling out very strangely, as if they intended to fright him out of his sleepiness or neglect of them. After their prayer is ended,

* These appear to be tuned bells, similar perhaps to those used in more recent times by Olivier Messiaen and other western composers.

they spend some time in feasting before they take their re-
pose. Thus they do every day for a whole month at least; for
sometimes 'tis two or three days longer before the Ramadan
ends: for it begins at the new moon, and lasts till they see the
next new moon, which sometimes in thick hazy weather is
not till three or four days after the change, as it happened
while I was at Achin, where they continued the Ramadan till
the new moon's appearance. The next day after they have seen
the new moon, the guns are all discharged about noon, and
then the time ends.

A main part of their religion consists in washing often, to
keep themselves from being defiled; or after they are defiled
to cleanse themselves again. They also take great care to keep
themselves from being polluted, by tasting or touching anything that is accounted unclean; therefore swine's flesh is
very abominable to them; nay, anyone that has either tasted
of swine's flesh, or touched those creatures, is not permitted
to come into their houses in many days after, and there is
nothing will scare them more than a swine. Yet there are
wild hogs in the islands, and those so plentiful, that they will
come in troops out of the woods in the night into the very
city, and come under their houses, to rummage up and down
the filth that they find there. The natives therefore would
even desire us to lie in wait for the hogs to destroy them,
which we did frequently, by shooting them and carrying
them presently on board, but were prohibited their houses
afterwards.

And now I am on this subject, I cannot omit a story concerning the general. He once desired to have a pair of shoes
made after the English fashion, though he did very seldom
wear any: so one of our men made him a pair, which the
general liked very well. Afterwards somebody told him, that
the thread wherewith the shoes were sewn, were pointed
with hogs'-bristles. This put him into a great passion; so he
sent the shoes to the man that made them, and sent him withal
more leather to make another pair, with threads pointed with
some other hair, which was immediately done, and then he
was well pleased.

PUNISHMENTS

Rajah Laut was responsible for law and order in the kingdom. On one occasion he tried to flatter Captain Swan by asking him to decide on whether a certain criminal should live or die. But first the man received customary punishment.

He was stripped stark naked in the morning at sun-rising, and bound to a post, so that he could not stir hand nor foot, but as he was moved; and was placed with his face eastward against the sun. In the afternoon they turned his face towards the west, that the sun might still be in his face; and thus he stood all day, parched in the sun (which shines here excessively hot) and tormented with the mosquitoes or gnats: after this the general would have killed him, if Captain Swan had consented to it. I did never see any put to death; but I believe they are barbarous enough in it. The general told us himself that he put two men to death in a town where some of us were with him; but I heard not the manner of it. Their common way of punishing is to strip them in this manner, and place them in the sun; but sometimes they lay them flat on their backs on the sand, which is very hot; where they remain a whole day in the scorching sun, with the mosquitoes biting them all the time . . .

At this time one of the general's servants had offended, and was punished in this manner: he was bound fast flat on his belly, on a bamboo belonging to the proa, which was so near the water, that by the vessel's motion, it frequently delved under water, and the man along with it; and sometimes when hoisted up, he had scarce time to blow before he would be carried under water again.

A WAPPING BOURGEOIS GENTILHOMME

When the Ramadan time was over, and the dry time set in a little, the general, to oblige Captain Swan, entertained him every night with dances. The dancing women that are purposely bred up to it, and make it their trade, I have already described. But beside them all the women in general are much addicted to dancing. They dance forty or fifty at once; and that standing all round in a ring, joined hand in hand, and singing and keeping time. But they never budge out of their places, nor make any motion till the chorus is sung; then all at once they throw out one leg, and bawl out aloud; and sometimes they only clap their hands when the chorus is sung. Captain Swan, to retaliate the general's favours, sent for his violins, and some that could dance English dances; wherewith the general was very well pleased. They commonly spent the biggest part of the night in these sort of pastimes.

Among the rest of our men that did use to dance thus before the general, there was one John Thacker, who was a seaman bred, and could neither write nor read; but had formerly learnt to dance in the music-houses about Wapping. This man came into the South Seas with Captain Harris, and getting with him a good quantity of gold, and being a pretty good husband of his share, had still some left, besides what he laid out in a very good suit of clothes. The general supposed by his garb and his dancing, that he had been of noble extraction; and to be satisfied of his quality, asked of one of our men, if he did not guess aright of him? The man of whom the general asked this question told him, he was much in the right; and that most of our ship's company were of the like extraction; especially all those that had fine clothes; and that they came aboard only to see the world, having money enough to bear their expenses wherever they came; but that for the rest, those that had but mean clothes, they were only common seamen. After this, the general showed a great deal of respect to all that had good clothes, but especially to John Thacker, till Captain Swan came to know the business, and marred all; undeceiving the general, and drubbing the nobleman; for he was so much incensed against John Thacker, that he could never endure him afterwards; though the poor fellow knew nothing of the matter.

CONFIDENCES

While we stayed here, the general with his men went out

every morning betimes, and did not return till four or five
o'clock in the afternoon, and he would often compliment us,
by telling us what good trust and confidence he had in us,
saying that he left his women and goods under our protec-
tion, and that he thought them as secure with us six (for we
had all our arms with us) as if he had left a hundred of his
own men to guard them. Yet for all this great confidence, he
always left one of his principal men, for fear some of us
should be too familiar with his women.

They did never stir out of their own room when the
general was at home, but as soon as he was gone out, they
would presently come into our room, and sit with us all day,
and ask a thousand questions of us concerning our English
women, and our customs. You may imagine that before this
time, some of us had attained so much of their language as to
understand them, and give them answers to their demands.
I remember that one day they asked how many wives the
King of England had? We told them but one, and that our
English laws did not allow of any more. They said it was a
strange custom, that a man should be confined to one woman;
some of them said it was a very bad law, but others again said
it was a good law; so there was a great dispute among them
about it. But one of the general's women said positively,
that our law was better than theirs, and made them all silent
by the reason which she gave for it. This was the War Queen,
as we called her, for she did always accompany the general
whenever he was called out to engage his enemies, but the
rest did not.

By this familiarity among the women, and by often discoursing them, we came to be acquainted with their customs
and privileges. The general lies with his wives by turns, but
she by whom he had the first son, has a double portion of his
company; for when it comes to her turn, she has him two
nights, whereas the rest have him but one. She with whom he
is to lie at night, seems to have a particular respect shown
her by the rest all the precedent day; and for a mark of distinction, wears a striped silk handkerchief about her neck, by
which we knew who was queen that day.

SOME THOUGHTS ON DIFFERENCES IN TIME

A Discourse of Winds *is not the only book to contain Dampier's reflections on nature, science or navigation. Such ideas are also presented in* A New Voyage Round the World *and other of his publications. J. C. Beaglehole has rightly observed in* The Exploration of the Pacific (*1934*) *that 'as a continual investigator of hydrography and of the variation of the compass, of winds and the many minutiae of navigation, he is fundamental to all future discovery'.*

It was during our stay at Mindanao, that we were first made sensible of the change of time, in the course of our voyage. For having travelled so far westward, keeping the same course with the sun, we must consequently have gained something insensibly in the length of the particular days, but have lost in the tail, the bulk, or number, of the days or hours. According to the different longitudes of England and Mindanao, this isle being west from the Lizard, by common computation about 210°, the difference of time at our arrival at Mindanao ought to be about fourteen hours: and so much we should have anticipated our reckoning, having gained it by bearing the sun company. Now the natural day in every particular place must be consonant to itself: but this going about with, or against the sun's course, will of necessity make a difference in the calculation of the civil day between any two places. Accordingly, at Mindanao, and all other places in the East Indies, we found them reckoning a day before us, both natives and Europeans; for the Europeans coming eastward by the Cape of Good Hope, in a course contrary to the sun and us, wherever we met they were a full day before us in their accounts. So among the Indian Mahometans here, their Friday, the day of their Sultan's going to their mosques, was Thursday with us; though it were Friday also with those who came eastward from Europe. Yet at the Ladrone Islands, we found the Spaniards of Guam keeping the same computation with ourselves; the reason of which I take to be that they settled that colony by a course westward from Spain; the Spaniards going first to America, and thence to the Ladrones and Philippines. But how the reckoning was at Manila, and the rest of the Spanish colonies in the Philippine Islands, I know not; whether they keep it as they brought it, or corrected it by the accounts of the natives, and of the Portuguese, Dutch and English, coming the contrary way from Europe.

One great reason why seamen ought to keep the difference of time as exact as they can, is that they may be the more exact in their latitudes. For our tables of the sun's declination, being calculated for the meridians of the places in which they were made, differ about 12' from those parts of the world that lie on their opposite meridians, in the months of March and September; and in proportion to the sun's declination, at other times of the year also. And should they run farther as we did, the difference would still increase upon them, and be an occasion of great errors. Yet even able seamen in these voyages are hardly made sensible of this, though so necessary to be observed, for want of duly attending to the reason of it, as it happened among those of our crew; who after we had passed 180°, began to decrease the difference of declination, whereas they ought still to have increased it, for it all the way increased upon us.

CAPTAIN SWAN LOSES THE CYGNET

About this time some of our men, who were weary and tired with wandering, ran away into the country and absconded, they being assisted, as was generally believed, by Rajah Laut. There were others also, who, fearing we should not go to an English port, bought a canoe, and designed to go in her to Borneo . . .

The whole crew were at this time under a general disaffection, and full of very different projects; and all for want of action. The main division was between those that had money and those that had none. There was a great difference in the humours of these; for they that had money lived ashore, and did not care for leaving Mindanao; whilst those that were poor lived aboard, and urged Captain Swan to go to sea. These began to be unruly as well as dissatisfied, and sent ashore the merchants' iron to sell for arrack and honey, to make punch, wherewith they grew drunk and quarrelsome: which disorderly actions deterred me from going aboard; for I did ever abhor drunkenness, which now our men that were aboard abandoned themselves wholly to.

Yet these disorders might have been crushed, if Captain Swan had used his authority to suppress them . . . If he had yet come aboard, he might have dashed all their designs; but he neither came himself, as a captain of any prudence and courage would have done, nor sent till the time was expired.* So we left Captain Swan and about thirty-six men ashore in the city, and six or eight that run away; and about sixteen we had buried there, the most of which died by poison. The natives are very expert at poisoning, and do it upon small occasions: nor did our men want for giving offence, through their general rogueries, and sometimes by dallying too familiarly with their women, even before their faces. Some of their poisons are slow and lingering; for we had some now aboard who were poisoned there; but died not till some months after.

* Captain Swan had given warning to all his men to come aboard on 13 January 1687.

CHAPTER
FIVE

*Leaving Mindanao on 14 January 1687, the buccaneers elected John
Read, from Bristol, as their new captain, and shaped course for
Manila. Three weeks later they anchored off Negros, north-west of
Mindanao, where they made repairs and alterations to their ship.
They may have been near what is now called Dinosaur Island, next
to Tinagong Dagat (Hidden Sea) at Sipalay. Dampier calculates
the wingspan of the flying foxes he saw there to be at least seven or
eight feet, which may be correct, though today's flying fox measures
only five feet.*

In the middle of this bay, about a mile from the shore, there
is a small low woody island, not above a mile in circumference: our ship rode about a mile from it. This island was
the habitation of an incredible number of great bats, with
bodies as big as ducks, or large fowl, and with vast wings:
for I saw at Mindanao one of this sort, and I judge that the
wings stretched out in length, could not be less asunder than
seven or eight foot from tip to tip; for it was much more than
any of us could fathom with our arms extended to the utmost.
The wings are for substance like those of other bats, of a dun
or mouse colour. The skin or leather of them has ribs running along it, and draws up in three or four folds; and at the
joints of those ribs and the extremities of the wings, there are
sharp and crooked claws, by which they may hang on anything. In the evening as soon as the sun was set, these creatures would begin to take their flight from this island, in
swarms like bees, directing their flight over to the main
island; and whither afterwards I know not. Thus we should

see them rising up from the island till night hindered our sight; and in the morning as soon as it was light, we should see them returning again like a cloud, to the small island, till sunrising. This course they kept constantly while we lay here, affording us every morning and evening an hour's diversion in gazing at them, and talking about them; but our curiosity did not prevail with us to go ashore to them, ourselves and canoes being all the daytime taken up in business about our ship. At this isle also we found plenty of turtle and manatee, but no fish.

REASONABLY PRICED WOMEN AT CON SON

Captain Read proved an erratic commander, who announced his objective as the Manila–Acapulco galleon, yet wasted such time en route pursuing unimportant coasters that the Cygnet *reached Luzon too late. He decided to return in three months and intercept a sister ship from Mexico, meanwhile lying low lest the Spanish be put on their guard. All he could show for the voyage from Mindanao was booty of rice and sailcloth. The lying low, with comparable absurdity, consisted of sailing no less than a thousand miles across the South China Sea to the little island of Con Son, near the mouth of the Mekong, off what is now South Vietnam. Here, the pirate Dampier stuck to his religious principles.*

They are so free of their women, that they would bring them aboard and offer them to us; and many of our men hired them for a small matter. This is a custom used by several nations in the East Indies, as at Pegu,* Siam, Cochinchina [South Vietnam], and Cambodia, as I have been told. It is used at Tonquin [North Vietnam] also to my knowledge; for I did afterwards make a voyage thither, and most of our men had women aboard all the time of our abode there. In Africa also, on the coast of Guinea, our merchants, factors, and seamen that reside there, have their black misses. It is accounted a piece of policy to do it; for the chief factors and captains of ships have the great men's daughters offered them, the Mandarins' or noblemen's at Tonquin, and even

* In Burma.

the king's wives in Guinea; and by this sort of alliance the country people are engaged to a greater friendship. And if there should arise any difference about trade, or anything else, which might provoke the natives to seek some treacherous revenge (to which all these heathen nations are very prone), then these Delilahs could certainly declare it to their white friends, and so hinder their countrymen's design.

These people are idolaters; but their manner of worship I know not. There are a few scattering houses and plantations on the great island, and a small village on the south side of it, where there is a little idol temple, and an image of an elephant about five foot high, and in bigness proportionable, placed on one side of the temple; and a horse not so big, placed on the other side of it; both standing with their heads towards the south. The temple itself was low and ordinary, built of wood, and thatched like one of their houses, which are but very meanly.

The images of the horse and the elephant were the most general idols that I observed in the temples of Tonquin, when I travelled there. There were other images also, of beasts, birds and fish. I do not remember I saw any human shape there; nor any such monstrous representations as I have seen among the Chinese. Wherever the Chinese seamen or merchants come (and they are very numerous all over these seas) they have always hideous idols on board their junks or ships, with altars, and lamps burning before them. These idols they bring ashore with them: and beside those they have in common, every man has one in his own house. Upon some particular solemn days I have seen their *bonzes*, or priests, bring whole armfuls of painted papers, and burn them with a great deal of ceremony, being very careful to let no piece escape them. The same day they killed a goat which had been purposely fatting a month before; this they offer or present before their idol, and then dress it and feast themselves with it. I have seen them do this in Tonquin, where I have at the same time been invited to their feasts; and at Bengkulu, in the isle of Sumatra, they sent a shoulder of the sacrificed goat to the English, who eat of it, and asked me to do so too; but I refused.

THE CHINESE

The buccaneers remained on Con Son for five weeks, eating the rice they had seized. 'While we lay here two of our men died who were poisoned at Mindanao; they told us of it when they found themselves poisoned, and had lingered ever since. They were opened by our doctor, according to their own request before they died, and their livers were black, light and dry, like pieces of cork.' (John Masefield feels they may have died from cirrhosis, caused by heavy drinking.) Captain Read took the Cygnet *into the Gulf of Thailand and cruised aimlessly for a month before returning to Con Son. Dampier, 'being sufficiently weary of this mad crew', planned to leave them when the right moment arrived. On 4 June 1687 they weighed anchor for Manila, but strong winds blew them north-east to the coast of China, where they sheltered for a week on the island of Sanchuan Dao, south-west of Hong Kong. Dampier visited the mainland every day to mix with the Chinese.*

The Chinese in general are tall, straight-bodied, raw-boned men. They are long-visaged, and their foreheads are high; but they have little eyes. Their noses are pretty large, with a rising in the middle. Their mouths are of a mean size, pretty thin lips. They are of an ashy complexion; their hair is black, and their beards thin and long, for they pluck the hair out by the roots, suffering only some few very long straggling hairs to grow about their chin, in which they take great pride, often combing them, and sometimes tying them up in a knot, and they have such hairs too growing down from each side of their upper lip like whiskers. The ancient Chinese were very proud of the hair of their heads, letting it grow very long, and stroking it back with their hands curiously, and then winding the plaits all together round a bodkin, thrust through it at the hinderpart of the head; and both men and women did thus. But when the Tatars conquered them, they broke them of this custom they were so fond of by main force; insomuch that they resented this imposition worse than their subjection, and rebelled upon it; but being still worsted, were forced to acquiesce; and to this day they follow the fashion of their masters the Tatars, and shave all their

'The Chinese in general are tall, straight-bodied,
raw-boned men. They are long-visaged, and
their foreheads are high; but they have little eyes'

heads, only reserving one lock, which some tie up, others let it hang down to a great or small length as they please. The Chinese in other countries still keep their old custom, but if any of the Chinese is found wearing long hair in China, he forfeits his head; and many of them have abandoned their country to preserve their liberty of wearing their hair, as I have been told by themselves.

The Chinese have no hats, caps, or turbans; but when they walk abroad, they carry a small umbrella in their hands, wherewith they fence their head from the sun or the rain, by holding it over their heads. If they walk but a little way, they carry only a large fan made of paper, or silk, of the same fashion as those our ladies have, and many of them are brought over hither; one of these every man carries in his hand if he do but cross the street, screening his head with it, if he has not an umbrella with him.

The common apparel of the men is a loose frock and breeches. They seldom wear stockings, but they have shoes, or a sort of slipper rather. The men's shoes are made diversly. The women have very small feet, and consequently but little shoes; for from their infancy their feet are kept swathed up with bands, as hard as they can possibly endure them; and from the time they can go till they have done growing they bind them up every night. This they do purposely to hinder them from growing, esteeming little feet to be a great beauty. But by this unreasonable custom they do in a manner lose the use of their feet, and instead of going they only stumble about their houses, and presently squat down on their breeches again, being as it were confined to sitting all days of their lives. They seldom stir abroad, and one would be apt to think, that as some have conjectured, their keeping up their fondness for this fashion were a stratagem of the men's, to keep them from gadding and gossiping about, and confine them at home. They are kept constantly to their work, being fine needlewomen, and making many curious embroideries, and they make their own shoes; but if any stranger be desirous to bring away any for novelty's sake, he must be a great favourite to get a pair of shoes of them, though he give twice their value. The poorer sort of women trudge about streets, and to the market, without shoes or stockings; and these cannot afford to have little feet, being to get their living with them.

The Chinese, both men and women, are very ingenious; as may appear by the many curious things that are brought from thence, especially the porcelain, or china earthenware. The Spaniards of Manila, that we took on the coast of Luzon, told me, that this commodity is made of conchshells; the inside of which looks like mother-of-pearl. But the Portuguese lately mentioned, who had lived in China, and spoke that and the neighbouring languages very well, said that it was made of a fine sort of clay that was dug in the province of Canton. I have often made enquiry about it, but could never be well satisfied in it: but while I was on the coast of Canton I forgot to enquire about it. They make very fine lacquerware also, and good silks; and they are curious at painting and carving.

China affords drugs in great abundance, especially Chinaroot;* but this is not peculiar to that country alone; for there is much of this root growing at Jamaica, particularly at Sixteen Mile Walk, and in the Bay of Honduras it is very plentiful. There is a great store of sugar made in this country; and tea in abundance is brought from thence; being much used there, and in Tonquin and Cochinchina as common drinking; women sitting in the streets, and selling dishes of tea hot and ready made; they call it *chau,*† and even the poorest people sip it. But the tea at Tonquin or Cochinchina seems not so good, or of so pleasant a bitter, or of so fine a colour, or such virtue as this in China; for I have drank of it in these countries; unless the fault be in their way of making it, for I made none there myself; and by the high red colour it looks as if they made a decoction of it, or kept it stale. Yet at Japan I was told there is a great deal of pure tea, very good.

The Chinese are very great gamesters, and they will never be tired with it, playing night and day, till they have lost all their estates; then it is usual with them to hang themselves. This was frequently done by the Chinese factors at Manila,

* Ginseng.
† More precisely, *ch'a* or *char.*

as I was told by Spaniards that lived there. The Spaniards themselves are much addicted to gaming, and are very expert at it; but the Chinese are too subtle for them, being in general a very cunning people.

TYPHOON AND WATERSPOUT

The buccaneers' stay at Sanchuan Dao was cut short by the onset of the monsoon season. Dampier's account of the ensuing typhoon is another well-known passage, still quoted complete in as recent a publication as Sir William Napier Shaw's Manual of Meteorology *(1919–31). Dampier was the first to suggest that hurricane and typhoon were one and the same, writing in* A Discourse of Winds, *'I know no difference between a hurricane among the Caribbean Islands in the West Indies and a typhoon on the coast of China in the East Indies, but only the name.' This opinion was scientifically confirmed in the nineteenth century by Henry Piddington's work on cyclones. The description here of St Elmo's fire is also among the first to appear in English.*

The Cygnet *had to weather a further terrible storm two months later and then a waterspout. Piddington gave Dampier credit for 'showing that waterspouts are really whirlwinds'.*

It was now the time of the year for the south-west monsoon, but the wind had been whiffling about from one part of the compass to another for two or three days, and sometimes it would be quite calm. This caused us to put to sea, that we might have sea-room at least; for such flattering weather is commonly the forerunner of a tempest.

Accordingly we weighed anchor, and set out; yet we had very little wind all the next night. But the day ensuing, which was 4 July, about four o'clock in the afternoon, the wind came to the NE and freshened upon us, and the sky looked very black in that quarter, and the black clouds began to rise apace and moved towards us; having hung all the morning in the horizon. This made us take in our topsails, and the wind still increasing, about nine o'clock we reefed our mainsail and foresail; at ten we furled our foresail, keeping under a mainsail and mizzen. At eleven o'clock we furled our mainsail, and ballasted our mizzen; at which time it began to rain, and by twelve o'clock at night it blew exceeding hard, and the rain poured down as through a sieve. It thundered and lightened prodigiously, and the sea seemed all afire about us; for every sea that broke sparkled like lightning. The violent wind raised the sea presently to a great height, and it ran very short, and began to break in on our deck. One sea struck away the rails of our head, and our sheet-anchor, which was stowed with one fluke or bending of the iron over the ship's gunwale, and lashed very well down to the side, was violently washed off, and had like to have struck a hole in our bow, as it lay beating against it. Then we were forced to put right before the wind to stow our anchor again; which we did with much ado; but afterwards we durst not adventure to bring our ship to the wind again, for fear of foundering, for the turning the ship either to or fro from the wind is danger-ous in such violent storms. The fierceness of the weather continued till four o'clock that morning; in which time we did cut away two canoes that were towing astern.

After four o'clock the thunder and the rain abated, and then we saw a corposant at our main topmast-head, on the very top of the truck of the spindle. This sight rejoiced our men exceedingly; for the height of the storm is commonly over when the corposant is seen aloft; but when they are seen lying on the deck, it is generally accounted a bad sign.

A corposant is a certain small glittering light; when it appears as this did, on the very top of the mainmast or at a yardarm, it is like a star; but when it appears on the deck, it resembles a great glow-worm. The Spaniards have another name for it (though I take even this to be a Spanish or Portuguese name,* and a corruption only of Corpus Sanc-tum) and I have been told that when they see them, they presently go to prayers, and bless themselves for the happy sight. I have heard some ignorant seamen discoursing how they have seen them creep, or, as they say, travel about in the scuppers, telling many dismal stories that happened at such times: but I did never see any one stir out of the place where

---

* In Portuguese, *corpo santo* – holy body. This was St Elmo's fire, an electrical discharge forming a glow about a mast-head.

it was first fixed, except upon deck, where every sea washes it about: neither did I ever see any but when we have had hard rain as well as wind; and therefore do believe it is some jelly: but enough of this.

We continued scudding right before wind and sea from two till seven o'clock in the morning, and then the wind being much abated, we set our mizzen again, and brought our ship to the wind, and lay under a mizzen till eleven. Then it fell flat calm, and it continued so for about two hours:* but the sky looked very black and rueful, especially in the southwest and the sea tossed us about like an eggshell, for want of wind. About one o'clock in the afternoon the wind sprung up at SW out of the quarter from whence we did expect it: therefore we presently brailed up our mizzen and wore our ship. But we had no sooner put our ship before the wind, but it blew a storm again, and rained very hard, though not so violently as the night before: but the wind was altogether as boisterous, and so continued till ten or eleven o'clock at night. All which time we scudded, and ran before the wind very swift, though only with our bare poles, that is, without any sail abroad. Afterwards the wind died away by degrees, and before day we had but little wind, and fine clear weather.

I was never in such a violent storm in all my life; so said all the company. This was near the change of the moon: it was two or three days before the change. The sixth day in the morning, having fine handsome weather, we got up our yards again, and began to dry ourselves and our clothes, for we were all well sopped. This storm had deadened the hearts of our men so much, that instead of going to buy more provision at the same place from whence we came before the storm, or of seeking any more from the island Pratas,† they thought of going somewhere to shelter before the full moon, for fear of another such storm at that time: for commonly, if there is any very bad weather in the month, it is about two or three days before or after the full or change of the moon . . .

A spout is a small ragged piece or part of a cloud hanging

* They were now in the eye of the storm.
† Also called Dongshao Qundao, about 200 miles south-east of Hong Kong, where several treasure ships had been lost on the rocks.

down about a yard, seemingly from the blackest part thereof. Commonly it hangs down sloping from thence, or sometimes appearing with a small bending, or elbow in the middle. I never saw any hang perpendicularly down. It is small at the lower end, seeming no bigger than one's arm, but is still fuller towards the cloud, from whence it proceeds.

When the surface of the sea begins to work, you shall see the water, for about a hundred paces in circumference, foam and move gently round till the whirling motion increases: and then it flies upward in a pillar, about a hundred paces in compass at the bottom, but lessening gradually upwards to the smallness of the spout itself, there where it reaches the lower end of the spout, through which the rising sea-water seems to be conveyed into the clouds. This visibly appears by the clouds increasing in bulk and blackness. Then you shall presently see the cloud drive along, although before it seemed to be without any motion: the spout also keeping the same course with the cloud, and still sucking up the water as it goes along, and they make a wind as they go. Thus it continues for the space of half an hour, more or less, until the sucking is spent, and then breaking off, all the water which was below the spout, or pendulous piece of cloud, falls down again into the sea, making a great noise with its fall and clashing motion in the sea.

It is very dangerous for a ship to be under a spout when it breaks, therefore we always endeavour to shun it, by keeping at a distance, if possibly we can. But for want of wind to carry us away, we are often in great fear and danger, for it is usually calm when spouts are at work; except only just where they are. Therefore men at sea, when they see a spout coming, and know not how to avoid it, do sometimes fire shot out of their great guns into it, to give it air or vent, that so it may break; but I did never hear that it proved to be of any benefit.

THE BATAN ISLANDS

Sailing towards Manila, the buccaneers visited the Batan Islands, south of Taiwan. The people here 'inhabit together in small villages built on the sides and tops of rocky hills, three or four rows of houses one above another, and on such steep precipices that they go up to the first row with a wooden ladder, and so with a ladder still from every storey up to that above it, there being no way to ascend . . . there is no coming at them from below but by climbing up as against a perpendicular wall.'

The common employment for the men is fishing; but I did never see them catch much: whether it is more plenty at other times of the year I know not. The women do manage their plantations.

I did never see them kill any of their goats or hogs for themselves, yet they would beg the paunches of the goats that they themselves did sell to us: and if any of our surly seamen did heave them into the sea, they would take them up again and the skins of the goats also. They would not meddle with hogs'-guts, if our men threw away any besides what they made chitterlings and sausages of. The goatskins these people would carry ashore, and making a fire they would singe off all the hair, and afterwards let the skin lie and parch on the coals, till they thought it eatable; and then they would gnaw it, and tear it in pieces with their teeth, and at last swallow it. The paunches of the goats would make them an excellent dish; they dressed it in this manner. They would turn out all the chopped grass and crudities found in the maw into their pots, and set it over the fire, and stir it about often. This would smoke and puff, and heave up as it was boiling; wind breaking out of the ferment, and making a very savoury stink. While this was doing, if they had any fish, as commonly they had two or three small fish, these they would make very clean (as hating nastiness belike) and cut the flesh from the bone, and then mince the flesh as small as possibly they could, and when that in the pot was well boiled, they would take it up, and strewing a little salt into it, they would eat it, mixed with their raw minced flesh. The dung in the maw would look like so much boiled herbs minced very small; and they took up their mess with their fingers, as the Moors do their pilau, using no spoons.

They had another dish made of a sort of locusts, whose

bodies were about an inch and an half long, and as thick as the top of one's little finger; with large thin wings, and long and small legs. At this time of the year these creatures came in great swarms to devour their potato-leaves, and other herbs; and the natives would go out with small nets, and take a quart at one sweep. When they had enough, they would carry them home, and parch them over the fire in an earthen pan; and then their wings and legs would fall off, and their heads and backs would turn red like boiled shrimps, being before brownish. Their bodies being full, would eat very moist, their heads would crackle in one's teeth. I did once eat of this dish, and liked it well enough; but their other dish my stomach would not take.

These men had wooden lances, and a few lances headed with iron; which are all the weapons that they have. Their armour is a piece of buffalo-hide, shaped like our carters' frocks, being without sleeves, and sewed both sides together, with holes for the head and the arms to come forth. This buff-coat reaches down to their knees: it is close about their shoulders, but below it is three foot wide, and as thick as a board.

I could never perceive them to worship anything, neither had they any idols; neither did they seem to observe any one day more than other. I could never perceive that one man was of greater power than another; but they seemed to be all equal; only every man ruling in his own house, and the children respecting and honouring their parents.

Yet 'tis probable that they have some law, or custom, by which they are governed; for while we lay here we saw a young man buried alive in the earth; and 'twas for theft, as far as we could understand from them. There was a great deep hole dug, and abundance of people came to the place to take their last farewell of him. Among the rest, there was one woman who made great lamentation, and took off the condemned person's earrings. We supposed her to be his mother. After he had taken his leave of her and some others, he was put into the pit, and covered over with earth. He did not struggle, but yielded very quietly to his punishment; and they rammed the earth close upon him, and stifled him . . .

Notwithstanding the seeming nastiness of their dish of goat's-maw, they are in their persons a very neat cleanly people, both men and women: and they are withal the quietest and civillest people that I did ever meet with. I could never perceive them to be angry with one another. I have admired to see twenty or thirty boats aboard our ship at a time, and yet no difference among them; but all civil and quiet, endeavouring to help each other on occasion: no noise, nor appearance of distaste: and although sometimes cross accidents would happen, which might have set other men together by the ears, yet they were not moved by them. Sometimes they will also drink freely, and warm themselves with their drink; yet neither then could I ever perceive them out of humour. They are not only thus civil among themselves, but very obliging and kind to strangers; nor were their children rude to us, as is usual. Indeed the women, when we came to their houses, would modestly beg any rags or small pieces of cloth, to swaddle their young ones in, holding out their children to us; and begging is usual among all these wild nations. Yet neither did they beg so importunately as in other places; nor did the men ever beg anything at all.

NEW HOLLAND

Most of the buccaneers were so frightened by the storms in the South China Sea and Philippines that Captain Read abandoned schemes of intercepting the Manila treasure ships and set out for India, shaping course south towards the Moluccas and Timor, thence to bear west through the Indian Ocean. As a means of avoiding the South China Sea, 'this seemed to be a very tedious way about', says Dampier, but 'I was well enough satisfied, knowing that the farther we went, the more knowledge and experience I should get, which was the main thing that I regarded, and should also have the more variety of places to attempt an escape from them, being fully resolved to take the first opportunity of giving them the slip.' When they were near the east coast of Mindanao, he broached the idea of picking up Captain Swan, but Captain Read quickly dismissed this suggestion 'and made all possible haste'. After passing Timor, Captain Read determined to have a look at New Holland, 'to see what that country would afford us'. Thus it was that William Dampier became the first Englishman to set foot in Australia and write about the experience. The visit is thought to have taken place in the King Sound area of Western Australia, and is commemorated by Buccaneer Archipelago and Cygnet Bay.

The day of 4 January 1688, we fell in with the land of New Holland in the latitude of 16° 50' having, as I said before, made our course due south from the shoal that we passed by the 31 December. We ran in close by it, and finding no convenient anchoring, because it lies open to the north-west we ran along shore to the eastward, steering NE by E. for so the land lies. We steered thus about twelve leagues; and then came to a point of land, from whence the land trends east and southerly, for ten or twelve leagues; but how afterwards I know not. About three leagues to the eastward of this point, there is a pretty deep bay, with abundance of islands in it, and a very good place to anchor in, or to haul ashore. About a league to the eastward of that point we anchored 5 January 1688, two mile from the shore, in twenty-nine fathom, good hard sand, and clean ground.

New Holland is a very large tract of land. It is not yet determined whether it is an island or a main continent; but I am certain that it joins neither to Asia, Africa, nor America. This part of it that we saw is all low even land, with sandy banks against the sea, only the points are rocky, and so are some of the islands in this bay.

The land is of a dry sandy soil, destitute of water, except you make wells; yet producing divers sorts of trees; but the woods are not thick, nor the trees very big. Most of the trees that we saw are dragon trees as we supposed; and these too are the largest trees of any there. They are about the bigness of our large apple trees, and about the same height; and the rind is blackish, and somewhat rough. The leaves are of a dark colour; the gum distils out of the knots or cracks that are in the bodies of the trees. We compared it with some gum-dragon or dragon's blood that was aboard, and it was of the same colour and taste.* The other sorts of trees were not known by any of us. There was pretty long grass growing under the trees; but it was very thin. We saw no trees that bore fruit or berries.

We saw no sort of animal, nor any track of beast, but once; and that seemed to be the tread of a beast as big as a great mastiff dog. Here are a few small land-birds, but none bigger than a blackbird; and but few sea-fowls. Neither is the sea very plentifully stored with fish, unless you reckon the manatee and turtle as such. Of these creatures there is plenty; but they are extraordinary shy; though the inhabitants cannot trouble them much having neither boats nor iron.

The inhabitants of this country are the miserablest people in the world. The Hodmadods of Monomotapa,† though a nasty people, yet for wealth are gentlemen to these; who have no houses, and skin garments, sheep, poultry, and fruits of the earth, ostrich eggs, etc. as the Hodmadods have. And setting aside their human shape, they differ but little from brutes. They are tall, straight-bodied, and thin, with small long limbs. They have great heads, round foreheads, and great brows. Their eyelids are always half closed, to keep the flies out of their eyes; they being so troublesome here, that no fanning will keep them from coming to one's face; and without the assistance of both hands to keep them off, they will creep into one's nostrils, and mouth too, if the lips are not shut very close; so that from their infancy being thus annoyed with these insects, they do never open their eyes as other people: and therefore they cannot see far, unless they hold up their heads, as if they were looking at somewhat over them.

They have great bottle-noses, pretty full lips, and wide mouths. The two fore-teeth of their upper jaw are wanting in all of them, men and women, old and young; whether they draw them out, I know not. Neither have they any beards. They are long-visaged, and of a very unpleasing aspect, having no one graceful feature in their faces. Their hair is black,

* The dragon tree is a source of dragon's blood, which is a resin once used medicinally, but now restricted to varnishes and lacquers.
† In southern Africa, visited by Dampier in 1691.

short and curled, like that of the Negroes; and not long and
lank like the common Indians. The colour of their skins,
both of their faces and the rest of their body, is coal-black,
like that of the Negroes of Guinea.

They have no sort of clothes, but a piece of the rind of a
tree tied like a girdle about their waists, and a handful of long
grass, or three or four small green boughs full of leaves,
thrust under their girdle, to cover their nakedness.

They have no houses, but lie in the open air without any
covering; the earth being their bed, and the heaven their
canopy. Whether they cohabit one man to one woman, or
promiscuously, I know not; but they do live in companies,
twenty or thirty men, women, and children together.* Their
only food is a small sort of fish, which they get by making
weirs of stone across little coves or branches of the sea; every
tide bringing in the small fish, and there leaving them for a
prey to these people, who constantly attend there to search
for them at low water. This small fry I take to be the top of
their fishery: they have no instruments to catch great fish,
should they come; and such seldom stay to be left behind at
low water: nor could we catch any fish with our hooks and
lines all the while we lay there. In other places at low water
they seek for cockles, mussels, and periwinkles. Of these
shellfish there are fewer still; so that their chiefest dependance
is upon what the sea leaves in their weirs; which, be it much
or little they gather up, and march to the places of their
abode. There the old people that are not able to stir abroad
by reason of their age, and the tender infants, wait their
return; and what providence has bestowed on them, they
presently broil on the coals, and eat it in common. Sometimes they get as many fish as makes them a plentiful banquet;
and at other times they scarce get everyone a taste: but be it
little or much that they get, everyone has his part, as well the
young and tender, the old and feeble, who are not able to go
abroad, as the strong and lusty. When they have eaten they

* When Gulliver visits New Holland in Chapter XI of *A Voyage to the
Houyhnhnms,* he sees 'twenty or thirty natives upon a height, not above
five hundred yards from me. They were stark naked, men, women and
children round a fire, as I could discover by the smoke.'

lie down till the next low water, and then all that are able march out, be it night or day, rain or shine, 'tis all one; they must attend the weirs, or else they must fast: for the earth affords them no food at all. There is neither herb, root, pulse nor any sort of grain for them to eat, that we saw; nor any sort of bird or beast that they can catch, having no instruments wherewithal to do so.

I did not perceive that they did worship anything. These poor creatures have a sort of weapon to defend their weir, or fight with their enemies, if they have any that will interfere with their poor fishery. They did at first endeavour with their weapons to frighten us, who lying ashore deterred them from one of their fishing-places. Some of them had wooden swords, others had a sort of lance. The sword is a piece of wood shaped somewhat like a cutlass. The lance is a long straight pole sharp at one end, and hardened afterwards by heat. I saw no iron, nor any other sort of metal; therefore it is probable they use stone hatchets, as some Indians in America do.

How they get their fire I know not; but probably as Indians do, out of wood. I have seen the Indians of Bonaire do it, and have myself tried the experiment: they take a flat piece of wood that is pretty soft, and make a small dent in one side of it, then they take another hard round stick, about the bigness of one's little finger, and sharpening it at one end like a pencil, they put that sharp end in the hole or dent of the flat soft piece, and then rubbing or twirling the hard piece between the palms of their hands, they drill the soft piece till it smokes, and at last takes fire.

These people speak somewhat through the throat; but we could not understand one word that they said. We anchored, as I said before, 5 January, and, seeing men walking on the shore, we presently sent a canoe to get some acquaintance with them; for we were in hopes to get some provision among them. But the inhabitants, seeing our boat coming, run away and hid themselves. We searched afterwards three days in hopes to find their houses, but found none; yet we saw many places where they had made fires. At last, being out of hopes to find their habitations, we searched no farther;

but left a great many toys ashore, in such places where we thought that they would come. In all our search we found no water, but old wells on the sandy bays.

At last we went over to the islands, and there we found a great many of the natives: I do believe there were forty on one island, men, women and children. The men at our first coming ashore, threatened us with their lances and swords; but they were frightened by firing one gun, which we fired purposely to scare them. The island was so small that they could not hide themselves; but they were much disordered at our landing, especially the women and children; for we went directly to their camp. The lustiest of the women, snatching up their infants, ran away howling, and the little children run after squeaking and bawling; but the men stood still. Some of the women, and such people as could not go from us, lay still by a fire, making a doleful noise, as if we had been coming to devour them: but when they saw we did not intend to harm them, they were pretty quiet, and the rest that fled from us at our first coming, returned again. This their place of dwelling was only a fire, with a few boughs before it, set up on that side the wind was of.

After we had been here a little while, the men began to be familiar, and we clothed some of them, designing to have had some service of them for it: for we found some wells of water here, and intended to carry two or three barrels of it aboard. But it being somewhat troublesome to carry to the canoes, we thought to have made these men to have carried it for us, and therefore we gave them some old clothes; to one an old pair of breeches, to another a ragged shirt, to the third a jacket that was scarce worth owning; which yet would have been very acceptable at some places where we had been, and so we thought they might have been with these people. We put them on them, thinking that this finery would have brought them to work heartily for us; and our water being filled in small long barrels, about six gallons in each, which were made purposely to carry water in, we brought these our new servants to the wells, and put a barrel on each of their shoulders for them to carry to the canoe. But all the signs we could make were to no purpose, for they stood like statues, without motion, but grinned like so many monkeys, staring one upon another: for these poor creatures seem not accustomed to carry burthens; and I believe that one of our shipboys of ten years old, would carry as much as one of them. So we were forced to carry our water ourselves, and they very fairly put the clothes off again, and laid them down, as if clothes were only to work in. I did not perceive that they had any great liking to them at first, neither did they seem to admire anything that we had.

At another time our canoe being among these islands seeking for game, espied a drove of these men swimming from one island to another; for they have no boats, canoes, or bark-logs. They took up four of them, and brought them aboard; two of them were middle-aged, the other two were young men about eighteen or twenty years old. To these we gave boiled rice, and with it turtle and manatee boiled. They did greedily devour what we gave them, but took no notice of the ship, or anything in it, and when they were set on land again, they ran away as fast as they could. At our first coming, before we were acquainted with them, or they with us, a company of them who lived on the main, came just against our ship, and standing on a pretty high bank, threatened us with their swords and lances, by shaking them at us: at last the captain ordered the drum to be beaten, which was done of a sudden with much vigour, purposely to scare the poor creatures. They hearing the noise, ran away as fast as they could drive; and when they ran away in haste, they would cry 'Gurry, gurry', speaking deep in the throat. Those inhabitants also that live on the main, would always run away from us; yet we took several of them. For, as I have already observed, they had such bad eyes, that they could not see us till we came close to them. We did always give them victuals, and let them go again, but the islanders, after our first time of being among them, did not stir for us.

When we had been here about a week, we hauled our ship into a small sandy cove, at a spring tide, as far as she would float; and at low water she was left dry, and the sand dry without us near half a mile; for the sea rises and falls here about five fathom. The flood runs north by east, and the ebb south by west. All the neap tides* we lay wholly aground, for the sea did not come near us by about a hundred yards. We had therefore time enough to clean our ship's bottom, which we did very well. Most of our men lay ashore in a tent, where our sails were mending; and our strikers brought home turtle and manatee every day, which was our constant food.

While we lay here, I did endeavour to persuade our men to go to some English factory;† but was threatened to be turned ashore, and left here for it. This made me desist, and patiently wait for some more convenient place and opportunity to leave them.

---

* The spring tides occur just after the new moon and full moon, causing the highest rise in tidal levels. The neap tides take place during the first and last quarters of the moon, producing the lowest rise.
† Elsewhere in the East Indies.

CHAPTER
SIX

AN END TO BUCCANEERING

From New Holland the buccaneers sailed north-west to Christmas Island, which Dampier was again the first to describe, and up the west coast of Sumatera. In reality they were now no longer buccaneers seeking to harass Spanish shipping, but common-or-garden pirates preying on anything that came their way. The nadir of such aspirations was reached when Captain Read ordered the capture of a native proa, with crew of four, carrying coconuts. He then sank the little boat. Next stop was Great Nicobar, north-west of Sumatera.

It was the 5th day of May, about ten in the morning, when we anchored at this island: Captain Read immediately ordered his men to heel the ship in order to clean her; which was done this day and the next. All the water vessels were filled. They intended to go to sea at night: for the winds being yet at NNE the captain was in hopes to get over to Cape Comorin* before the wind shifted. Otherwise it would have been somewhat difficult for him to get thither, because the westerly monsoon was now at hand.

I thought now was my time to make my escape, by getting leave, if possible, to stay here: for it seemed not very feasible to do it by stealth; and I had no reason to despair of getting leave; this being a place where my stay could, probably, do our crew no harm, should I design it. Indeed one reason that put me on the thoughts of staying at this particular place, besides the present opportunity of leaving Captain Read, which I did always intend to do as soon as I could, was that I had here also a prospect of advancing a profitable trade for

* Off the southernmost tip of India.

ambergris with these people, and of gaining a considerable fortune to myself: for in a short time I might have learned their language, and by accustoming myself to row with them in the proas or canoes, especially by conforming myself to their customs and manners of living, I should have seen how they got their ambergris, and have known what quantities they get, and the time of the year when most is found. And then afterwards I thought it would be easy for me to have transported myself from thence, either in some ship that passed this way, whether English, Dutch, or Portuguese; or else to have gotten one of the young men of the island, to have gone with me in one of their canoes to Achin; and there to have furnished myself with such commodities, as I found most coveted by them; and therewith, at my return, to have bought their ambergris.

I had, till this time, made no open show of going ashore here; but now, the water being filled, and the ship in a readiness to sail, I desired Captain Read to set me ashore on this island. He, supposing that I could not go ashore in a place less frequented by ships than this, gave me leave: which probably he would have refused to have done, if he thought I should have gotten from hence in any short time; for fear of my giving an account of him to the English or Dutch. I soon got up my chest and bedding, and immediately got some to row me ashore; for fear lest his mind should change again.

The canoe that brought me ashore, landed me on a small sandy bay, where there were two houses, but no person in them. For the inhabitants were removed to some other house, probably, for fear of us; because the ship was close by: and yet both men and women came aboard the ship without any sign of fear. When our ship's canoe was going aboard again, they met the owner of the houses coming ashore in his boat. He made a great many signs to them to fetch me off again: but they would not understand him. Then he came to me, and offered his boat to carry me off; but I refused it. Then he made signs for me to go up into the house, and, according as I did understand him by his signs, and a few Malayan words that he used, he intimated that somewhat would come out of the woods in the night, when I was asleep, and kill me, meaning probably some wild beast. Then I carried my chest and clothes up into the house.*

I had not been ashore an hour before Captain Teat and one John Damarell, with three or four armed men more, came to fetch me aboard again. They need not have sent an armed posse for me; for had they but sent the cabin-boy ashore for me, I would not have denied going aboard. For though I could have hid myself in the woods, yet then they would have abused, or have killed some of the natives, purposely to incense them against me. I told them therefore that I was ready to go with them, and went aboard with all my things.

When I came aboard I found the ship in an uproar; for there were three men more, who taking courage by my example, desired leave also to accompany me. One of them was the surgeon Mr Coppinger, the others were Mr Robert Hall, and one named Ambrose; I have forgot his surname. These men had always harboured the same designs as I had. The two last were not much opposed; but Captain Read and his crew would not part with the surgeon. At last the surgeon leapt into the canoe, and taking up my gun, swore he would go ashore, and that if any man did oppose it, he would shoot him: but John Oliver, who was then quartermaster, leapt into the canoe, taking hold of him, took away the gun, and with the help of two or three more, they dragged him again into the ship.

Then Mr Hall and Ambrose and I were again sent ashore; and one of the men that rowed us ashore stole an axe, and gave it to us, knowing it was a good commodity with the Indians. It was now dark, therefore we lighted a candle, and I being the oldest stander in our new country, conducted them into one of the houses, where we did presently hang up our hammocks. We had scarce done this before the canoe came ashore again and brought the four Malayan men belonging to Achin (which we took in the proa we took off of Sumatra), and the Portuguese that came to our ship out of

* In the original manuscript there follows: 'As soon as my friends were gone, I kneeled down and gave thanks to God Almighty for this deliverance.'

the Siam junk at Pulo Condore [Con Son]. The crew having no occasion for these, being leaving the Malayan parts, where the Portuguese spark served as an interpreter; and not fearing now that the Achinese could be serviceable to us in bringing us over to their country, forty leagues off; nor imagining that we durst make such an attempt, as indeed it was a bold one. Now we were men enough to defend ourselves against the natives of this island, if they should prove our enemies: though if none of these men had come ashore to me, I should not have feared any danger: nay, perhaps less, because I should have been cautious of giving any offence to the natives. And I am of the opinion, that there are no people in the world so barbarous as to kill a single person that falls accidentally into their hands, or comes to live among them; except they have before been injured, by some outrage or violence committed against them. Yet even then, or afterwards, if a man could but preserve his life from their first rage, and come to treat with them (which is the hardest thing, because their way is usually to abscond, and rushing suddenly upon his enemy to kill him at unawares), one might, by some sleight, insinuate one's self into their favours again; especially by showing some toy or knack that they did never see before: which any European, that has seen the world, might soon contrive to amuse them withal: as might be done, generally even with a lit fire struck with a flint and steel.

As for the common opinion of Anthropophagi, or man-eaters, I did never meet with any such people: all nations or families in the world, that I have seen or heard of, having some sort of food to live on, either fruit, grain, pulse or roots, which grow naturally, or else planted by them; if not fish and land-animals besides (yea, even the people of New Holland had fish amidst all their penury); and would scarce kill a man purposely to eat him. I know not what barbarous customs may formerly have been in the world; and to sacrifice their enemies to their gods, is a thing has been much talked of, with relation to the savages of America. I am a stranger to that also, if it be, or have been customary in any nation there; and yet, if they sacrifice their enemies, it is not necessary they should eat them too. After all, I will not be peremptory in the negative, but I speak as to the compass of my own knowledge, and know some of these cannibal stories to be false, and many of them have been disproved since I first went to the West Indies. At that time how barbarous were the poor Florida Indians accounted, which now we find to be civil enough? What strange stories have we heard of the Indians, whose islands were called the Isles of Cannibals? Yet we find that they do trade very civilly with the French and Spaniards; and have done so with us. I do own that they have formerly endeavoured to destroy our plantations at Barbados, and have since hindered us from settling in the island Santa Loca [Saint Lucia] by destroying two or three colonies successively of those that were settled there; and even the island Tobago has been often annoyed and ravaged by them, when settled by the Dutch, and still lies waste (though a delicate fruitful island) as being too near the Caribs on the continent, who visit it every year. But this was to preserve their own right, by endeavouring to keep out any that would settle themselves on those islands, where they had planted themselves; yet even these people would not hurt a single person, as I have been told by some that have been prisoners among them. I could instance also the Indians of Bocca Toro, and Bocca Drago,* and many other places where they do live, as the Spaniards call it, wild and savage: yet there they have been familiar with privateers, but by abuses have withdrawn their friendship again. As for these Nicobar people, I found them affable enough, and therefore I did not fear them; but I did not much care whether I had gotten any more company or no.

But however I was very well satisfied, and the rather, because we were now men enough to row ourselves over to the island Sumatra; and accordingly we presently consulted how to purchase a canoe of the natives.

It was a fine clear moonlight night, in which we were left ashore. Therefore we walked on the sandy bay to watch when the ship would weigh and be gone, not thinking our-

* Bocas del Toro and Bocas del Drago are the two entrances to Bahia de Almirante in north-west Panama, near the Costa Rica border.

selves secure in our new-gotten liberty till then. About eleven or twelve o'clock we saw her under sail, and then we returned to our chamber, and so to sleep. This was the 6 May.

The next morning betimes, our landlord, with four or five of his friends, came to see his new guests, and was somewhat surprised to see so many of us, for he knew of no more but myself. Yet he seemed to be very well pleased, and entertained us with a large calabash of toddy, which he brought with him. Before he went away again (for wheresoever we came they left their houses to us, but whether out of fear or superstition I know not), we bought a canoe of him for an axe, and we did presently put our chests and clothes in it, designing to go to the south end of the island, and lie there till the monsoon shifted, which we expected every day.

When our things were stowed away, we with the Achinese entered with joy into our new frigate, and launched off from the shore. We were no sooner off, but our canoe overset, bottom upwards. We preserved our lives well enough by swimming, and dragged also our chests and clothes ashore; but all our things were wet. I had nothing of value but my journal and some drafts of land of my own taking, which I much prized, and which I had hitherto carefully preserved. Mr Hall had also such another cargo of books and drafts, which were now like to perish. But we presently opened our chests and took out our books, which, with much ado, we did afterwards dry; but some of our drafts that lay loose in our chests were spoiled.

We lay here afterwards three days, making great fires to dry our books. The Achinese in the meantime fixed our canoe, with outriggers on each side; and they also cut a good mast for her, and made a substantial sail with mats.

The canoe being now very well fixed, and our books and clothes dry, we launched out a second time, and rowed towards the east side of the island, leaving many islands to the north of us. The Indians of the island accompanied us with eight or ten canoes against our desire; for we thought that these men would make provision dearer at that side of the island we were going to, by giving an account what rates we gave for it at the place from whence we came, which was owing to the ship's being there; for the ship's crew were not so thrifty in bargaining (as they seldom are) as single persons, or a few men might be apt to be, who would keep to one bargain. Therefore to hinder them from going with us, Mr Hall scared one canoe's crew by firing a shot over them. They all leapt overboard, and cried out, but seeing us row away, they got into their canoe again and came after us.

The firing of that gun made all the inhabitants of the island to be our enemies. For presently after this we put ashore at a bay where were four houses, and a great many canoes: but they all went away, and came near us no more for several days. We had then a great loaf of melory* which was our constant food; and if we had a mind of coconuts, or toddy, our Malayans of Achin would climb the trees, and fetch as many nuts as we would have, and a good pot of toddy every morning. Thus we lived till our melory was almost spent; being still in hopes that the natives would come to us, and sell it as they had formerly done. But they came not to us; nay, they opposed us wherever we came, and often shaking their lances at us, made all the show of hatred that they could invent.

At last, when we saw that they stood in opposition to us, we resolved to use force to get some of their food, if we could not get it other ways. With this resolution we went into our canoe to a small bay on the north part of the island; because it was smooth water there and good landing; but on the other side, the wind being yet on that quarter, we could not land without jeopardy of oversetting our canoe, and wetting our arms, and then we must have lain at the mercy of our enemies, who stood two or three hundred men in every bay, where they saw us coming, to keep us off.

When we set out, we rowed directly to the north end, and presently were followed by seven or eight of their canoes. They, keeping at a distance, rowed away faster than we did, and got to the bay before us; and there, with about twenty more canoes full of men, they all landed, and stood to hinder us from landing. But we rowed in, within a hundred yards of them. Then we lay still, and I took my gun, and presented at

* Like breadfruit.

them; at which they all fell down flat on the ground. But I turned myself about, and to show that we did not intend to harm them, I fired my gun off towards the sea; so that they might see the shot graze on the water. As soon as my gun was loaded again, we rowed gently in; at which some of them withdrew. The rest standing up, did still cut and hew the air, making signs of their hatred; till I once more frightened them with my gun, and discharged it as before. Then more of them sneaked away, leaving only five or six men on the bay. Then we rowed in again, and Mr Hall taking his sword in his hand, leaped ashore; and I stood ready with my gun to fire at the Indians, if they had injured him: but they did not stir, till he came to them and saluted them.

He shook them by the hand, and by such signs of friendship as he made, the peace was concluded, ratified and confirmed by all that were present: and others that were gone, were again called back, and they all very joyfully accepted of a peace. This became universal over all the island, to the great joy of the inhabitants.

A LINGERING VIEW OF APPROACHING DEATH

On 15 May 1688 Dampier and his seven companions left Great Nicobar for the second time in their native canoe equipped with four paddles and square-rigged mast. By the following day they had made little progress. The author's reflections on his former life and belief in God's providence are often cited as a model for similar passages in Robinson Crusoe.

In the afternoon at four o'clock, we had a gentle breeze at WSW which continued so till nine, all which time we laid down our oars, and steered away SSE. I was then at the helm, and I found by the rippling of the sea, that there was a strong current against us. It made a great noise that might be heard near half a mile. At nine o'clock it fell calm, and so continued till ten. Then the wind sprung up again, and blew a fresh breeze all night.

The 17th day in the morning we looked out for the island Sumatra, supposing that we were now within twenty leagues

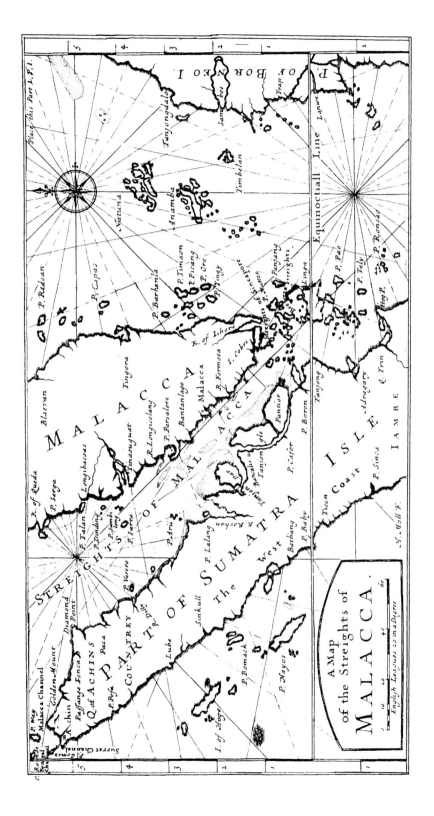

A Map
of the Streights of
MALACCA.

English Leagues 20 in a Degree

of it; for we had rowed and sailed, by our reckoning, twenty-four leagues from Nicobar Island; and the distance from Nicobar to Achin is about forty leagues. But we looked in vain for the island Sumatra; for turning ourselves about, we saw, to our grief, Nicobar Island lying west-north-west and not above eight leagues distant. By this it was visible, that we had met a very strong current against us in the night. But the wind freshened on us, and we made the best use of it while the weather continued fair. At noon we had an observation of the sun, my latitude was 6° 55′ and Mr Hall's was 7° N.

The 18th day the wind freshened on us again, and the sky began to be clouded. It was indifferent clear till noon, and we thought to have had an observation; but we were hindered by the clouds that covered the face of the sun, when it came on the meridian. This often happens that we are disappointed of making observations, by the sun's being clouded at noon, though it shines clear both before and after, especially in places near the sun; and this obscuring of the sun at noon, is commonly sudden and unexpected, and for about half an hour or more.

We had then also a very ill presage, by a great circle about the sun (five or six times the diameter of it) which seldom appears, but storms of wind, or much rain ensue. Such circles about the moon are more frequent, but of less import. We do commonly take great notice of these that are about the sun, observing if there be any breach in the circle, and in what quarter the breach is; for from thence we commonly find the greatest stress of the wind will come. I must confess that I was a little anxious at the sight of this circle, and wished heartily that we were near some land. Yet I showed no sign of it to discourage my comrades, but made a virtue of necessity, and put a good countenance on the matter.

I told Mr Hall that if the wind became too strong and violent, as I feared it would, it being even then very strong, we must of necessity steer away before the wind and sea, till better weather presented; and that as the winds were now, we should, instead of about twenty leagues to Achin, be driven sixty or seventy leagues to the coast of Kedah, a kingdom, and town, and harbour of trade on the coast of Malacca [Malaya].

The winds therefore bearing very hard, we rolled up the foot of our sail on a pole fastened to it, and settled our yard within three foot of the canoe sides, so that we had now but a small sail; yet it was still too big, considering the wind; for the wind being on our broadside, pressed her down very much, though supported by her outriggers; insomuch that the poles of the outriggers going from the sides of the vessel, bent as if they would break; and should they have broken, our overturning and perishing had been inevitable. Besides, the sea increasing, would soon have filled the vessel this way. Yet thus we made a shift to bear up with the side of the vessel against the wind for a while: but the wind still increasing, about one o'clock in the afternoon we put away right before wind and sea, continuing to run thus all the afternoon, and part of the night ensuing. The wind continued increasing all the afternoon, and the sea still swelled higher, and often broke, but did us no damage; for the ends of the vessel being very narrow, he that steered received and broke the sea on his back, and so kept it from coming in so much as to endanger the vessel: though much water would come in, which we were forced to keep heaving out continually. And by this time we saw it was well that we had altered our course, every wave would else have filled and sunk us, taking the side of the vessel: and though our outriggers were well lashed down to the canoe's bottom with rattans, yet they must probably have yielded to such a sea as this; when even before they were plunged under water, and bent like twigs.

The evening of this 18th day was very dismal. The sky looked very black, being covered with dark clouds, the wind blew hard, and the seas ran high. The sea was already roaring in a white foam about us, a dark night coming on, and no land in sight to shelter us, and our little ark in danger to be swallowed by every wave; and, what was worst of all, none of us thought ourselves prepared for another world. The reader may better guess than I can express the confusion that we were all in. I had been in many imminent dangers before now, some of which I have already related, but the worst of them all was but a play-game in comparison with this. I must confess that I was in great conflicts of mind at this time. Other dangers came not upon me with such a leisurely and dreadful solemnity. A sudden skirmish or engagement, or so, was nothing when one's blood was up, and pushed forwards with eager expectations. But here I had a lingering view of approaching death, and little or no hopes of escaping it; and I must confess that my courage, which I had hitherto kept up, failed me here; and I made very sad reflections on my former life, and looked back with horror and detestation on actions which before I disliked, but now I trembled at the remembrance of. I had long before this repented me of that roving course of life, but never with such concern as now. I did also call to mind the many miraculous acts of God's providence towards me in the whole course of my life, of which kind I believe few men have met with the like. For all these I returned thanks in a peculiar manner, and this once more desired God's assistance, and composed my mind as well as I could in the hopes of it, and as the event showed I was not disappointed of my hopes.

Submitting ourselves therefore to God's good providence, and taking all the care we could to preserve our lives, Mr Hall and I took turns to steer, and the rest took turns to heave out the water, and thus we provided to spend the most doleful night I ever was in. About ten o'clock it began to thunder, lighten and rain; but the rain was very welcome to us, having drank up all the water we brought from the island.

The wind at first blew harder than before, but within half an hour it abated, and became more moderate; and the sea also assuaged of its fury; and then by a lighted match, of which we kept a piece burning on purpose,* we looked on our compass, to see how we steered, and found our course to be still east. We had no occasion to look on the compass before, for we steered right before the wind, which if it shifted we had been obliged to have altered our course accordingly. But now it being abated, we found our vessel

---

* This was probably a piece of twisted and tarred hemp cord, soaked in saltpetre and lime water, which burned at the rate of about a foot an hour and was generally used to touch off the priming pans of firearms.

lively enough with that small sail which was then aboard, to haul to our former course SSE which accordingly we did, being now in hopes again to get to the island Sumatra.

But about two o'clock in the morning of the 19th day, we had another gust of wind, with much thunder, lightning and rain, which lasted till day, and obliged us to put before the wind again, steering thus for several hours. It was very dark, and the hard rain soaked us so thoroughly, that we had not one dry thread about us. The rain chilled us extremely; for any fresh water is much colder than that of the sea. For even in the coldest climates the sea is warm, and in the hottest climates the rain is cold and unwholesome for man's body. In this wet starveling plight we spent the tedious night. Never did poor mariners on a lee-shore more earnestly long for the dawning light than we did now. At length the day appeared; but with such dark black clouds near the horizon, that the first glimpse of the dawn appeared 30 or 40° high; which was dreadful enough; for it is a common saying among seamen, and true, as I have experienced, that 'a high dawn will have high winds, and a low dawn small winds'.

We continued our course still east, before wind and sea, till about eight o'clock in the morning of this 19th day; and then one of our Malayan friends cried out, 'Pulo Way'. Mr Hall, and Ambrose and I, thought the fellow had said 'Pull away', an expression usual among English seamen when they are rowing. And we wondered what he meant by it, till we saw him point to his comrades; and then we looking that way, saw land appearing, like an island, and all our Malayans said it was an island at the north-west end of Sumatra, called Way; for Pulo Way is the island Way.* We, who were dropping with wet, cold and hungry, were all overjoyed.

A VOYAGE TO TONQUIN

Dampier and his companions were so ill after their voyage from Great Nicobar to Sumatera that two of them died. Treated by a Malayan doctor, Dampier began to recover, but suffered from fever

* Now spelt We.

and dysentery for the next year. He was offered a position on a merchant ship commanded by Captain Weldon and in July 1688 sailed to Tonquin (North Vietnam). They docked a little way up the Red River, transferring their goods to local vessels for the rest of the journey to Cachao (now Hanoi), where he stayed for a week before returning to his ship.

We went from our ships in the country boats we had hired, with the tide of flood, and anchored in the ebb: for the tide runs strong for thirty or forty miles beyond the place where we left our ships. Our men contented themselves with looking after their goods (the Tonquinese being very light-fingered) and left the management of the boats entirely to the boat's crew. Their boats have but one mast; and when the wind is against them they take it down, and ply their oars. As we advanced thus up the river, sometimes rowing, sometimes sailing, we had a delightful prospect over a large level fruitful country. It was generally either pasture or rice-fields; and void of trees, except only about the villages, which stood thick, and appeared mighty pleasant at a distance. There are many of these villages standing close to the banks of the rivers, encompassed with trees on the backside only, but open to the river.

When we came near any of these villages, we were commonly encountered with beggars, who came off to us in little boats made of twigs, and plastered over both inside and outside with clay, but very leaky. These were a poor leprous people, who for that reason are compelled by the rest to live by themselves, and are permitted to beg publicly. As soon as they spied us they set up a loud doleful cry, and as we passed by them we threw them out some rice, which they received with great appearance of joy . . .

There is a kind of locust in Tonquin, in great abundance. This creature is about the bigness of the top of a man's finger, and as long as the first joint. It breeds in the earth, especially in the banks of rivers and ditches in the low country. In the months of January and February, which is the season of taking them, being then only seen, this creature first comes out of the earth in huge swarms. It is then of a

whitish colour, having two small wings, like the wings of a
bee: at its first coming out of the earth it takes its flight; but
for want of strength or use falls down again in a short time.
Such as strive to fly over the river, do commonly fall down
into the water and are drowned, or become a prey to the fish
of the river, or are carried out into the sea to be devoured
there: but the natives in these months watch the rivers, and
take up thence multitudes, skimming them from off the water
with little nets. They eat them fresh, broiled on the coals; or
pickle them to keep. They are plump and fat, and are much
esteemed by rich and poor as good wholesome food, either
fresh or pickled.

The rivers and ponds are stored with divers sorts of excellent fish, besides abundance of frogs, which they angle for,
being highly esteemed by the Tonquinese. The sea too contributes much towards the support of poor people, by yielding plentiful stores of fish, that swarm on this coast in their
seasons, and which are commonly preferred before the river
fish. Of these here are divers sorts, besides sea-turtle, which
frequently come ashore on the sandy bays in their seasons to
lay their eggs. Here are also both land-crabs and sea-crabs in
good store, and other shellfish, viz. crawfish, shrimps, and
prawns. Here is one sort of small fish much like an anchovy,
both in shape and size, which is very good pickled. There
are other sorts of small fish, which I know not the names of.
One sort of them comes in great shoals near the shore, and
these the fishermen with their nets take so plentifully as to
load their boats with them. Among these they generally take
a great many shrimps in their nets, which they carry ashore
mixed together as they take them, and make balichow with
them.

Balichow is a composition of a strong savour; yet a very
delightsome dish to the natives of this country. To make it,
they throw the mixture of shrimps and small fish into a sort
of weak pickle* made with salt and water, and put it into a
tight earthen vessel or jar. The pickle being thus weak, it
keeps not the fish firm and hard, neither is it probably so
designed, for the fish are never gutted. Therefore in a short

---

* Containing mostly onion.

time they turn all to a mash in the vessel; and when they have lain thus a good while, so that the fish is reduced to a pap, they then draw off the liquor into fresh jars, and preserve it for use. The mashed fish that remains behind is called balichow, and the liquor poured off is called nuoc mam. The poor people eat the balichow with their rice. 'Tis rank-scented, yet the taste is not altogether unpleasant; but rather savoury, after one is a little used to it. The nuoc mam is of a pale brown colour, inclining to grey, and pretty clear. It is also very savoury and used as a good sauce for fowls, not only by the natives, but also by many Europeans, who esteem it equal with soy. I have been told that soy is made partly with a fishy composition, and it seems most likely by the taste: though a gentleman of my acquaintance, who was very intimate with one that sailed often from Tonquin to Japan, from whence the true soy comes, told me that it was made only with wheat, and a sort of beans mixed with water and salt* . . .

For all these sorts of provision there are markets duly kept all over Tonquin once a week, in a neighbourhood of four or five villages; and held at each of them successively in its order: so that the same village has not the market returned to it till four or five weeks after. These markets are abundantly more stored with rice (as being their chief subsistence, especially the poorer sort) than either with flesh or fish, yet wants there not for pork, and young pigs in good store, ducks and hens, plenty of eggs, fish great and small, fresh and salted balichow and nuoc mam; with all sorts of roots, herbs and fruits, even in these country markets. But at Cachao, where there are markets kept every day, they have besides these, beef of bullocks, buffaloes' flesh, goats' flesh, horseflesh, cats and dogs (as I have been told), and locusts.

They dress their food very cleanly, and make it savoury; for which they have several ways unknown in Europe: but they have many sorts of dishes that would turn the stomach of a stranger, which yet they themselves like very well, as particularly a dish of raw pork, which is very cheap and com-

* Soy sauce is made by fermenting soya beans and wheat kernels, mixed with water and salt.

mon. This is only pork cut and minced very small, fat and
lean together; which being afterwards made up in balls, or
rolls like sausages, and pressed very hard together, is then
neatly wrapped up in clean leaves, and without more ado
served up to the table. Raw beef is another dish, much
esteemed at Cachao. When they kill a bullock they singe the
hair off with fire, as we singe bacon-hogs in England. Then
they open it, and, while the flesh is yet hot, they cut good
collops from off the lean parts, and put them into a very tart
vinegar, where it remains three or four hours longer, till it
is sufficiently soaked, and then, without more trouble, they
take it out, and eat it with great delight. As for horseflesh, I
know not whether they kill any purposely for the shambles
[market]; or whether they only do it, when they are not
likely to live; as I have seen them do their working bullocks
at Galicia in Old Spain; where the cattle falling down with
labour, and being so poor and tired that they cannot rise,
they are slaughtered, and sent to market; and I think I never
ate worse beef than at the Groin [La Coruña]. The horseflesh
comes to market at Cachao very frequently, and is as much
esteemed as beef. Elephants they eat also; and the trunk of
this beast is an acceptable present for a nobleman, and that
too though the beast dies with age or sickness. For here are
but few wild elephants, and those so shy that they are not
easily taken. But the king having a great number of tame
elephants, when one of these dies, 'tis given to the poor, who
presently fetch away the flesh, but the trunk is cut in pieces,
and presented to the mandarins. Dogs and cats are killed
purposely for the shambles, and their flesh is much esteemed
by people of the best fashion, as I have been credibly informed. Great yellow frogs also are much admired, especially
when they come fresh out of the pond. They have many other
such choice dishes: and in all the villages, at any time of the
day, be it market-day or not, there are several to be sold by
poor people, who make it their trade. The most common
sorts of cookeries, next to boiled rice, is to dress little bits of
pork, spitted five or six of them at once on a small skewer,
and roasted. In the markets also, and daily in every village,
there are women sitting in the streets, with a pipkin over a

small fire, full of *chau,* as they call it, a sort of very ordinary tea, of a reddish brown colour, and 'tis their ordinary drink.

The kingdom of Tonquin is in general healthy enough, especially in the dry season, when also it is very delightsome. For the seasons of the year at Tonquin and all the countries between the Tropics, are distinguished into wet and dry, as properly as others are into winter and summer: but as the alteration from winter to summer, and vice versa is not made of a sudden, but with the interchangeable weather of spring and autumn; so also towards the end of the dry season, there are some gentle showers now and then, that precede the violent wet months; and again toward the end of these, several fair days that introduce the dry time. These seasons are generally much alike at the same time of the year in all places of the Torrid Zone, on the same side of the Equator: but for two or three degrees on each side of it, the weather is more mixed and uncertain (though inclining to the wet extreme), and is often contrary to that which is then settled on the same side of the Equator more toward the Tropic. So that even when the wet season is set in, in the northern parts of the Torrid Zone, it may yet be dry weather for two or three degrees north of the Line: and the same may be said of the contrary latitudes and seasons. This I speak with respect to the dryness or moisture of countries in the Torrid Zone: but it may also hold good of their heat or cold generally: for as to all these qualities there is a further difference arises from the make or situation of the land, or other accidental causes, besides what depends on the respective latitude or regard to the sun. Thus the Bay of Campeachy in the West Indies, and that of Bengal in the east, in much the same latitude, are exceeding hot and moist; and whether their situation, being very low countries, and the scarcity and faintness of the sea-breezes, as in most bays, may not contribute hereunto, I leave others to judge. Yet even as to the latitudes of these places, lying near the Tropics they are generally upon that account alone more inclined to great heats, than places near the Equator. This is what I have experienced in many places in such latitudes both in the East and West Indies, that the hottest parts of the world are these near the Tropics, especially 3 or 4° within them; sensibly hotter than under the Line itself. Many reasons may be assigned for this, beside the accidental ones from the make of the particular countries, tropical winds, or the like. For the longest day at the Equator never exceeds twelve hours, and the night is always at the same length: but near the Tropics the longest day is about thirteen hours and an half; and an hour and an half being also taken from the night, what with the length of the day, and the shortness of the night, there is a difference of three hours: which is very considerable. Besides which, at such places as are about 3° within the Tropics, or in the latitude of 20° N. the sun comes within 2 or 3° of the Zenith in the beginning of May; and having passed the Zenith, goes not above 2 or 3° beyond it, before it returns and passes the Zenith once more; and by this means is at least three months within 4° of the Zenith; so that they have the sun in a manner over their heads, from the beginning of May till the latter end of July. Whereas when the sun comes under the Line, in March or September, it immediately posts away to the north or the south, and is not twenty days in passing from 3° on one side, to 3° on the other side of the Line. So that by his small stay there, the heat cannot be answerable to what it is near the Tropic, where he so long continues in a manner vertical at noon, and is so much longer above the horizon each particular day, with the intervening of a shorter night.

But to return to Tonquin. During the wet months there 'tis excessive hot, especially whenever the sun breaks out of the clouds, and there is then but little wind stirring: and I have been told by a gentleman who lived there many years, that he thought it was the hottest place that ever he was in, though he had been in many other parts of India.* And as to the rains, it has not the least share of them, though neither altogether the greatest of what I have met with in the Torrid Zone; and even in the same latitude, and on the same side of the Equator. The wet season begins here the latter end of April, or the beginning of May; and holds till the latter end of August, in which time are very violent rains, some of many hours, others of two or three days' continuance. Yet

* In this context, Dampier is referring to the Orient.

are not these rains without some considerable intervals of fair weather, especially toward the beginning or end of the season.

By these rains are caused those land-floods which never fail in these countries between the Tropics at their annual periods; all the rivers then overflowing their banks. This is a thing so well known to all who are any way acquainted with the Torrid Zone, that the cause of the overflowing of the Nile, to find out which the ancients set their wits so much upon the rack, and fancied melting of snows, and blowing of Etesia,* and I know not what, is now no longer a secret. For these floods must needs discharge themselves upon such low lands as lie in their way; as the land of Egypt does with respect to the Nile, coming a great way from within the Torrid Zone, and falling down from the higher Ethiopia. And anyone who will be at the pains to compare the time of the land-flood in Egypt with that of the Torrid Zone in any of the parts of it along which the Nile runs, will find that of Egypt so much later than the other, as 'twill be thought reasonable to allow for the daily progress of the waters along so vast a tract of ground. They might have made the same wonderment of any other rivers which run any long course from out the Torrid Zone: but they, knowing only the North Temperate Zone, and the Nile being the only great river known to come thither a great way from a country near the Line, they made that only the subject of their enquiry: but the same effect must also follow from any great river that should run from out of the Torrid Zone into the South Temperate Zone. And as to the Torrid Zone, the yearly floods, and their cause, are everywhere as well known by people there, as the rivers themselves. In America particularly, in Campeachy rivers, in Rio Grande, and others, 'tis a vast havoc is made by these floods; bringing down sometimes trees of an incredible bigness; and these floods always come at the stated season of the year. In the dry part of Peru, along the coasts of the Pacific Sea, where it never rains, as it seldom does in Egypt, they have not only floods, but rivers themselves, made by the annual falling of rain on the mountains within land; the channels of which are dry all the rest of the year. This I have

* A Mediterranean wind that blows mainly from the north.

observed concerning the river Ilo, on the coast of Peru, in my former volume. But it has this difference from the floods of Egypt, that besides its being a river in the Torrid Zone, 'tis also in south latitude, and so overflows at a contrary season of the year; to wit at such time as the sun being in southern signs, causes the rains and floods on that side of the Line.

But to return from this digression, in August the weather at Tonquin is more moderate, as to heat or wet, yet not without some showers, and September and October are more temperate still: yet the worst weather in all the year for seamen, is in one of the three months last mentioned: for then the violent storms, called typhoons are expected. These winds are so very fierce, that for fear of them the Chinese that trade thither, will not stir out of harbour till the end of October: after which month there is no more danger of any violent storms, till the next year.

Typhoons are a particular kind of violent storms, blowing on the coast of Tonquin and the neighbouring coasts in the months of July, August, and September. They commonly happen near the full or change of the moon, and are usually preceded by very fair weather, small winds and a clear sky. Those small winds veer from the common Trade of that time of the year, which is here at SW and shuffles about to the N. and NE. Before the storm comes there appears a boding cloud in the NE which is very black near the horizon, but towards the upper edge it looks of a dark copper-colour, and higher still it is brighter, and afterwards it fades to a whitish glaring colour, at the very edge of the cloud. This cloud appears very amazing and ghastly, and is sometimes seen twelve hours before the storm comes. When that cloud begins to move apace, you may expect the wind presently. It comes on fierce, and blows very violent at NE twelve hours more or less. It is also commonly accompanied with terrible claps of thunder, large and frequent flashes of lightning, and excessive hard rain. When the wind begins to abate it dies away suddenly, and falling flat calm, it continues so an hour, more or less: then the wind comes about to the SW and it blows and rains as fierce from thence, as it did before at NE and as long.

November and December are two very dry, wholesome, warm, and pleasant months. January, February, and March are pretty dry: but then you have thick fogs in the morning, and sometimes drizzling cold rains: the air also in these three months, particularly in January and February, is very sharp, especially when the wind is at NE, or NNE, whether because of the quarter it blows from, or the land it blows over, I know not; for I have elsewhere observed such winds to be colder, where they have come from over land. April is counted a moderate month, either as to heat or cold, dryness or moisture.

This is ordinarily the state of their year: yet are not these various seasons so exact in the returns, but that there may sometimes be the difference of a month or more. Neither yet are the several seasons, when they do come, altogether alike in all years. For sometimes the rains are more violent and lasting, at other times more moderate; and some years they are not sufficient to produce reasonable crops, or else they come so unseasonably as to injure and destroy the rice, or at least to advance it but little. For the husbandry of this country, and other countries in the Torrid Zone depends on the annual floods, to moisten and fatten the land; and if the wet seasons prove more dry than ordinary, so as that the rice-land is not well drenched with the overflowing of the rivers, the crops will be but mean: and rice being their bread, the staff of life with them, if that fails, such a populous country as this cannot subsist without being beholden to its neighbours. But when it comes to that pass, that they must be supplied by sea, many of the poorer sort sell their children to relieve their wants, and so preserve their lives, whilst others that have not children to sell, may be famished and die miserable in the streets. This manner of parents dealing with their children is not peculiar to this kingdom alone, but is customary in other places of the East Indies, especially on the coasts of Malabar and Coromandel. There a famine happens more frequently, and rages sometimes to a degree beyond belief: for those countries are generally very dry, and less productive of rice than Tonquin. Neither are there such large rivers to fatten the land; but all their crop depends on seasons of rains only, to moisten the earth; and when those seasons fail, as they do very often, then they can have no crop at all. Sometimes they have little or no rain in three or four years, and then they perish at a lamentable rate. Such a famine as this happened two or three years before my going to Fort St George, which raged so sore, that thousands of people perished for want, and happy were they that could hold out till they got to the sea-port towns, where the Europeans lived, to sell themselves to them, though they were sure to be transported from their own country presently. But the famine does never rage so much at Tonquin, neither may their greatest scarcity be so truly called a famine: for in the worst of times there is rice, and 'tis through the poverty of the meaner people, that so many perish or sell their children, for they might else have rice enough, had they money to buy it with: and when their rice is thus dear, all other provisions are so proportionably.

THE PEOPLE OF TONQUIN

Tonquin is very populous, being thick-set with villages; and the natives in general are of a middle stature, and clean limbed. They are of a tawny Indian colour; but I think the fairest and clearest that I ever saw of that complexion; for you may perceive a blush or change of colour in some of their faces, on any sudden surprise of passion, which I could never discern in any other Indians. Their faces are generally flattish, and of an oval form. Their noses and lips are proportionable enough, and altogether graceful. Their hair is black, long and lank, and very thick; and they wear it hanging down to their shoulders.

Their teeth are as black as they can make them; for this being accounted a great ornament, they dye them of that colour, and are three or four days doing it. They do this when they are about twelve or fourteen years old, both boys and girls: and during all the time of the operation they dare not take any nourishment, besides water, *chau*, or some liquid thing, and not much of that neither, for fear, I judge, of being poisoned by the dye, or pigment. So that while this is doing

The Vietnamese: 'Their hair is black, long and lank, and
very thick; and they wear it hanging to their shoulders'

they undergo very severe penance; but as both sexes, so all qualities, the poor as well as the rich, must be in this fashion: they say they should else be like brutes; and that would be a great shame to them to be like elephants or dogs; which they compare those to that have white teeth.

They are generally dextrous, nimble, and active, and ingenious in any mechanic science they profess. This may be seen by the multitude of fine silks that are made here; and the curious lacquerwork, that is yearly transported from thence. They are also laborious and diligent in their callings; but the country being so very populous, many of them are extreme poor for want of employment: and though the country is full of silk, and other materials to work on, yet little is done, but when strange ships arrive. For 'tis the money and goods that are brought hither, especially by the English and Dutch, that puts life into them: for the handicrafts men have not money to set themselves to work; and the foreign merchants are therefore forced to trust them with advance-money, to the value of at least a third, or half their goods; and this for two or three months or more, before they have made their goods, and brought them in. So that they having no goods ready by them, till they have money from the merchant strangers, the ships that trade hither must of necessity stay here all the time that their goods are making, which are commonly five or six months.

The Tonquinese make very good servants; I think the best in India. For as they are generally apprehensive and docile, so are they faithful when hired, diligent and obedient. Yet they are low spirited: probably by reason of their living under an arbitrary government. They are patient in labour, but in sickness they are mightily dejected. They have one great fault extreme common among them, which is gaming. To this they are so universally addicted, servants and all, that neither the awe of their masters, nor anything else, is sufficient to restrain them, till they have lost all they have, even their very clothes. This is a reigning vice among the eastern nations, especially the Chinese, as I said in my former volume. And I may add that the Chinese I found settled at Tonquin, were no less given to it than those I met with elsewhere. For after they have lost their money, goods and clothes, they will stake down their wives and children: and lastly, as the dearest thing they have, will play upon tick, and mortgage their hair upon honour: and whatever it cost them they will be sure to redeem it. For a free Chinese as these are, who have fled from the Tartars, would be as much ashamed of short hair, as a Tonquinese of white teeth.

The clothes of the Tonquinese are made either of silk or cotton. The poor people and the soldiers do chiefly wear cotton cloth dyed to a dark tawny colour. The rich men and mandarins commonly wear English broadcloth: the chief colours are red or green. When they appear before the king, they wear long gowns which reach down to their heels: neither may any man appear in his presence but in such a garb. The great men have also long caps made of the same that their gowns are made of: but the middle sort of men and the poor commonly go bare-headed. Yet the fishermen, and such labourers as are by their employments more exposed to the weather, have broad-brimmed hats made of reeds, straw, or palmetto-leaves. These hats are as stiff as boards, and sit not pliant to their heads: for which reason they have band-strings or necklaces fastened to their hats, which, coming under their chins are there tied, to keep their hats fast to their heads. These hats are very ordinary things; they seldom wear them but in rainy weather. Their other clothes are very few and mean: a ragged pair of breeches commonly suffices them. Some have bad jackets, but neither shirt, stockings, nor shoes.

The Tonquinese buildings are but mean. Their houses are small and low: the walls are either mud, or wattle bedaubed over: and the roofs are thatched, and that very ill, especially in the country. The houses are too low to admit of chambers: yet they have here two or three partitions on the ground floor, made with a wattling of canes or sticks, for their several uses; in each of which there is a window to let in the light. The windows are very small square holes in the walls, which they shut up at night with a board fitted for that purpose. The rooms are but meanly furnished; with a poor bed or two (or more, according to the bigness of the family) in the inner room. The outer rooms are furnished with stools, benches, or chairs to sit on. There is also a table, and on one side a little altar, with two incense pots on it; nor is any house without its altar. One of these incense pots has a small bundle of rushes in it; the ends of which I always took notice had been burnt, and the fire put out. This outer room is the place where they commonly dress their food: yet in fair weather they do it as frequently in the open air, at their doors, or in their yards; as being thereby the less incommoded by heat or smoke.

They dwell not in lone houses, but together in villages: 'tis rare to see a single house by itself. The country villages commonly consist of twenty, thirty, or forty houses, and are thick-seated over all the country; yet hardly to be seen till you come to their very doors, by reason of the trees and groves they are surrounded with. And 'tis as rare to see a grove without a village, in the low country near the sea, as to see a village without a grove: but the high lands are full of woods, and the villages there stand all as in one great forest. The villages and land about them do most belong to great men, and the inhabitants are tenants that manure and cultivate the ground.

The villages in the low land are also surrounded with great banks and deep ditches. These encompass the whole grove in which each village stands.

The banks are to keep the water from overflowing their gardens, and from coming into their houses in the wet time, when all the land about them is under water, two or three foot deep. The ditches or trenches are to preserve the water in the dry time, with which they water their gardens when need requires. Every man lets water at pleasure, by little drains that run inward from the town ditch, into his own garden; and usually each man's yard or garden is parted from his neighbours' by one of these little drains on each side. The houses lie scattering up and down in the grove; nowhere joining to one another, but each apart, and fenced in with a small hedge. Every house has a small gate or stile to enter into the garden first, for the house stands in the middle of it: and the gardens run also from the backside of the house to the town ditch, with its drain and hedge on each side. In the gardens every man has his own fruit trees, as oranges, limes, betel; his pumpkins, melons, pineapples, and a great many herbs. In the dry season these grovy dwellings are very pleasant; but in the wet season they are altogether uncomfortable: for though fenced in thus with banks, yet are they like so many duck-houses all wet and dirt: neither can they pass from one village to another, but mid-leg or to their knees in water, unless sometimes in boats, which they keep for this purpose. But notwithstanding these, they are seldom out of mire and wet, even in the midst of the village or garden, so long as that season lasts. The inhabitants of the higher part of the kingdom are not troubled with such inconveniences, but live more cleanly and comfortably, forasmuch as their land is never overflown with water: and though they live also in villages or towns as the former, yet they have no occasion to surround them with banks or trenches, but lie open to the forest.

The capital city Cachao, which stands in the high country about eighty miles from the sea, on the west side of the river, and on a pretty level, yet rising ground, lies open in the same manner, without wall, bank, or ditch. There may be in Cachao about 20,000 houses. The houses are generally low, the walls of the houses are of mud, and the covering thatch, yet some are built with brick, and the covering with pantiles. Most of these houses have a yard, or backside belonging to them. In each yard you shall see a small arched building made somewhat like an oven, about six foot high, with the mouth on the ground. It is built from top to bottom with brick, all over daubed thick with mud and dirt. If any house wants a yard, they have nevertheless such a kind of oven as this, but smaller, set up in the middle of the house itself; and there is scarce a house in the city without one. The use of it is to thrust their chiefest goods into when a fire happens: for these low-thatched houses are very subject to take fire, especially in the dry times, to the destruction of many houses in an instant, that often they have scarce time to secure their goods in the arched ovens, though so near them.

As every private person has this contrivance, to secure his

own goods, when a fire happens, so the government has carefully ordered necessary means to be used for the preventing of fire, or extinguishing it before it gets too great a head. For in the beginning of the dry season every man must keep a great jar of water, on the top of his house, to be ready to pour down as occasion shall serve. Besides this, he is to keep a long pole, with a basket or bowl at the end of it, to throw water out of the channels upon the houses. But if the fire gets to such a head, that both these expedients fail, then they cut the straps that hold the thatch of the houses, and let it drop from the rafters to the ground. This is done with little trouble; for the thatch is not laid on as ours, neither is it tied on by single leaves, as in the West Indies, and many parts of the East Indies, where they thatch with palmetto or palm tree leaves: but this is made up in panes of seven or eight foot square, before it is laid on; so that four or six panes, more or less, according to the bigness of the house, will cover one side of it: and these panes being only fastened in a few places to the rafters with rattans, they are easily cut, and down drops half the covering at once. These panes are also better than loose thatch, as being more manageable, in case any of them should fall on or near the oven where the goods are; for they are easily dragged off to another place. The neighbouring houses may this way be soon uncovered, before the flames come to 'em; and the thatch either carried away, or at least laid where it may burn by itself. And for this purpose every man is ordered to keep a long pole or bamboo at his door, with a cutting-hook at the end of it, purposely for uncovering the houses: and if any man is found without his jar upon the house, and his bucket pole and long hook at his door, he will be punished severely for his neglect. They are rigorous in exacting this: for even with all this caution they are much and often damaged by fire.

The principal streets in this city are very wide, though some are but narrow. They are most of them paved, or patched rather, with small stones; but after a very ill manner. In the wet season they are very dirty; and in the dry time there are many stagnant ponds, and some ditches full of black stinking mud, in and about the city. This makes it unpleasant, and a man would think unwholesome too: yet it is healthy enough, as far as I perceived, or could ever learn.

The kings of Tonquin, who make this city their constant residence, have two or three palaces in it, such as they be. Two of them are very mean: they are built with timber, yet have they many great guns planted in houses near them, stables for the king's elephants and horses, and pretty large square spots of ground for the soldiers to draw themselves up regularly before him. The third palace is called the palace royal. It is more magnificently built than the other two: yet built also with timber, but all open as the divans in Turkey are said to be. The wall that encompasses it is most remarkable. It is said to be three leagues in circumference. The height of this wall is about fifteen or sixteen foot, and almost as many broad or thick. It is faced up on both sides with brick: there are several small gates to go in and out at, but the main gate faces to the city. This they say is never opened, but when the Boua or emperor goes in or comes out. There are two smaller gates adjoining to it, one on each side, which are opened on all occasions, for any concerned there to pass in and out; but strangers are not permitted this liberty. Yet they may ascend to the top of the wall, and walk round it, there being stairs at the gate to go up by: and in some places the walls are fallen down . . .

There is nothing more in or about the city worth noting, but only a piece of work on the south side, up the river. This is a massy frame of timber, ingeniously put together, and very skilfully placed on great piles that are set upright in the river, just by its banks. The piles are driven firmly into the ground, close one by another, and all the space between them and the bank is filled up with stones, and on them great trees laid across, and pinned fast at each end to the piles, so that the whole fabric must be moved before any part of it will yield. This piece of work is raised about sixteen or seventeen foot above the water in the dry time, but in the wet season the floods come within two or three foot of the top. It was made to resist the violence of the water in the rainy season; for the stream then pressed so hard against this place, that before this pile was built it broke down the bank, and threatened to carry all before it, even to the ruining of the city, if this course had not timely been taken to prevent it. And so much the rather, because there is a large pond just within land, and low ground between it and the city: so that had it made but a small breach into the pond, it would have come even to the skirts of the city. And though the city stands so high as that the land-floods never reach it, yet the land on which it stands being a sort of yielding sand, could not be thought capable of always resisting such violence. For the natural floods do very often make great changes in the river, breaking down one point of land, and making another point in the opposite side of the river; and that chiefly in this part of the country, where it is bounded with high banks: for nearer the sea, where it presently overflows, the floods do seldom make any considerable change, and move more quietly.

But to return to the people. They are courteous and civil to strangers, especially the trading people; but the great men are proud, haughty, and ambitious; and the soldiers very insolent. The poorer sort are very thievish, insomuch that the factors and strangers that traffic hither are forced to keep good watch in the night to secure their goods, notwithstanding the severe punishments they have against thieving. They have indeed great opportunities of thieving, the houses being so slightly built: but they will work a way underground, rather than fail; and use many subtle stratagems. I am a stranger to any ceremonies used by them in marriage, or at the birth of a child or the like, if they use any. Polygamy is allowed of in this country, and they buy their wives of the parents. The king and great men keep several, as their inclinations lead them, and their ability serves. The poor are stinted for want of means more than desire: for though many are not able to buy, much less to maintain one wife; yet most of them make a shift to get one, for here are some very low-prized ones, that are glad to take up with poor husbands. But then in hard times, the man must sell both wife and children, to buy rice to maintain himself. Yet this is not so common here as in some places; as I before observed of the Malabar and Coromandel coasts. This custom among them of buying wives, easily degenerates into that other of hiring misses, and gives great liberty to the young women, who offer themselves of their own accord to any strangers, who will go to their price. There are of them of all prices, from a hundred dollars to five dollars, and the refuse of all will be caressed by the poor seamen, such as the Lascars, who are Moors of India, coming hither in vessels from Fort St George and other places; who yet have nothing to give them, but such fragments of food, as their commons will afford. Even the great men of Tonquin will offer their daughters to the merchants and officers, though their stay is not likely to be above five or six months in the country: neither are they afraid to be with child by white men, for their children will be much fairer than their mothers, and consequently of greater repute when they grow up, if they be girls. Nor is it any charge to breed them here: and at the worst, if their mothers are not able to maintain them, 'tis but selling them when they are young. But to return, the women who thus let themselves to hire, if they have been so frugal as to save what they have got by these loose amours, they soon procure husbands, that will love and esteem them well enough: and themselves also will prove afterwards obedient and faithful wives. For 'tis said, that even while they are with strangers, they are very faithful to them; especially to such as remain long in the country, or make annual returns hither, as the Dutch generally do. Many of these have gotten good estates by their Tonquin ladies, and that chiefly by trusting them with money and goods. For in this poor country 'tis a great advantage to watch the market; and these female merchants having stocks will mightily improve them, taking their opportunities of buying raw silk in the dead time of the year. With this they will employ the poor people, when work is scarce; and get it cheaper and better done than when ships are here: for then every man being employed and in a hurry of business, he will have his price according to the haste of work. And by this means they will get their goods ready against the ships arrive, and before the ordinary working season, to the profit both of the merchant and the *pagally*.

When a man dies he is interred in his own land, for here

are no common burying-places: and within a month afterwards the friends of the deceased, especially if he was the
master of the family, must make a great feast of flesh and fruit
at the grave. 'Tis a thing belonging to the priest's office to
assist at this solemnity; they are always there, and take care
to see that the friends of the deceased have it duly performed.
To make this feast they are obliged to sell a piece of land,
though they have money enough otherways, which money
they bestow in such things as are necessary for the solemnity,
which is more or less according to the quality of the deceased.
If he was a great man, there is a tower of wood erected over
the grave: it may be seven or eight foot square, and built
twenty or twenty-five foot high. About twenty yards from
the tower, are little sheds built with stalls, to lay the provisions on, both of meat and fruits of all sorts, and that in great
plenty. Thither the country people resort to fill their bellies,
for the feast seems to be free for all comers, at least of the
neighbourhood. How it is dressed or distributed about, I
know not; but there the people wait till 'tis ready. Then the
priest gets within the tower, and climbs up to the top, and,
looking out from thence, makes an oration to the people
below. After this the priest descends, and then they set fire
to the foundation of the tower, burning it down to the
ground: and when this is done they fall to their meat. I saw
one of these grave-feasts, which I shall have elsewhere occasion to mention.

The Tonquinese have two annual feasts. The chief is at the
first new moon of the New Year:* and their New Year begins
with the first new moon that falls out after the middle of
January, for else that moon is reckoned to the Old Year. At
this time they make merry and rejoice ten or twelve days, and
then there is no business done, but every man makes himself
as fine as may be, especially the common sort. These spend
their time in gaming or sporting, and you shall see the streets
full of people, both citizens and countryfolk, gazing at several
diverting exercises. Some set up swings in the streets, and
get money of those that will swing in them. The frames are
contrived like ours in the fields about London in holiday

* The lunar New Year, or Tet.

times: but they who swing stand upright in the lower part
of the swing, which is only a stick standing on each end,
being fastened to a pendulous rope, which they hold fast
with their hands on each side; and they raise themselves to
such a prodigious height, that if the swing should break they
must needs break their limbs at best, if not kill themselves
outright. Others spend their time in drinking. Their ordinary
drink is tea: but they make themselves merry with hot arrack,
which sometimes also they mix with their tea. Either way it
has an odd nasty taste, but is very strong; and is therefore
much esteemed by them, especially at this time when they
so much devote themselves to mirth, or madness, or even
bestial drunkenness. The richer sort are more reserved; yet
they will also be very merry at this time. The nobles treat
their friends with good cheer and the best arrack; but indeed
there is none good in this country. Yet such as they have they
esteem as a great cordial; especially when snakes and scorpions have been infused therein, as I have been informed.
This is not only accounted a great cordial, but an antidote
against the leprosy, and all sorts of poison; and 'tis accounted
a great piece of respect to anyone to treat him with his liquor.
I had this relation from one that had been treated thus by
many of the great men. They also at this time more especially
chew abundance of betel, and make presents thereof to one
another.

The betel-leaf is the great entertainment in the East for all
visitants; and 'tis always given with the areca folded up in it.
They make up the areca in pellets fit for use, by first peeling
off the outer green hard rind of the nuts, and then splitting it
lengthways in three or four parts, more or less, according to
its bigness. Then they daub the leaf all over with chunam or
lime made into a mortar or paste, and kept in a box for this
purpose, spreading it thin.

And here by the way I shall take notice of a slip in my
former volume, which I desire may be corrected: the nut
being there by mistake called the betel, and the areca tree
called the betel tree, whereas betel is the name of the leaf
they chew. In this leaf thus spread with chunam, they roll up
a slice of areca-nut, very neatly, and make a pellet of about an

inch long, and as big as the top of one's finger. Every man here has a box that will hold a great many of these pellets, in which they keep a store ready made up: for all persons, of what quality soever, from the prince to the beggar, chew abundance of it. The poorer sort carry a small pouchful about with them: but the mandarins, or great men, have curious oval boxes, made purposely for this use, that will hold fifty or sixty betel pellets. These boxes are neatly lacquered and gilded, both inside and outside, with a cover to take off; and if any stranger visits them, especially Europeans, they are sure, among other good entertainment, to be treated with a box of betel. The attendant that brings it, holds it to the left hand of the stranger; who therewith taking off the cover, takes with his right hand the nuts out of the box. 'Twere an affront to take them, or give or receive anything with the left hand, which is confined all over India to the viler uses.

It is accounted good breeding to commend the taste or neatness of this present; and they all love to be flattered. You thereby extremely please the master of the house, and engage him to be your friend: and afterwards you may be sure he will not fail to send his servant with a present of betel once in two or three mornings, with a compliment to know how you do. This will cost you a small gratuity to the servant, who joyfully acquaints his master how gratefully you received the present: and this still engages him more; and he will compliment you with great respect whenever he meets you. I was invited to one of these New Year's feasts by one of the country, and accordingly went ashore, as many other seamen did upon like invitations. I know not what entertainment they had; but mine was like to be but mean, and therefore I presently left it. The staple dish was rice, which I have said before is the common food: besides which, my friend, that he might the better entertain me and his other guests, had been in the morning a-fishing in a pond not far from his house, and had caught a huge mess of frogs, and with great joy brought them home as soon as I came to his house. I wondered to see him turn out so many of these creatures into a basket; and asked him what they were for? He told me, to eat: but how he dressed them I know not; I did not like his dainties so well as to stay and dine with him. The other great feast* they have, is after their May crop is housed, about the beginning of June. At this feast also they have public rejoicing; but much inferior to those of their New Year's feast.

Their religion is paganism, and they are great idolaters: nevertheless they own an omnipotent, supreme, over-ruling power, that beholds both them and their actions, and so far takes notice of them, as to reward the good, and punish the bad in the other world. For they believe the immortality of the soul: but the notion that they have of the deity is very obscure. Yet by the figures which they make representing this god, they manifestly show that they do believe him to excel in sight, strength, courage and wisdom, justice, etc. For though their idols, which are made in human shapes, are very different in their forms; yet they all represent somewhat extraordinary, either in the countenance, or in the make of the body or limbs. Some are very corpulent and fat, others are very lean; some also have many eyes, others as many hands, and all grasping somewhat. Their aspects are also different, and in some measure representing what they are made to imitate, or there is somewhat in their hands or lying by them, to illustrate the meaning of the figure. Several passions are also represented in the countenance of the image, as love, hatred, joy, grief. I was told of one image that was placed sitting on his hams, with his elbows resting on his knees, and his chin resting on his two thumbs, for the supporting his head, which looked drooping forwards: his eyes were mournfully lifted up towards heaven, and the figure was so lean, and the countenance and whole composure was so sorrowful, that it was enough to move the beholder with pity and compassion. My friend said he was much affected with the sight thereof.

There are other images also, that are in the shape of beasts, either elephants or horses, for I have not seen them in any other shape. The pagodas or idol temples, are not sumptuous and magnificent, as in some of the neighbouring kingdoms. They are generally built with timber, and are but small and

* Tet Doan Ngo.

low: yet mostly covered with pantiles, especially the city pagodas; but in the country some of them are thatched. I saw the horse and elephant idols only in the country: and indeed I saw none of the idols in the city Cachao, but was told they were generally in human shapes.

The horse and elephant images I saw were both sorts about the bigness and height of a good horse, each standing in the midst of a little temple, just big enough to contain them, with their heads towards the door: and sometimes one, sometimes two together in a temple, which was always open. There were up and down in the country other buildings, such as pagodas, or temples, tombs or the like, less than these; and not above the height of a man: but these were always shut so close, that I could not see what was within them.

There were many pagan priests belonging to these pagodas, and 'tis reported that they are by the laws tied to strict rules of living, as abstinence from women and strong drink especially, and enjoined a poor sort of life. Yet they don't seem to confine themselves much to these rules: but their subsistence being chiefly from offerings, and there being many of them, they are usually very poor. The offering to the priest is commonly two or three handfuls of rice, a box of betel, or some suchlike present. One thing the people resort to them for is fortune-telling, at which they pretend to be very expert, and will be much offended if any dispute their skill in that, or the truth of their religion. Their habitations are very little and mean, close by the pagodas, where they constantly attend to offer the petitions of the poor people, that frequently resort thither on some such errand. For they have no set times of devotion, neither do they seem to esteem one day above another, except their annual feasts. The people bring to the priest in writing what petition they have to make: and he reads it aloud before the idol, and afterwards burns it in an incense pot, the supplicant all the while lying prostrate on the ground.

CHAPTER
SEVEN

BOUA AND CHOUA

This kingdom is an absolute monarchy, but of such a kind as is not in the world again; for it has two kings, and each supreme in his particular way: the one is called Boua, the other Choua; which last name I have been told signifies master. The Boua and his ancestors were the sole monarchs of Tonquin; though I know not whether as independent sovereigns, or as tributaries to China, of which they have been thought to have been a frontier province, if not a colony: for there is a great affinity between them in their language, religion, and customs. These two kings they have at present, are not any way related in their descent or families: nor could I learn how long their government has continued in the present form; but it appears to have been for some successions. The occasion is variously reported; but some give this account of it.

The Bouas, or ancient kings of Tonquin, were formerly masters of Cochinchina, and kept that nation in subjection by an army of Tonquinese constantly kept there, under a general or deputy, who ruled them. When Cochinchina threw off the Tonquinese yoke, the king had two great generals, one in Cochinchina, and another in Tonquin itself. These two generals differing, he who was in Cochinchina revolted from his sovereign of Tonquin, and by his power over the army there, made himself King of Cochinchina: since when these two nations have always been at war; yet each nation of late is rather on the defensive part than on the offensive. But when the general who commanded in Cochinchina had been thus successful in his revolt from under the

Boua, the Tonquinese general took the courage to do so too; and having gained the affections of his army, deprived the king his master of all the regal power, and kept it with all the revenues of the crown in his own hands: yet leaving the other the title of king; probably, because of the great zeal the people had for that family. And thus the kingdom came wholly into the power of this Tonquinese general, and his heirs, who carry the title of Choua; the Bouas of the ancient family having only the shadow of that authority they were formerly masters of. The Boua lives the life of a kind of a prisoner of state, within the old palace, with his women and children; and diverts himself in boats among his fishponds within the palace walls, but never stirs without those bounds. He is held in great veneration by all the Tonquinese, and seemingly by the Choua also; who never offers any violence to him, but treats him with all imaginable respect. The people say they have no king but Boua; and seem to have sad apprehensions of the loss they should have, if he should die without an heir: and whenever the Choua comes into his presence, which is two or three times in the year, he uses abundance of compliments to him, and tells him, that his very life is at his service, and that he governs and rules wholly to do him a kindness: and always gives him the upper hand. So also when any ambassadors are sent from the emperor of China, they will deliver their message to none but the Boua, and have their audience of him. Yet after all this pageantry, the Boua has only a few servants to attend him, none of the mandarins make their court to him, nor is he allowed any guards. All the magistracy and soldiery, treasure, and the ordering of all matters of peace or war, are entirely at the Choua's disposal; all preferment is from him, and the very servants who attend the Boua, are such only as the Choua places about him. Besides these servants are never suffered to see the Boua, much less strangers; so that I could learn nothing as to his person. But as to the Choua, I have been informed that he is an angry, ill-natured, leprous person. He lives in the second palace, where he has ten or twelve wives; but what children I know not. He governs with absolute authority over the subjects, and with great tyranny: for their lives, goods, and estates are at his command.

The Choua has always a strong guard of soldiers about his palace, and many large stables for his horses and elephants. The horses are about thirteen or fourteen hands high, and are kept very fat: there are two or three hundred of them. The elephants are kept in long stables by themselves, each having a peculiar room or partition, with a keeper to dress and feed him. The number of the king's elephants are about 150 or 200. They are watered and washed every day in the river. Some of the elephants are very gentle and governable, others are more indocile and unruly. When these rude ones are to pass through the streets, though only to be watered, the rider or dresser orders a gong or drum to be beaten before him, to warn people that an unruly elephant is coming; and they presently clear the streets and give a passage for the beast; who will do mischief to any that are in the way, and their riders or keepers cannot restrain him.

Before the Choua's palace, there is a large parade, or square place, for the soldiers to be drawn up. On one side there is a place for the mandarins to sit, and see the soldiers exercise, on the other side there is a shed, wherein all the cannon and heavy guns are lodged. There be fifty or sixty iron guns from falcon to demi-culverin,* two or three whole culverin or demi-cannon, and some old iron mortars lying on logs. The guns are mounted on their carriages, but the carriages of these guns are old and very ill made. There is one great brass gun, much bigger than the rest, supposed to be eight or nine thousand pound weight. It is of a taper bore; of a foot diameter at the mouth, but much smaller at the breech. It is an ill shaped thing, yet much esteemed by them, probably because it was cast here, and the biggest that ever they made. It was cast about twelve or thirteen years ago, and it being so heavy, they could not contrive to mount it, but were beholden to the English, to put it into the carriage; where it now stands more for a show than service. But though this is but an ordinary piece of workmanship, yet the Tonquinese understand how to run metals, and are very expert in tempering the earth, wherewith they make their mould.

* Types of light–medium cannon.

These are all the great guns, that I saw or heard of in this kingdom, neither are here any forts, yet the king keeps always a great many soldiers. 'Tis said that he has always seventy or eighty thousand constantly in pay. These are most foot, they are armed with curtanas or swords, and hand-guns of three foot and an half or four foot in the barrel. The bore is about the bigness of our horse pistols, they are all matchlocks, and they are very thick and heavy. The soldiers do all make their own powder. They have little engines for mixing the ingredients, and make as small a quantity as they please. They know not how to corn it, and therefore it is in unequal lumps, some as big as the top of a man's thumb, and some no bigger than a white pea: neither have I seen any powder well corned, that has been made in any of these eastern nations.

The soldiers have each a cartridge box covered with leather, after the manner of the West Indian privateers: but instead of paper cartridges, these are filled with small hollow canes, each containing a load or charge of powder; which they empty out of the cane into the gun; so that each box has in it, as it were, so many bandoleers. Their arms are kept very bright and clean; for which purpose every one of them has a hollow bamboo to lay over the barrel of his gun; and to keep the dust from it as it lies over the rack in his house. When they march also in rainy weather, they have another bamboo to cover their guns. This is large enough to cover the whole barrel, and very well lacquered; so that it is not only handsome, but also preserves the gun dry.

The soldiers when they march are led by an officer, who is leader of the file; and every file consists of ten men: but as I have been informed by one who has seen them march, they don't keep their ranks in marching. The soldiers are most of them lusty, strong well-made men, for 'tis that chiefly recommends them to the king's service. They must also have good stomachs, for that is a greater recommendation than the former; neither can any man be entertained as a soldier, that has not a greater stroke than ordinary at eating: for by this they judge of his strength and constitution. For which reason, when a soldier comes to be listed, his stomach is first proved with rice, the common subsistence of the ordinary people in this kingdom: and according as he acquits himself in this first trial of his manhood, so he is either discharged or entertained in the service. 'Tis reported, that at these trials they commonly eat eight or nine cups of rice, each containing a pint, and they are ever afterwards esteemed and advanced, according to the first day's service: and the greatest eaters are chiefly employed as guards to the king, and commonly attend on his person. The province of Nguyen breeds the lustiest men, and the best eaters: for that reason those of that province are generally employed as soldiers. After thirty years' service a soldier may petition to be disbanded; and then the village where he was born must send another man to serve in his place . . .

PUNISHMENTS

Some of the soldiers are employed also in keeping watch and ward, for the security of private men, as well as in the king's business: and the Tonquinese are observed to keep good orders in the night in all towns and villages; but more particularly in the great cities, and especially at Cachao. There every street is guarded with a strong watch, as well to keep silence, as to hinder any disorder. The watchmen are armed with staves, and stand in the street by the watch-houses, to examine every one that passes by. There is also a rope stretched cross the street breast high, and no man may pass this place till he is examined, unless he will venture to be soundly banged by the watch. These men can handle their weapons so well, that if they design mischief, they will dextrously break a leg or thigh-bone, that being the place which they commonly strike at. There is a pair of stocks by every watch-house, to secure night ramblers in: but for a small piece of money a man may pass quiet enough, and for the most part only the poor are taken up. These watchmen are soldiers, but belong to the governor or some other men of great power, who will hear no complaints against them, though never so justly made: and therefore they often put men in the stocks at their pleasure, and in the morning carry them before a magistrate; who commonly fines the prisoners to pay somewhat, and be it more or less, it falls part to the magistrate. Neither dares any man complain of injustice upon such usage, in this case especially; though his cause be never so just: and therefore patience is in this country as necessary for poor people as in any part of the world.

But notwithstanding these abuses, they have one custom in the administering justice that is pleasing enough. For if a difference or quarrel at any time happens between two mean men, and they are not to be reconciled without going before a magistrate, he, usually considering their poverty, lays no heavy mulct on the offender, but enjoins him this as his penalty, that he shall treat the injured person with a jar of arrack and a fowl, or a small porker, that so feasting together they may both drown all animosity in good liquor, and renew their friendship.

But if it be a controversy about a debt, they take a very different method. For the debtors are many times ordered to be prisoners in their creditors' houses, where they are beaten, or kept with a log of wood made fast to their legs, to hinder them from running away. These poor prisoners eat nothing but rice and drink water, and are tyrannically insulted over by their rigid creditors till the debt is satisfied. Their corporal punishments upon malefactors, and sometimes upon others, are very severe. Some are loaden with iron chains fastened to their legs, with logs also like the debtors but now mentioned. Others have their necks enclosed between two great heavy planks made like a pillory, but moveable, for they carry it about with them wherever they go, and even when they go to rest they are forced to lie down and sleep in it as they can.

There is another sort of punishing instrument not unlike this, called a *gongo*. This also is made to wear about the neck, but is shaped like a ladder. The sides of it are two large bamboos, of about ten or twelve foot long, with several such rounds or sticks as ladders have to keep the sides asunder; but much shorter: for the two side bamboos are no farther asunder than to admit of a narrow room for the neck; and the two rounds in the middle are much at the same distance from each other, on each side of the neck, forming a little square, through which the man looks as if he were carrying a ladder on his shoulders, with his head through the rounds. If either of these yokes were to be taken off in a short time, as in six, nine, or twelve hours, it would be no great matter: but to wear one of them a month, two, three, or longer, as I have been informed they sometimes do, seems to be a very severe punishment. Yet 'tis some comfort to some, that they have the liberty to walk abroad where they will: but others are both yoked and imprisoned: and the prisoners in public prisons are used worse than a man would use a dog, they being half starved, and soundly beaten to boot.

They have a particular punishment for such as are suspected to fire houses, or who are thought to have occasioned the fire through their neglect. The master of the house, where the fire first breaks out, will hardly clear himself from suspicion and the severity of the law. The punishment in this case is to sit in a chair of twelve or fourteen foot high, bareheaded three whole days successively in the hot scorching sun: this chair is set, for his greater disgrace, before the place where his house stood.

Other smaller crimes are punished with blows; which we call bambooing. The criminal is laid flat on his belly on the ground, with his breeches plucked down over his hams: in which posture a lusty fellow bangs his bare breech with a split bamboo, about four fingers broad, and five foot long. The number of his blows are more or less, according to the nature of the crime, or the pleasure of the magistrate; yet money will buy favour of the executioner, who knows how to moderate his strokes for a fee beforehand. Otherwise his blows usually fall so heavy, that the poor offender may be lamed a month or two. After a man has suffered any of these punishments, he can never obtain any public favour or employment.

They have no courts of judicature, but any single magistrate issues out his warrants for the apprehending of malefactors, and, upon taking them, immediately tries them: and as the sentence is final, and without appeal, so 'tis no sooner passed, but 'tis executed also without more ado. Their punishment in capital crimes is usually beheading. The criminal is carried immediately from the magistrate's house to his own;

for there is no common place of execution, but the male-factor suffers near his own house, or where the fact was committed. There he is placed sitting on the ground, with his body upright, and his legs stretched out: and the executioner being provided with a large curtana or back-sword, and striking a full back blow on the neck, at one stroke he severs the head from the body; the head commonly tumbling down into the owner's lap, and the trunk falling backward on the ground.

Theft is not thought worthy of death, but is punished with cutting off some member, or part of a member, according to the degree of the offence. For sometimes only one joint of a finger is chopped off, for other crimes a whole finger, or more, and for some the whole hand.

The magistrates and other great men of this kingdom are called mandarins. Most of them in office about the king are eunuchs, and not only gelded, but also their members cut off quite flat to their bellies. These, as I have been informed, are all very learned men after their way, especially in the laws of the country. They rise gradually by their merit or favour, from one degree to another, as well they who are employed in civil as in military affairs: and scarce a place of trust or profit goes beside them. No man is permitted to walk familiarly about the king's palace without the leave of the eunuch mandarins; and for this reason having such free access to the king themselves, and excluding whom they will, they engross his favour. This is taken so much to heart by some, that through envy and discontent they often pine away, as is commonly said, even to death: and I heard of such a one, who was called Ungee Thuan Ding: Ungee seems a title of honour among them. He was a man of great learning in the laws, extremely politic, and mighty high-spirited. This man sought all the means imaginable to be preferred, but could not for want of being an eunuch. He fretted to see his inferiors raised; but plainly seeing that there was no rising without removing that objection, he one day in a rage took up a sharp knife, and qualified himself effectually. He had a wife and six or eight children who were all in great fear of his life: but he was not at all dismayed, though in that condition, and the king advanced him. He was living when I was there, and was a great mandarin. He had the care of the armory and artillery, being great master of the king's ordnance.

CHOPSTICKS

In their entertainments, and at their ordinary eating, instead of forks and spoons, they use two small round sticks about the length and bigness of a tobacco pipe. They hold them both in the right hand, one between the forefinger and thumb, the other between the middle-finger and the forefinger, as our boys do their snappers. They use them very dextrously, taking up the smallest grain of rice with them; nor is it accounted mannerly to touch the food after it is dressed, with their hands: and though it be difficult for strangers to use them, being unaccustomed to them, yet a little use will overcome that difficulty; and persons that reside here ought to learn this, as well as other customs of the country, that are innocent, that so their company may be more acceptable. All the Tonquinese keep many of these sticks in their houses, as well for their own use as to entertain strangers at meals: they are as ordinarily placed at the table here as knives, forks, and spoons are in England: and a man that cannot dextrously handle these instruments makes but an odd figure at their tables. The richer sort of people, especially the mandarins, have them tipped with silver. In China also these things are constantly used: they are called by the English seamen chopsticks.

A SOCIAL BLUNDER

After a week at Cachao, Dampier went back to his ship, remaining there for a month while Captain Weldon tried to negotiate new business in north-east Vietnam, near Mong Cai on the Chinese border. Despite persistent attacks of dysentery, Dampier made daily trips out and about, eventually using half his meagre savings to hire a guide and undertake an extended journey.

We found no houses of entertainment on the road, yet at

every village we came we got houseroom, and a barbecue [bed] of split bamboo to sleep on. The people were very civil, lending us an earthen pot to dress rice, or anything else. Usually after supper, if the day was not shut in, I took a ramble about the village, to see what was worth taking notice of, especially the pagoda of the place. These had the image of either a horse, an elephant, or both, standing with the head looking out of the doors: the pagodas themselves were but small and low. I still made it dark night before I returned to my lodging, and then I laid me down to sleep. My guide carried my sea-gown, which was my covering in the night, and my pillow was a log of wood: but I slept very well, though the weakness of my body did now require better accommodation.

The third day after my setting out, about three o'clock in the afternoon, I saw before me a small tower, such as I mentioned before; as erected for a time in honour of some great person deceased. But I knew not then the meaning of it, for I had not seen the like before in the country. As I came nearer to it, I saw a multitude of people, most of them men and boys; and, coming nearer still, I saw a great deal of meat on the stalls that were placed at a small distance from the tower. This made me conclude that it was some great market, and that the flesh I saw was for sale: therefore I went in among the crowd, as well to see the tower as to buy some of the meat for my supper, it being now between four and five o'clock in the afternoon. My guide could not speak English, neither could I speak the Tonquinese language: so I asked him no questions about it; and he too went readily in with me, it may be not knowing my intent was to buy. First I went round the tower and viewed it: it was four-square, each side about eight foot broad at the ground; the height of it was about twenty-six foot, but at the top somewhat narrower than at the bottom. I saw no door to enter into it: it seemed to be very slightly built, at least covered with thin boards, which were all joined close together, and painted of a dark reddish colour. I then went on to the stalls, which had sheds built over them: and there I viewed the fruits and flesh, each of which was ranged in order apart. I passed by abundance of oranges packed up in baskets, which I think were the fairest I ever saw, and for quantity more than I had seen gathered all the time I was at Tonquin. I passed by these, and seeing no other fruit, I came to the flesh-stalls, where was nothing but pork, and this also was all cut into quarters and sides of pork: I thought there might be fifty or sixty hogs cut up thus, and all seemed to be very good meat. When I saw that there was none of it in small pieces fit for my use, I, as was customary in the markets, took hold of a quarter, and made signs to the master of it, as I thought, to cut me a piece of two or three pound. I was ignorant of any ceremony they were about, but the superstitious people soon made me sensible of my error; for they assaulted me on all sides, buffeting me and rending my clothes, and one of them snatched away my hat. My guide did all he could to appease them, and dragged me out of the crowd: yet some surly fellows followed us, and seemed by their countenance and gestures to threaten me; but my guide at last pacified them and fetched my hat, and we marched away as fast as we could. I could not be informed of my guide what this meant; but some time after, when I was returned to our ship, the guide's brother, who spoke English, told me it was a funeral feast, and that the tower was the tomb which was to be burned; and some Englishmen who lived there told me the same. This was the only funeral feast that ever I was at among them, and they gave me cause to remember it: but this was the worst usage I received from any of them all the time that I was in the country.

THE NEW PROMETHEUS

On the way to Cachao again Dampier stopped at Pho Hien in Hai Hung province, where there was a substantial Roman Catholic mission, which he visited to acquire more information.

When I came hither I entered the gate, and seeing nobody in the yard, I went into that room. At the door thereof, I found a small line hanging down, which I pulled; and a bell ringing within gave notice of my being there: yet nobody appearing presently, I went in and sat down. There was a table in the middle of the room, and handsome chairs, and several European pictures hung upon the walls.

It was not long before one of the priests came into the room to me, and received me very civilly. With him I had a great deal of discourse: he was a Frenchman by nation, but spoke Spanish and Portuguese very well. It was chiefly in Spanish that we entertained each other, which I understood much better than I could speak: yet I asked him questions, and made a shift to answer him to such questions as he asked me; and when I was at a loss in my Spanish, I had recourse to Latin, having still some smatterings of what I learnt of it at school in my youth. He was very free to talk with me, and first asked me my business thither? I told him that my business was to Cachao, where I had been once before; that then I went by water, but now I was moved by my curiosity to travel by land, and that I could not pass by any Europeans without a visit, especially such a famous place as this. He asked me many other questions, and particularly if I was a Roman Catholic? I told him no; but falling then into a discourse about religion, he told me what progress the Gospel was like to make in these Eastern nations . . .

As things stand at present, it seems very improbable that Christianity should fructify there: for as the English and Dutch in these parts of the world are too loose livers to gain reputation to their religion, so are the other Europeans, I mean the missionary priests, especially the Portuguese, but very blind teachers. But indeed as the Romanists are the only men who compass sea and land to gain proselytes, so they may seem to have one advantage over Protestant ministers in these idolatrous countries, that they present them with such kind of objects for religious worship as they have been used to already. For the exchange is not great from pagan idols to images of saints, which may serve altogether as well for the poor souls they convert, who are guided only by sense. But then even here also, these people, having been bred up in the belief of the goodness of their own gods or heroes, will more hardly be brought over to change their own idols for new ones, without some better arguments to prove these to be more valuable than the missionaries ordinarily are able to afford them. And if I may freely speak my opinion, I am apt to think that the gross idolatry of the papists is rather a prejudice than advantage to their missions, and that their first care should be to bring the people to be virtuous and considerate, and their next, to give them a plain history and scheme of the fundamental truths of Christianity, and show them how agreeable they are to natural light, and how worthy of God.

But to return to the French priest; he at length asked me if any of our English ships brought powder to sell? I told him, I thought not. Then he asked me if I knew the composition of powder? I answered that I had receipts how to make either cannon or fine powder, and told him the manner of the composition. Said he, I have the same receipts from France, and have tried to make powder, but could not; and therefore I think the fault is in our coals. Then he asked me many questions about the coals, what were proper to be used, but that I could not satisfy him in. He desired me to try to make a pound, and withal told me that he had all the ingredients, and an engine to mix them. I was easily persuaded to try my skill, which I had never yet tried, not knowing what I might be put to before I got to England; and having drank a glass or two of wine with him, I went to work; and it succeeded so well, that I pleased him extremely, and satisfied my own desire of trying the receipt, and the reader shall have the history of the operation, if he pleases. He brought me sulphur and saltpetre, and I weighed a portion of each of these, and of coals I gathered up in the hearth and beat to powder. While his man mixed these in a little engine, I made a small sieve of parchment, which I pricked full of holes, with a small iron made hot, and this was to corn it. I had two large coconuts to roll in the sieve, and work it through the holes to corn it. When it was dry we proved it, and it answered our expectation. The receipt I had out of Captain Sturmy's *Magazine of Arts.**

---

* *The Mariners Magazine* by Samuel Sturmy.

A BUCCANEER'S REFLECTIONS ON TRADE

Also at Pho Hien was a branch of the East India Company, whose manager Dampier found unenterprising, particularly in his failure to develop business with Japan.

For while I was there, there were merchants came every year from Japan to Tonquin; and by some of these our English factory might probably have settled a correspondence and traffic, but he who was little qualified for the station he was in was less fit for any new undertaking: and though men ought not to run inconsiderately into new discoveries or undertakings, yet where there is a prospect of profit, I think it not amiss for merchants to try for a trade, for if our ancestors had been as dull as we have been of late, 'tis probable we had never known the way so much as to the East Indies, but must have been beholden to our neighbours for all the product of those Eastern nations. What care was formerly taken to get us a trade into the East Indies, and other countries? What pains particularly did some take to find out the Muscovites by doubling the North Cape, and away thence by land trade into Persia? But now, as if we were cloyed with trade, we sit still contented, saying with Cato, '*Non minor est virtus quam quaerere parta tueri.*'* This was the saying of an eminent merchant of the East India Company to me: but by his leave, our neighbours have encroached on us, and that in our times too. However, 'tis certainly for the interest of our merchants to employ fit men in their factories, since the reputation of the company rises or falls by the discreet management, or the ill conduct, of the agents. Nor is it enough for the chief of a factory to be a good merchant, and an honest man: for though these are necessary qualifications, yet the governor, or chief of the factory, ought to know more than barely how to buy, sell, and keep accounts, especially where other European merchants reside among them, or trade to the same places: for they keep a diligent eye on the management of our affairs, and are always ready to take all

* 'Courage is nothing less than seeking to determine the course of future events.'

advantages of our misimprovements. Neither ought this care to be neglected where we have the trade to ourselves, for there ought to be a fair understanding between us and the natives, and care taken that they should have no reason to complain of unjust dealings, as I could show where there has been; but 'tis an invidious subject, and all that I aim at is to give a caution . . . The more trade, the more civilisation; and on the contrary, the less trade, the more barbarity and inhumanity. For trade has a strong influence upon all people, who have found the sweet of it, bringing with it so many of the conveniences of life as it does. And I believe that even the poor Americans, who have not yet tasted the sweetness of it, might be allured to it by an honest and just commerce: even such of them as do yet seem to covet no more than a bare subsistence of meat and drink, and a clout to cover their nakedness. That large continent has yet millions of inhabitants, both on the Mexican and Peruvian parts, who are still ignorant of trade: and they would be fond of it, did they once experience it; though at the present they live happy enough, by enjoying such fruits of the earth as nature has bestowed on those places, where their lot is fallen: and it may be they are happier now, than they may hereafter be, when more known to the avaricious world. For with trade they will be in danger of meeting with oppression: men not being content with a free traffic and a just and reasonable gain, especially in these remote countries: but they must have the current run altogether in their own channel, though to the depriving the poor natives they deal with of their natural liberty: as if all mankind were to be ruled by their laws. The islands of Sumatra and Java can sufficiently witness this; the Dutch having in a manner engrossed all the trade of those, and several of the neighbouring countries, to themselves – not that they are able to supply the natives with a quarter of what they want, but because they would have all the produce of them at their own disposal.

SUMATERANS

After returning with Captain Weldon, via Melaka, to Sumatera,

Dampier stayed at Banda Aceh for six months, still trying to shake off his dysentery. Achin, as it was then called, was one of the most prosperous cities in the East. Merchants of many nations settled there, and foreign scholars thronged the Achinese academies. The city's importance led both Elizabeth I and James I to send letters to the princes of Achin to help promote trade. From 1641 four queens reigned successively, but in 1699 the kingdom's fanatical Arab party managed to abolish female rule and put a leader of their own blood on the throne. Achin's fortunes thereafter declined.

They are people of a middle stature, straight, and well shaped, and of a dark Indian copper colour. Their hair is black and lank, their faces generally pretty long, yet graceful enough. They have black eyes, middling noses, thin lips, and black teeth, by the frequent use of betel. They are very lazy, and care not to work or take pains. The poorer sort are addicted to theft, and are often punished severely for it. They are otherwise good-natured in general, and kind enough to strangers.

The better sort of them wear caps fitted to their heads, of red or other coloured woollen cloth, like the crown of a hat without any brim; for none of the Eastern people use the compliment of uncovering their heads when they meet, as we do. But the general wear for all sorts of people is a small turban, such as the Mindanaoans wear. They have small breeches, and the better sort will have a piece of silk thrown loosely over their shoulders; but the poor go naked from the waist upwards. Neither have they the use of stockings and shoes, but a sort of sandals are worn by the better sort.

Their houses are built on posts, as those of Mindanao, and they live much after the same fashion: but by reason of their gold mines, and the frequent resort of strangers, they are richer, and live in greater plenty. Their common food is rice, and the better sort have fowls and fish, with which the markets are plentifully stored, and sometimes buffaloes' flesh, all which is dressed very savoury with pepper and garlic, and tinctured yellow with turmeric, to make it pleasant to the eye, as the East Indians generally love to have their food look yellow: neither do they want good chutneys or sauces to give it a relish.

The city of Achin is the chief in all this kingdom. It is seated on the banks of a river, near the north-west end of the island, and about two miles from the sea. This town consists of seven or eight thousand houses, and in it there are always a great many merchant strangers, viz. English, Dutch, Danes, Portuguese, Chinese, Guzrats, etc. The houses of this city are generally larger than those I saw at Mindanao, and better furnished with household goods. The city has no walls, nor so much as a ditch about it. It has a great number of mosques, generally square built, and covered with pantiles, but neither high nor large. Every morning a man made a great noise from thence; but I saw no turrets or steeples for them to climb up into for that purpose, as they have generally in Turkey. The queen has a large palace here, built handsomely with stone; but I could not get into the inside of it. 'Tis said there are some great guns about it, four of which are of brass, and are said to have been sent hither as a present by our King James I.

The chief trades at Achin are carpenters, blacksmiths, goldsmiths, fishermen, and money-changers: but the country people live either on breeding heads of cattle, but most for their own use, or fowls, especially they who live near the city, which they send weekly thither to sell: others plant roots, fruits, etc. and of late they have sown pretty large fields of rice. This thrives here well enough, but they are so proud that it is against their stomach to work: neither do they themselves much trouble their heads about it, but leave it to be managed by their slaves: and they were the slaves brought lately by the English and Danes from the coast of Coromandel in the time of a famine there, I spoke of before, who first brought this sort of husbandry into such request among the Achinese. Yet neither does the rice they have this way supply one quarter of their occasions, but they have it brought to them from their neighbouring countries.

The fishermen are the richest working people: I mean such of them as can purchase a net; for thereby they get great profit; and this sort of employment is managed also by their slaves. In fair weather you shall have eight or ten great boats, each with a seine or hauling net: and when they see a shoal of fish, they strive to encompass them with these nets, and all the boats that are near assist each other to drag them ashore. Sometimes they draw ashore this way fifty, sixty, or a hundred large fish, as big as a man's leg, and as long: and then they rejoice mightily, and scamper about, making a great shout. The fish is presently sent to the market in one of their boats, the rest looking out again for more. Those who fish with hook and line, go out in small proas, with about one or two slaves in each proa. These also get good fish of other sorts, which they carry home to their masters.

The carpenters use such hatchets as they have at Mindanao. They build good houses after their fashion: and they are also ingenious enough in building proas, making very pretty ones, especially of that sort which are flying proas; which are built long, deep, narrow and sharp, with both sides alike, and outriggers on each side, the head and stern like other boats. They carry a great sail, and when the wind blows hard, they send a man or two to sit at the extremity of the windward outrigger, to poise the vessel. They build also some vessels of ten to twenty tons burthen, to trade from one place to another: but I think their greatest ingenuity is in building their flying proas; which are made very smooth, kept neat and clean, and will sail very well: for which reason they had that name given them by the English . . .

There are but few of them resort daily to their mosques; yet they are all stiff in their religion, and so zealous for it, that they greatly rejoice in making a proselyte. I was told, that while I was at Tonquin, a Chinese inhabiting here turned from his paganism to Mahometanism, and, being circumcised, he was thereupon carried in great state through the city on an elephant, with one crying before him, that he was turned believer. This man was called the captain of the China Camp; for, as I was informed, he was placed there by his countrymen as the chief factor or agent, to negotiate their affairs with the people of the country. Whether he had dealt falsely, or was only envied by others, I know not: but his countrymen had so entangled him in law, that he had been ruined, if he had not made use of this way to disingage himself; and then his religion protected him, and they could not meddle with him.

The laws of this country are very strict, and offenders are punished with great severity. Neither are there any delays of justice here; for as soon as the offender is taken, he is immediately brought before the magistrate, who presently hears the matter, and according as he finds it, so he either acquits, or orders punishment to be inflicted on the party immediately. Small offenders are only whipped on the back, which sort of punishment they call *chaubuck*.* A thief for his first offence, has his right hand chopped off at the wrist; for the second offence off goes the other; and sometimes instead of one of their hands, one or both their feet are cut off; and sometimes (though very rarely) both hands and feet. If after the loss of one or both hands or feet, they still prove incorrigible, for they are many of them such very rogues, and so arch that they will steal with their toes, then they are banished to Pulo Way, during their lives: and if they get thence to the city, as sometimes they do, they are commonly sent back again; though sometimes they get a licence to stay.

On Pulo Way there are none but this sort of cattle: and though they all of them want one or both hands, yet they so order matters, that they can row very well, and do many things to admiration, whereby they are able to get a livelihood: for if they have no hands, they will get somebody or other to fasten ropes or withes about their oars, so as to leave loops wherein they may put the stumps of their arms; and therewith they will pull an oar lustily. They that have one hand can do well enough: and of these you shall see a great many even in the city. This sort of punishment is inflicted for greater robberies; but for small pilfering the first time thieves are only whipped; but after this a petty larceny is looked on as a great crime. Neither is this sort of punishment peculiar to the Achinese government, but probably used by the other princes of this island, and on the island Java also, especially at Banten. They formerly, when the King of

* This seems to have found its way, via the Dutch, to South Africa, as *sjambok*.

Banten was in his prosperity, deprived men of the right hand
for theft, and may still for aught I know. I knew a Dutchman
so served: he was a seaman belonging to one of the King of
Banten's ships. Being thus punished, he was dismissed from
his service, and when I was this time at Achin he lived there.
Here at Achin, when a member is thus cut off, they have a
broad piece of leather or bladder ready to clap on the wound.
This is presently applied, and bound on so fast that the blood
cannot issue forth. By this means the great flux of blood is
stopped, which would else ensue; and I never heard of anyone who died of it. How long this leather is kept on the
wound I know not: but it is so long, till the blood is perfectly staunched; and when it is taken off, the clods of blood
which were pressed in the wound by the leather, peel all off
with it, leaving the wound clean. Then, I judge, they use
cleansing or healing plasters, as they see convenient, and cure
the wound with a great deal of ease.

I never heard of any that suffered death for theft. Criminals
who deserve death are executed divers ways, according to
the nature of the offence, or the quality of the offender. One
way is by impaling on a sharp stake, which passes up right
from the fundament through the bowels, and comes out at
the neck. The stake is about the bigness of a man's thigh,
placed upright, one end in the ground very firm; the upper
sharp end is about twelve or fourteen foot high. I saw one
man spitted in this manner, and there he remained two or
three days: but I could not learn his offence.

Noblemen have a more honourable death; they are allowed
to fight for their lives: but the numbers of those with whom
they are to engage soon put a period to the combat, by the
death of the malefactor. The manner of it is thus; the person
condemned is brought bound to the place of execution. This
is a large plain field, spacious enough to contain thousands
of people. Thither the Achinese, armed as they usually go,
with their krisses, but then more especially, resort in troops,
as well to be spectators, as actors in the tragedy. These make
a very large ring, and in the midst of the multitude the
criminal is placed, and by him such arms as are allowed on
such occasions: which are a sword, a kris, and a lance. When

the time is come to act, he is unbound, and left at his liberty to take up his fighting weapons. The spectators being all ready, each man with his arms in his hand, stand still in their places, till the malefactor advances. He commonly sets out with a shriek, and daringly faces the multitude: but he is soon brought to the ground, first by lances thrown at him, and afterwards by their swords and krisses. One was thus executed while I was there: I had not the fortune to hear of it till it was ended; but had this relation the same evening it was done, from Mr Dennis Driscal, who was then one of the spectators.

This country is governed by a queen, under whom there are twelve *Oronkeyes*, or great lords. These act in their several precincts with great power and authority. Under these there are other inferior officers, to keep the peace in the several parts of the queen's dominions . . .

The Queen of Achin, as 'tis said, is always an old maid, chosen out of the royal family. What ceremonies are used at the choosing her I know not: nor who are the electors; but I suppose they are the *Oronkeyes*. After she is chosen, she is in a manner confined to her palace; for by report she seldom goes abroad, neither is she seen by any people of inferior rank and quality; but only by some of her domestics: except that once a year she is dressed all in white, and placed on an elephant, and so rides to the river in state to wash herself: but whether any of the meaner sort of people may see her in that progress I know not; for it is the custom of most Eastern princes to screen themselves from the sight of their subjects. Or if they sometimes go abroad for their pleasure, yet the people are then ordered either to turn their backs towards them while they pass by, as formerly at Banten, or to hold their hands before their eyes, as at Siam. At Mindanao, they may look on their prince: but from the highest to the lowest they approach him with the greatest respect and veneration, creeping very low, and oft-times on their knees, with their eyes fixed on him: and when they withdraw, they return in the same manner, creeping backwards, and still keeping their eyes on him, till they are out of his sight.

But to return to the Queen of Achin, I think Mr Hakluyt

or Purchas,* makes mention of a king here in our King James I's time. But at least of later years there has always been a queen only, and the English who reside there, have been of the opinion that these people have been governed by a queen *ab origine*.

THE PAINTED PRINCE

In September 1689 Dampier sailed as mate aboard a merchantman bound for Melaka with a cargo of 'three or four hundred pound' of contraband opium. His next voyage was to Madras, where he stayed for five months, 'but 'tis not my design to enter into a description of a place so well known to my countrymen'. Here he learnt of the death of Captain Swan, who was murdered by order of Rajah Laut. Returning once more to Sumatera, he became chief gunner and engineer at the English fort in Bengkulu, and after making a deal with Mr Moody, who was appointed to run the East India Company branch further up the west coast at Indrapura, took part-ownership of two tattooed Philippinos, a royal mother and son from the Miangas, south-east of Mindanao, whom Mr Moody had bought out of slavery in the capital, now Cotabato. The son, Jeoly, who was so marvellously decorated that Dampier planned to exhibit him in England, must have been in his mid-twenties.

He told me that his father was rajah of the island where they lived: that there were not above thirty men on the island, and about one hundred women: that he himself had five wives and eight children, and that one of his wives painted him.

He was painted all down the breast, between his shoulders behind; on his thighs (mostly) before; and in the form of several broad rings, or bracelets round his arms and legs. I cannot liken the drawings to any figure of animals, or the like; but they were very curious, full of great variety of lines, flourishes, chequered-work, etc. keeping a very graceful proportion, and appearing very artificial, even to wonder, especially that upon and between his shoulder-blades. By the

---

* Richard Hakluyt (?1552–1616) and Samuel Purchas (1577–1626), compilers of travel books. The source here is Purchas.

Prince Jeoly 'was painted all down the breast,
between his shoulders behind . . .'

account he gave me of the manner of doing it, I understood that the painting was done in the same manner as the Jerusalem cross is made in men's arms, by pricking the skin, and rubbing in a pigment. But whereas powder is used in making the Jerusalem cross, they at Miangas use the gum of a tree beaten to powder, called by the English, dammar, which is used instead of pitch in many parts of India. He told me that most of the men and women on the island were thus painted: and also that they had all earrings made of gold, and gold shackles about their legs and arms: that their common food, of the produce of the land, was potatoes and yams: that they had plenty of cocks and hens; but no other tame fowl. He said that fish (of which he was a great lover, as wild Indians generally are) was very plentiful about the island; and that they had canoes, and went a-fishing frequently in them; and that they often visited the other two small islands, whose inhabitants spoke the same language as they did; which was so unlike the Malayan, which he had learnt while he was a slave at Mindanao, that when his mother and he were talking together in their Miangan tongue, I could not understand one word they said . . .

He said also that the customs of those other isles, and their manner of living, was like theirs, and that they were the only people with whom they had any converse: and that one time as he, with his father, mother and brother, with two or three men more were going to one of these other islands, they were driven by a strong wind on the coast of Mindanao, where they were taken by the fishermen of that island, and carried ashore, and sold as slaves; they being first stripped of their gold ornaments . . .

Prince Jeoly lived thus a slave at Mindanao [city] four or five years, till at last Mr Moody bought him and his mother for sixty dollars . . . Jeoly and his mother lived in a house by themselves without the fort. I had no employment for them; but they both employed themselves. She used to make and mend their own clothes, at which she was not very expert, for they wear no clothes in the Miangas, but only a cloth about their waists: and he busied himself in making a chest with four boards, and a few nails that he begged of me. It was but an ill-shaped odd thing, yet he was as proud of it as if it had been the rarest piece in the world. After some time they were both taken sick, and though I took as much care of them as if they had been my brother and sister, yet she died. I did what I could to comfort Jeoly; but he took on extremely, insomuch that I feared for him also. Therefore I caused a grave to be made presently, to hide her out of his sight. I had her shrouded decently in a piece of new calico; but Jeoly was not so satisfied, for he wrapped all her clothes about her, and two new pieces of chintz that Mr Moody gave her, saying that they were his mother's, and she must have 'em. I would not disoblige him for fear of endangering his life; and I used all possible means to recover his health; but I found little amendment while we stayed here.

In the little printed relation that was made of him when he was shown for a sight in England, there was a romantic story of a beautiful sister of his a slave with them at Mindanao; and of the sultan's falling in love with her; but these were stories indeed. They reported also that this paint was of such virtue, that serpents and venomous creatures would flee from him, for which reason, I suppose, they represented so many serpents scampering about in the printed picture that was made of him. But I never knew any paint of such virtue: and as for Jeoly, I have seen him as much afraid of snakes, scorpions, or centipedes, as myself.

THE DEATH SHIP

Dampier came to dislike his boss at Bengkulu. 'I saw so much ignorance in him with respect to his charge, being much fitter to be a book-keeper than governor of a fort; and yet so much insolence and cruelty with respect to those under him, and rashness in his management of the Sumatran neighbourhood, that I soon grew weary of him, not thinking myself very safe indeed under a man whose humours were so brutish and barbarous.' Accordingly, after being granted and then refused permission to leave, he 'slipped away at midnight' and joined a ship heading for England under command of Captain Heath. 'I brought with me my journal and most of my written papers, but some papers and books of value I left in haste.' Jeoly had gone aboard earlier in the day. The following morning, 25 January 1691, Captain Heath weighed anchor, with first port of call the Cape of Good Hope.

We had not been at sea long before our men began to droop, in a sort of distemper that stole insensibly on them, and proved fatal to above thirty, who died before we arrived at the Cape. We had sometimes two, and once three men thrown overboard in a morning. This distemper might probably arise from the badness of the water which we took in at Bengkulu: for I did observe while I was there that the river water, wherewith our ships were watered, was very unwholesome, it being mixed with the water of many small creeks, that proceeded from low land, and whose streams were always very black, they being nourished by the water that drained out of the low swampy unwholesome ground.

I have observed, not only there, but in other hot countries also both in the East and West Indies, that the land-floods which pour into the channels of the rivers, about the season of the rains, are very unwholesome. For when I lived in the Bay of Campeachy, the fish were found dead in heaps on the shores of the rivers and creeks, at such a season; and many we took up half dead; of which sudden mortality there appeared no cause, but only the malignity of the waters draining off the land. This happens chiefly, as I take it, where the water drains through thick woods and savannahs of long grass, and swampy grounds, with which some hot countries abound: and I believe it receives a strong tincture from the roots of several kinds of trees, herbs, etc. And especially where there is any stagnancy of the water, it soon corrupts; and possibly the serpents and other poisonous vermin and insects may not a little contribute to its bad qualities: at such times it will look very deep-coloured, yellow, red, or black, etc. The season of the rains was over, and the land-floods were abating upon the taking up this water in the river of Bengkulu: but would the seamen have given themselves the trouble they might have filled their vessels with excellent good water at a spring on the backside of the fort, not above two or three hundred paces from the landing-place; and with which the fort is served. And I mention this as a caution to any ships that shall go to Bengkulu for the future; and withal I think it worth the care of the owners or governors of the factory, and that it would tend much to the preservation of their seamen's lives, to lay pipes to convey the fountain water to the shore, which might easily be done with a small charge: and had I stayed longer there I would have undertaken it. I had a design also of bringing it into the fort, though much higher: for it would be a great convenience and security to it, in case of a siege.

Besides the badness of our water, it was stowed among the pepper in the hold, which made it very hot. Every morning when we came to take our allowance, it was so hot that a man could hardly suffer his hands in it, or hold a bottle full of it in his hand. I never anywhere felt the like, nor could have thought it possible that water should heat to that degree in a ship's hold. It was exceeding black too, and looked more like ink than water. Whether it grew so black with standing, or was tinged with the pepper, I know not, for this water was not so black when it was first taken up. Our food also was very bad; for the ship had been out of England upon this voyage above three years; and the salt provision brought from thence, and which we fed on, having been so long in salt, was but ordinary food for sickly men to feed on.

Captain Heath, when he saw the misery of his company, ordered his own tamarinds, of which he had some jars aboard, to be given some to each mess, to eat with their rice. This was a great refreshment to the men, and I do believe it contributed much to keep us on our legs.

This distemper was so universal, that I do believe there was scarce a man in the ship, but languished under it; yet it stole so insensibly on us, that we could not say we were sick, feeling little or no pain, only a weakness, and but little stomach. Nay, most of those that died in this voyage, would hardly be persuaded to keep their cabins, or hammocks, till they could not stir about; and when they were forced to lie down, they made their wills, and peaked off in two or three days.

'These Hottentots are people of a middle stature,
with small limbs and thin bodies, full of activity'

HODMADODS

*Despite lacking sufficient fit men to run the ship, Captain Heath
succeeded in reaching Table Bay safely towards the middle of April
1691. He remained there six weeks, provisioning and searching for
additional hands. As usual, Dampier put the time to good account.*

The natural inhabitants of the Cape are the Hodmadods, as
they are commonly called, which is a corruption of the word
Hottentot; for this is the name by which they call to one
another, either in their dances, or on any occasion; as if every
one of them had this for his name. The word probably has
some signification or other in their language, whatever it is.

These Hottentots are people of a middle stature, with
small limbs and thin bodies, full of activity. Their faces are
of a flat oval figure, of the Negro make, with great eyebrows,
black eyes, but neither are their noses so flat, nor their lips
so thick, as the Negroes of Guinea. Their complexion is
darker than the common Indians; though not so black as
the Negroes or New Hollanders; neither is their hair so
much frizzled.

They besmear themselves all over with grease, as well to
keep their joints supple, as to fence their half-naked bodies
from the air, by stopping up their pores. To do this the more
effectually, they rub soot over the greased parts, especially
their faces, which adds to their natural beauty, as painting
does in Europe; but withal sends from them a strong smell,
which though sufficiently pleasing to themselves, is very unpleasant to others. They are glad of the worst of kitchen stuff
for this purpose, and use it as often as they can get it.

This custom of anointing the body is very common in
other parts of Africa, especially on the coast of Guinea, where
they generally use palm-oil, anointing themselves from head
to foot; but when they want oil, they make use of kitchen
stuff, which they buy of the Europeans that trade with them.
In the East Indies also, especially on the coast of Kedah and
Malacca, and in general, on almost all the easterly islands,
as well on Sumatra, Java, etc. as on the Philippines and
Spice Islands, the Indian inhabitants anoint themselves with

coconut oil two or three times a day, especially mornings and evenings. They spend sometimes half an hour in chafing the oil, and rubbing it into their hair and skin, leaving no place unsmeared with oil, but their face, which they daub not like these Hottentots. The Americans also in some places do use this custom, but not so frequently, perhaps for want of oil and grease to do it. Yet some American Indians in the North Seas frequently daub themselves with a pigment made with leaves, roots, or herbs, or with a sort of red earth, giving their skins a yellow, red, or green colour, according as the pigment is. And these smell unsavoury enough to people not accustomed to them; though not so rank as those who use oil or grease.

The Hottentots do wear no covering on their heads, but deck their hair with small shells. Their garments are sheepskins wrapped about their shoulders like a mantle, with the woolly sides next their bodies. The men have besides this mantle a piece of skin like a small apron, hanging before them. The women have another skin tucked about their waists, which comes down to their knees like a petticoat; and their legs are wrapped round with sheep's guts two or three inches thick, some up as high as to their calves, others even from their feet to their knees, which at a small distance seems to be a sort of boot. These are put on when they are green; and so they grow hard and stiff on their legs, for they never pull them off again, till they have occasion to eat them; which is when they journey from home, and have no other food; then these guts which have been worn, it may be, six, eight, ten or twelve months, make them a good banquet: this I was informed of by the Dutch. They never pull off their sheepskin garments, but to louse themselves, for by continual wearing them they are full of vermin, which obliges them often to strip and sit in the sun two or three hours together in the heat of the day, to destroy them. Indeed most Indians that live remote from the Equator, are molested with lice, though their garments afford less shelter for lice than these Hottentots' sheepskins do. For all those Indians who live in cold countries, as in the north and south parts of America, have some sort of skin or other to cover their bodies, as deer,

The Hottentots 'traced to and fro promiscuously,
often clapping their hands and singing aloud'

otter, beaver or sealskins, all which they as constantly wear, without shifting themselves, as these Hottentots do their sheepskins. And hence they are lousy too, and strong scented, for though they do not daub themselves at all, or but very little, even by reason of their skins they smell strong. The Hottentots' houses are the meanest that I did ever see. They are about nine or ten foot high, and ten or twelve from side to side. They are in a manner round, made with small poles stuck into the ground, and brought together at the top, where they are fastened. The sides and top of the house are filled up with boughs coarsely wattled between the poles, and all is covered over with long grass, rushes, and pieces of hides; and the house at a distance appears just like a haycock. They leave only a small hole on one side about three or four foot high, for a door to creep in and out at; but when the wind comes in at this door, they stop it up, and make another hole in the opposite side. They make the fire in the middle of the house, and the smoke ascends out of the crannies, from all parts of the house. They have no beds to lie on, but tumble down at night round the fire . . .

Their religion, if they have any, is wholly unknown to me; for they have no temple nor idol, nor any place of worship that I did see or hear of. Yet their mirth and nocturnal pastimes at the new and full of the moon, looked as if they had some superstition about it. For at the full especially they sing and dance all night, making a great noise: I walked out to their huts twice at these times, in the evening, when the moon arose above the horizon, and viewed them for an hour or more. They seemed all very busy, both men, women and children, dancing very oddly on the green grass by their houses. They traced to and fro promiscuously, often clapping their hands and singing aloud. Their faces were sometimes to the east, sometimes to the west: neither did I see any motion or gesture that they used when their faces were toward the moon, more than when their backs were toward it. After I had thus observed them for a while, I returned to my lodging, which was not above two or three hundred paces from their huts; and I heard them singing in the same manner all night. In the grey of the morning I walked out

again, and found many of the men and women still singing
and dancing; who continued their mirth till the moon went
down, and then they left off.

ZEBRA

There is a very beautiful sort of wild ass in this country,
whose body is curiously striped with equal lists of white and
black; the stripes coming from the ridge of his back, and
ending under the belly, which is white. These stripes are two
or three fingers broad, running parallel with each other, and
curiously intermixed, one white and one black, over from
the shoulder to the rump. I saw two of the skins of these
beasts, dried and preserved to be sent to Holland as a rarity.
They seemed big enough to enclose the body of a beast, as
big as a large colt of a twelvemonth old.

ST HELENA

*They left the Cape about 23 May 1691 and put into St Helena on
20 June, anchoring off Jamestown. The island had been captured by
the British eighteen years earlier; a charter of December 1673
ceded it to the East India Company.*

We stayed here five or six days; all which time the islanders
lived at the town, to entertain the seamen, who constantly
flock ashore to enjoy themselves among their country people.
Our touching at the Cape had greatly drained the seamen of
their loose coins, at which these islanders as greatly repined;
and some of the poorer sort openly complained against such
doings, saying, it was fit that the East India Company should
be acquainted with it, that they might hinder their ships from
touching at the Cape. Yet they were extremely kind, in hopes
to get what was remaining. They are most of them very poor:
but such as could get a little liquor to sell to the seamen at
this time got what the seamen could spare; for the punch-
houses were never empty. But had we all come directly
hither, and not touched at the Cape, even the poorest people

among them would have gotten something by entertaining sick men. For commonly the seamen coming home, are troubled, more or less with scorbutic distempers: and their only hopes are to get refreshment and health at this island; and these hopes seldom or never fail them, if once they get footing here. For the islands afford abundance of delicate herbs, wherewith the sick are first bathed to supple their joints, and then the fruits and herbs, and fresh food soon after cure them of their scorbutic humours. So that in a week's time men that have been carried ashore in hammocks, and they who were wholly unable to go, have soon been able to leap and dance. Doubtless the serenity and wholesomeness of the air contributes much to the carrying off of these distempers; for here is constantly a fresh breeze. While we stayed here, many of the seamen got sweethearts. One young man belonging to the *James and Mary*, was married, and brought his wife to England with him. Another brought his sweetheart to England, they being each engaged by bonds to marry at their arrival in England; and several other of our men were over head and ears in love with the Santa Helena maids, who though they were born there, yet very earnestly desired to be released from that prison, which they have no other way to compass, but by marrying seamen or passengers that touch here. The young women born here, are but one remove from English, being the daughters of such. They are well shaped, proper and comely, were they in a dress to set them off.

My stay ashore here was but two days, to get refreshments for myself and Jeoly, whom I carried ashore with me: and he was very diligent to pick up such things as the islands afforded, carrying ashore with him a bag, which the people of the isle filled with roots for him. They flocked about him, and seemed to admire him much. This was the last place where I had him at my own disposal, for the mate of the ship, who had Mr Moody's share in him, left him entirely to my management, I being to bring him to England. But I was no sooner arrived in the Thames, but he was sent ashore to be seen by some eminent persons; and I being in want of money, was prevailed upon to sell first, part of my share in him, and by degrees all of it. After this I heard he was carried about to be shown as a sight, and that he died of the smallpox at Oxford.

CHAPTER
EIGHT

THE PREFACE TO A VOYAGE TO NEW HOLLAND

Dampier reached England on 16 September 1691, a fortnight after his fortieth birthday, having been away for twelve and a half years. He brought home no sea chest stuffed with pieces of eight, no leather pouch bulging with diamonds, but only his battered, dog-eared notes and poor shivering Jeoly. Over the next five years he laboured at writing A New Voyage Round the World, *which was published in 1697 and won instant recognition. A second printing followed during the same year, and a third in 1698. He began preparing the companion volume,* Voyages and Descriptions, *and meanwhile gained a position as 'landcarriage man' in the Customs House. Then came an invitation from Lord High Admiral the Earl of Orford (one of Captain Kidd's secret sponsors in 1695) to lead a voyage of discovery to New Holland, also to identify trading and commercial opportunities. Thus it was as Captain Dampier of HMS* Roebuck *that the celebrated author and ex-buccaneer set sail from England at the start of 1699.*

The favourable reception my two former volumes of voyages and descriptions have already met with in the world, gives me reason to hope that notwithstanding the objections which have been raised against me by prejudiced persons, this third volume likewise may in some measure be acceptable to candid and impartial readers, who are curious to know the nature of the inhabitants, animals, plants, soil, etc. in those distant countries, which have either seldom or not at all been visited by any Europeans.

It has almost always been the fate of those who have made new discoveries, to be disesteemed and slightly spoken of, by such as either have had no true relish and value for the things themselves that are discovered, or have had some prejudice against the persons by whom the discoveries were made. It would be vain therefore and unreasonable in me to expect to escape the censure of all, or to hope for better treatment than far worthier persons have met with before me. But this satisfaction I am sure of having, that the things themselves in the discovery of which I have been employed, are most worthy of our diligentest search and inquiry; being the various and wonderful works of God in different parts of the world. And however unfit a person I may be in other respects to have undertaken this task, yet at least I have given a faithful account, and have found some things undiscovered by any before, and which may at least be some assistance and direction to better qualified persons who shall come after me.

It has been objected against me by some, that my accounts and descriptions of things are dry and jejune, not filled with variety of pleasant matter, to divert and gratify the curious reader. How far this is true, I must leave to the world to judge. But if I have been exactly and strictly careful to give only true relations and descriptions of things (as I am sure I have); and if my descriptions be such as may be of use not only to myself (which I have already in good measure experienced) but also to others in future voyages; and likewise to such readers at home as are more desirous of a plain and just account of the true nature and state of the things described, than of a polite and rhetorical narrative, I hope all the defects in my style, will meet with an easy and ready pardon.

Others have taxed me with borrowing from other men's journals; and with insufficiency, as if I was not myself the author of what I write, but published things digested and drawn up by others. As to the first part of this objection, I assure the reader I have taken nothing from any man without mentioning his name, except some very few relations and particular observations received from credible persons who desired not to be named; and these I have always expressly distinguished in my books, from what I relate as of my own observing. And as to the latter; I think it so far from being a diminution to one of my education and employment, to have what I write revised and corrected by friends; that on the contrary, the best and most eminent authors are not ashamed to own the same thing, and look upon it as an advantage.

Lastly, I know there are some who are apt to slight my accounts and descriptions of things, as if it was an easy matter and of little or no difficulty to do all that I have done, to visit little more than the coasts of unknown countries, and make short and imperfect observations of things only near the shore. But whoever is experienced in these matters, or considers things impartially, will be of a very different opinion. And anyone who is sensible, how backward and refractory the seamen are apt to be in long voyages when they know not whither they are going, how ignorant they are of the nature of the winds and the shifting seasons of the monsoons, and how little even the officers themselves generally are skilled in the variation of the needle and the use of the azimuth compass;* besides the hazard of all outward accidents in strange and unknown seas: anyone, I say, who is sensible of these difficulties, will be much more pleased at the discoveries and observations I have been able to make, than displeased with me, that I did not make more.

Thus much I thought necessary to premise in my own vindication, against the objections that have been made to my former performances. But not to trouble the reader any further with matters of this nature; what I have more to offer, shall be only in relation to the following voyage.

TENERIFE

I sailed from the Downs early on Saturday, 14 January 1699, with a fair wind, in His Majesty's Ship the *Roebuck*; carrying but twelve guns in this voyage, and fifty men and boys, with twenty months' provision. We had several of the king's ships in company, bound for Spithead and Plymouth; and by noon we were off Dungeness. We parted from them that night, and stood down the Channel, but found ourselves next morning nearer the French coast than we expected; Cape la

* A compass used for taking a bearing based on a celestial body.

Hague bearing SE and by E. six leagues. There were many other ships, some nearer, some farther off the French coast, who all seemed to have gone nearer to it than they thought they should. My master, who was somewhat troubled at it at first, was not displeased however to find that he had company in his mistake; which, as I have heard, is a very common one, and fatal to many ships. The occasion of it is the not allowing for the change of the variation since the making of the charts; which Captain Halley* has observed to be very considerable. I shall refer the reader to his own account of it which he caused to be published in a single sheet of paper, purposely for a caution to such as pass to and fro the English Channel. And my own experience thus confirming to me the usefulness of such a caution, I was willing to take this occasion of helping towards the making it the more public.

Not to trouble the reader with every day's run, nor with the winds or weather (but only in the remoter parts, where it may be more particularly useful) standing away from Cape la Hague, we made the Start about five that afternoon; which being the last land we saw of England, we reckoned our departure from thence: though we had rather have taken it from the Lizard, if the hazy weather would have suffered us to have seen it.

The first land we saw after we were out of the Channel was Cape Finisterre, which we made on the 19th; and on the 28th made Lanzarote, one of the Canary Islands; of which, and of Alegranza, another of them, I have here given the sights, as they both appeared to us at two several bearings and distances.

We were now standing away for the island Tenerife, where I intended to take in some wine and brandy for my voyage. On Sunday, half an hour past three in the afternoon, we made the island, and crowded in with all our sails till five; when the north-east point of the isle bore WSW distance seven leagues: but being then so far off that I could not expect to get in before night, I lay by till next morning,

* Edmond Halley (1656–1742), astronomer, mathematician and hydro-grapher, after whom the comet is named.

deliberating whether I should put in at Santa Cruz, or at Orotava, the one on the east the other on the west side of the island; which lies mostly north and south; and these are the principal ports on each side. I chose Santa Cruz as the better harbour (especially at this time of the year) and as best furnished with that sort of wine which I had occasion to take in for my voyage. So there I come to an anchor 30 January, in thirty-three fathom water, black slimy ground; about half a mile from the shore; from which distance I took the sight of the town.

In the road, ships must ride in thirty, forty, or fifty fathom water, not above half a mile from the shore at farthest: and if there are many ships, they must ride close one by another. The shore is generally high land, and in most places steep too. This road lies so open to the east, that winds from that side make a great swell, and very bad going ashore in boats. The ships that ride here are then often forced to put to sea, and sometimes to cut or slip their anchors, not being able to weigh them. The best and smoothest landing is in a small sandy cove, about a mile to the north-east of the road, where there is good water, with which ships that lade here are supplied; and many times ships that lade at Orotava, which is the chief port for trade, send their boats hither for water. That is a worse port for westerly than this is for easterly winds; and then all ships that are there put to sea. Between this watering-place and Santa Cruz are two little forts; which with some batteries scattered along the coast command the road. Santa Cruz itself is a small unwalled town fronting the sea, guarded with two other forts to secure the road. There are about two hundred houses in the town, all two storeys high, strongly built with stone, and covered with pantiles. It has two convents and one church, which are the best buildings in the town. The forts here could not secure the Spanish galleons from Admiral Blake,* though they hauled in close under the main fort. Many of the inhabitants that are

* Robert Blake (1599–1657), like Dampier, was a Somerset man. He won a remarkable victory against the Spanish in Santa Cruz Bay in April 1657. Nelson lost his arm here during a less successful attack in July 1797.

now living remember that action; in which the English battered the town, and did it much damage; and the marks of the shot still remain in the fort walls. The wrecks of the galleons that were burnt here, lie in fifteen fathom water: and 'tis said that most of the plate lies there, though some of it was hastily carried ashore at Blake's coming in sight.

Soon after I had anchored I went ashore here to the governor of the town, who received me very kindly, and invited me to dine with him the next day. I returned on board in the evening, and went ashore again with two of my officers the next morning; hoping to get up the hill with time enough to see Laguna, the principal town, and to be back again to dine with the governor of Santa Cruz; for I was told that Laguna was but three miles off. The road is all the way up a pretty steep hill; yet not so steep but that carts go up and down laden. There are public houses scattering by the wayside, where we got some wine. The land on each side seemed to be but rocky and dry; yet in many places we saw spots of green flourishing corn. At farther distances there were small vineyards by the sides of the mountains, intermixed with abundance of waste rocky land, unfit for cultivation, which afforded only dildo bushes. It was about seven or eight in the morning when we set out from Santa Cruz; and it being fair clear weather, the sun shone very bright and warmed us sufficiently before we got to the city of Laguna; which we reached about ten o'clock, all sweaty and tired, and were glad to refresh ourselves with a little wine in a sorry tippling house: but we soon found out one of the English merchants that resided here; who entertained us handsomely at dinner, and in the afternoon showed us the town.

Laguna is a pretty large well-compacted town, and makes a very agreeable prospect. It stands part of it against a hill, and part on a level. The houses have mostly strong walls built with stone and covered with pantiles. They are not uniform, yet they appear pleasant enough. There are many fair buildings; among which are two parish churches, two nunneries, a hospital, four convents, and some chapels; besides many gentlemen's houses. The convents are those of St Austin, St Dominic, St Francis, and St Diego. The two

churches have pretty high square steeples, which top the rest
of the buildings. The streets are not regular, yet they are
mostly spacious and pretty handsome; and near the middle
of the town is a large parade, which has good buildings about
it. There is a strong prison on one side of it; near which is a
large conduit of good water, that supplies all the town. They
have many gardens which are set round with oranges, limes,
and other fruits; in the middle of which are pot-herbs,
salading, flowers, etc. And indeed, if the inhabitants were
curious this way, they might have very pleasant gardens: for
as the town stands high from the sea, on the brow of a plain
that is all open to the east, and has consequently the benefit
of the true Trade Wind, which blows here, and is most commonly fair; so there are seldom wanting at this town, brisk,
cooling, and refreshing breezes all the day . . .

The true malmsey wine grows in this island; and this here
is said to be the best of its kind in the world. Here is also
Canary wine, and Verdona, or green wine. The Canary grows
chiefly on the west side of the island; and therefore is commonly sent to Orotava; which being the chief sea-port for
trade in the island, the principal English merchants reside
there, with their consul; because we have a great trade for
this wine. I was told, that that town is bigger than Laguna;
that it has but one church, but many convents; that the port
is but ordinary at best, and is very bad when the NW winds
blow. These nor'westers give notice of their coming by a
great sea that tumbles in on the shore for some time before
they come, and by a black sky in the north-west. Upon these
signs ships either get up their anchors, or slip their cables
and put to sea, and ply off and on till the weather is over.
Sometimes they are forced to do so two or three times before
they can take in their lading; which 'tis hard to do here in
the fairest weather; and for fresh water, they send, as I have
said, to Santa Cruz. Verdona is green, strong-bodied wine,
harsher and sharper than Canary. 'Tis not so much esteemed
in Europe, but is exported to the West Indies, and will keep
best in hot countries; for which reason I touched here to take
in some of it for my voyage. This sort of wine is made chiefly
on the east side of the island, and shipped off at Santa Cruz.

GATHERING DISCONTENT

From the Canary Islands Dampier made for Pernambuco, now Recife, on the north coast of Brazil, where he could water and victual before taking advantage of certain winds and currents to sail almost due south across the Tropic of Cancer before bearing east for the Cape of Good Hope.

But notwithstanding these advantages I proposed to myself in going to Pernambuco, I was soon put by that design through the refractoriness of some under me, and the discontents and backwardness of some of my men. For the calms and shiftings of winds which I met with, as I was to expect, in crossing the line, made them, who were unacquainted with these matters, almost heartless as to the pursuit of the voyage, as thinking we should never be able to weather Cape St Augustine. And though I told them that by that time we should get to about 3° S. of the Line, we should again have a true brisk general Trade Wind from the northeast, that would carry us to what part of Brazil we pleased, yet they would not believe it till they found it so. This, with some other unforeseen accidents, not necessary to be mentioned in this place, meeting with the aversion of my men to a long unknown voyage, made me justly apprehensive of their revolting, and was a great trouble and hindrance to me. So that I was obliged partly to alter my measures, and met with many difficulties, the particulars of which I shall not trouble the reader with: but I mention thus much of it in general for my own necessary vindication, in my taking such measures sometimes for prosecuting the voyage as the state of my ship's crew, rather than my own judgment and experience, determined me to. The disorders of my ship made me think at present that Pernambuco would not be so fit a place for me; being told that ships ride there two or three leagues from the town, under the command of no forts; so that whenever I should have been ashore it might have been easy for my discontented crew to have cut or slipped their cables, and have gone away from me, many of them discovering already an intention to return to England, and some of them declaring openly that they would go no further onwards than Brazil. I altered my course therefore, and stood away for Bahia de todos los Santos, or the Bay of all Saints [Salvador], where I hoped to have the governor's help, if need should require, for securing my ship from any such mutinous attempt; being forced to keep myself all the way upon my guard, and to lie with my officers, such as I could trust, and with small arms upon the quarterdeck; it scarce being safe for me to lie in my cabin, by reason of the discontents among my men.

On 23 March we saw the land of Brazil; having had thither, from the time when we came into the true Trade Wind again after crossing the Line, very fair weather and brisk gales, mostly at ENE. The land we saw was about twenty leagues to the north of Bahia; so I coasted along shore to the southward.

THE RICHER SORT

Dampier put in to Bahia, now Salvador, jettisoning his deputy, Lieutenant Fisher, whom he deemed mutinous. Despite his responsibilities as captain, he found time to record an immense amount of information about Bahia and the surrounding country.

Besides merchants and others that trade by sea from this port, here are other pretty wealthy men, and several artificers and tradesmen of most sorts, who by labour and industry maintain themselves very well; especially such as can arrive at the purchase of a Negro slave or two. And indeed, excepting people of the lowest degree of all, here are scarce any but what keep slaves in their houses. The richer sort, besides the slaves of both sexes whom they keep for servile uses in their houses, have men slaves who wait on them abroad, for state; either running by their horses' sides when they ride out, or to carry them to and fro on their shoulders in the town when they make short visits near home. Every gentleman or merchant is provided with things necessary for this sort of carriage. The main thing is a pretty large cotton hammock of the West India fashion, but mostly dyed blue, with large fringes of the same, hanging down on each side. This is carried on the Negroes' shoulders by the help of a bamboo about twelve or fourteen foot long, to which the hammock is hung; and a covering comes over the pole, hanging down on each side like a curtain: so that the person so carried cannot be seen unless he pleases; but may either lie down, having pillows for his head; or may sit up by being a little supported with these pillows, and by letting both his legs hang out over one side of the hammock. When he has a mind to be seen, he puts by his curtain, and salutes every one of his acquaintance whom he meets in the streets; for they take a piece of pride in greeting one another from their hammocks, and will hold long conferences thus in the street. But then their two slaves who carry the hammock have each a strong well-made staff, with a fine iron fork at the upper end, and a sharp iron below, like the rest for a musket, which they stick fast in the ground, and let the pole or bamboo of the hammock rest upon them, till their master's business or the compliment is over. There is scarce a man of any fashion, especially a woman, will pass the streets but so carried in a hammock. The chief mechanic traders here, are smiths, hatters, shoemakers, tanners, sawyers, carpenters, coopers, etc. Here are also tailors, butchers, etc. which last kill the bullocks very dextrously, sticking them at one blow with a sharp-pointed knife in the nape of the neck, having first drawn them close to a rail; but they dress them very slovenly. It being Lent when I came hither, there was no buying any flesh till Easter Eve, when a great number of bullocks were killed at once in the slaughterhouses within the town, men, women and children flocking thither with great joy to buy, and a multitude of dogs, almost starved, following them, for whom the meat seemed fittest, it was so lean. All these tradesmen buy Negroes, and train them up to their several employments, which is a great help to them; and they having so frequent trade to Angola, and other parts of Guinea, they have a constant supply of blacks both for their plantations and town. These slaves are very useful in this place for carriage, as porters; for as here is a great trade by sea, and the landing-place is at the foot of a hill, too steep for drawing with carts, so there is great need of slaves to carry goods up into the town, especially for the inferior sort: but the merchants have also the convenience of a great crane that goes with ropes or pulleys, one end of which goes up while the other goes down. The house in which this crane is, stands on the brow of the hill towards the sea, hanging over the precipice; and there are planks set shelving against the bank from thence to the bottom, against which the goods lean or slide as they are hoisted up or let down. The Negro slaves in this town are so numerous, that they make up the greatest part or bulk of the inhabitants: every house, as I said, having some, both men and women, of them. Many of the Portuguese, who are bachelors, keep of these black women for misses, though they know the danger they are in of being poisoned by them, if ever they give them any occasion of jealousy. A gentleman of my acquaintance, who had been familiar with his cook-maid, lay under some such apprehensions from her when I was there. These slaves also of either sex will easily be engaged to do any sort of mischief; even to murder, if they are hired to do it, especially in the night; for which reason I kept my men on board as much as I could; for one of the French king's ships being here, had several men murdered by them in the night, as I was credibly informed.

SNAKES

Here are several sorts of serpents, many of them vastly great, and most of them very venomous: as the rattlesnake for one. And for venom, a small green snake is bad enough, no bigger than the stem of a tobacco-pipe, and about eighteen inches long, very common here.

They have here also the amphisbaena, or two-headed snake, of a grey colour, mixed with blackish stripes, whose bite is reckoned to be incurable. 'Tis said to be blind, though it has two small specks in each head like eyes: but whether it sees or not I cannot tell. They say it lives like a mole, mostly underground; and that when it is found above ground it is easily killed because it moves but slowly: neither is its sight (if it has any) so good as to discern anyone that comes near to kill it; as few of these creatures fly at a man, or hurt him but when he comes in their way. 'Tis about fourteen inches long, and about the bigness of the inner joint of a man's middle finger; being of one and the same bigness from one end to the other, with a head at each end (as they said; for I cannot vouch it, for one I had was cut short at one end), and both alike in shape and bigness; and 'tis said to move with either head foremost, indifferently; whence 'tis called by the Portuguese, cobra de dos cabezas, the snake with two heads.

The small black snake is a very venomous creature.

There is also a grey snake, with red and brown spots all over its back. 'Tis as big as a man's arm, and about three foot long, and is said to be venomous. I saw one of these.

Here are two sorts of very large snakes or serpents: one of 'em a land-snake, the other a water-snake. The land-snake is of a grey colour, and about eighteen or twenty foot long: not very venomous, but ravenous. I was promised the sight of one of their skins, but wanted opportunity.

The water-snake is said to be near thirty foot long. These live wholly in the water, either in large rivers, or great lakes, and prey upon any creature that comes within their reach, be it man or beast. They draw their prey to them with their tails: for when they see anything on the banks of the river or lake where they lurk, they swing about their tails ten or twelve foot over the bank; and whatever stands within their sweep is snatched with great violence into the river, and drowned by them. Nay, 'tis reported very credibly that if they see only a shade of any animal at all on the water, they will flourish their tails to bring in the man or beast whose shade they see, and are oftentimes too successful in it. Wherefore men that have business near any place where these water-monsters are suspected to lurk, are always provided with a gun, which they often fire, and that scares them away, or keeps them quiet. They are said to have great heads, and strong teeth about six inches long. I was told by an Irishman who lived here, that his wife's father was very near being taken by one of them about this time of my first arrival here,

when his father was with him up in the country: for the beast
flourished his tail for him, but came not nigh enough by a
yard or two; however it scared him sufficiently.

SUGAR

*The following extract is so interestingly detailed as to suggest that
Dampier played a more productive part on Squire Helyar's Jamaica
sugar plantation in 1674 than manager William Whaley contended.
It is intriguing to recall that, before being shipwrecked, Robinson
Crusoe lived for a few years in Bahia and initially 'acquainted
myself . . . with the manner of their planting and making of sugar'.*

The European ships carry from hence sugar, tobacco, either
in roll or snuff, never in leaf, that I know of: these are the
staple commodities. Besides which, here are dye-woods, such
as fustic, etc. with woods for other uses, as speckled wood,
brazil, etc. They also carry home raw hides, tallow, train-oil
of whales, etc. Here are also kept tame monkeys, parrots,
parakeets, etc. which the seamen carry home.

The sugar of this country is much better than that which
we bring home from our plantations: for all the sugar that
is made here is clayed, which makes it whiter and finer than
our muscovado, as we call our unrefined sugar. Our planters
seldom refine any with clay, unless sometimes a little to send
home as presents for their friends in England. Their way of
doing it is by taking some of the whitest clay and mixing it
with water, till 'tis like cream. With this they fill up the pans
of sugar, that are sunk two or three inches below the brim
by the draining of the molasses out of it: first scraping off
the thin hard crust of the sugar that lies at the top, and would
hinder the water of the clay from soaking through the sugar
of the pan. The refining is made by this percolation. For ten
or twelve days' time that the clayish liquor lies soaking down
the pan, the white water whitens the sugar as it passes
through it; and the gross body of the clay itself grows hard
on the top, and may be taken off at pleasure. When scraping
off with a knife the very upper part of the sugar, which will
be a little sullied, that which is underneath will be white

almost to the bottom: and such as is called Brazil sugar is thus whitened. When I was here this sugar was sold for 5os. per 100 lb. And the bottoms of the pots, which is very coarse sugar, for about 2os. per 100 lb., both sorts being then scarce; for here was not enough to lade the ships, and therefore some of them were to lie here till the next season.

PUZZLING COMPASS VARIATIONS

The Roebuck *weighed from Bahia on 23 April 1699, setting course for the Cape of Good Hope, which she cleared on 3 June. Dampier was surprised to reach the Cape earlier than his calculations indicated, 'but our reckonings are liable to such uncertainties from steerage, log, currents, half-minute glasses, and sometimes want of care, as in so long a run cause often a difference of many leagues in the whole account'.*

Another thing that stumbled me here was the variation, which, at this time, by the last amplitude I had I found to be but $7° 58'$ W. whereas the variation at the Cape (from which I found myself not thirty leagues distant) was then computed, and truly, about $11°$ or more: and yet a while after this, when I was got ten leagues to the eastward of the Cape, I found the variation but $10° 40'$ W. whereas it should have been rather more than at the Cape. These things, I confess, did puzzle me: neither was I fully satisfied as to the exactness of the taking the variation at sea; for in a great sea, which we often meet with, the compass will traverse with the motion of the ship; besides the ship may and will deviate somewhat in steering, even by the best helmsmen. And then when you come to take an azimuth,* there is often some difference between him that looks at the compass, and the man that takes the altitude height of the sun; and a small error in each, if the error of both should be one way, will make it wide of any great exactness. But what was most shocking to me, I found that the variation did not always increase or decrease in proportion to the degrees of longitude east or west; as I had a notion they might do to a certain number of degrees

* See note on p. 197.

of variation east or west, at such or such particular meridians. But finding in this voyage that the difference of variation did not bear a regular proportion to the difference of longitude, I was much pleased to see it thus observed in a scheme shown me after my return home, wherein are represented the several variations in the Atlantic Sea, on both sides the Equator; and there, the line of no variation in that sea is not a meridian line, but goes very oblique, as do those also which show the increase of variation on each side of it. In that draught there is so large an advance made as well towards the accounting for those seemingly irregular increases and decreases of variation towards the south-east coast of America, as towards the fixing a general scheme or system of the variation everywhere, which would be of such great use in navigation, that I cannot but hope that the ingenious author, Captain Halley, who to his profound skill in all theories of these kinds, has added and is adding continually personal experiments, will e'er long oblige the world with a fuller discovery of the course of the variation, which has hitherto been a secret. But since matter of fact, and whatever increases the history of the variation, may be of use towards the settling or confirming the theory of it, I shall here once for all insert a table of all the variations I observed beyond the Equator in this voyage, both in going out, and returning back; and what errors there may be in it I shall leave to be corrected by the observations of others.*

NEW HOLLAND AGAIN

By the last week in July the Roebuck *was almost across the Indian Ocean.*

. . . As we drew nigher the coast of New Holland, we saw frequently three or four whales together. When we were about ninety leagues from the land we began to see seaweeds,

* The table, covering five pages, was sufficiently accurate to help the famous navigator Matthew Flinders modify the ship's compass a century later with the addition of what are now known as Flinders' Bars.

all of one sort; and as we drew nigher the shore we saw them more frequently. At about thirty leagues distance we began to see some scuttlefish floating on the water; and drawing still nigher the land we saw greater quantities of them. On 25 July being in latitude 26° 14′ S. and longitude E. from the Cape of Good Hope 85° 52′, we saw a large garpike leap four times by us, which seemed to be as big as a porpoise. It was now very fair weather, and the sea was full of a sort of very small grass or moss, which as it floated in the water seemed to have been some spawn of fish; and there was among it some small fry. The next day the sea was full of small round things like pearl, some as big as white peas. They were very clear and transparent, and upon crushing any of them a drop of water would come forth: the skin that contained the water was so thin that it was but just discernible. Some weeds swam by us, so that we did not doubt but we should quickly see land. On the 27th also, some weeds swam by us, and the birds that had flown along with us all the way almost from Brazil, now left us, except only two or three shearwaters. On the 28th we saw many weeds swim by us, and some whales, blowing. On the 29th we had dark cloudy weather, with much thunder, lightning, and violent rains in the morning; but in the evening it grew fair. We saw this day a scuttlefish swim by us, and some of our young men a seal, as it should seem by their description of its head. I saw also some bonito, and some skipjack, a fish about eight inches long, broad, and sizeable, not much unlike a roach; which our seamen call so from their leaping about.

The 30 July, being still nearer the land, we saw abundance of scuttlefish and seaweed, more tokens that we were not far from it; and saw also a sort of fowl, the like of which we had not seen in the whole voyage, all the other fowl having now left us. These were as big as lapwings; of a grey colour, black about their eyes, with red sharp bills, long wings, their tails long and forked like swallows; and they flew flapping their wings like lapwings.* In the afternoon we met with a rippling like a tide or current, or the water of some shoal or overfall;

---

* Hubert Massey Whittell identifies these birds as Caspian terns.

but were past it before we could sound. The birds last mentioned and this were further signs of land. In the evening we had fair weather, and a small gale at west. At 8 o'clock we sounded again; but had no ground . . .

On 1 August, as we were standing in, we saw several large sea-fowls, like our gannets on the coast of England, flying three or four together; and a sort of white seamews, but black about the eyes, and with forked tails.* We strove to run in near the shore to seek for a harbour to refresh us after our tedious voyage; having made one continued stretch from Brazil hither of about 114° designing from hence also to begin the discovery I had a mind to make on New Holland and New Guinea. The land was low, and appeared even, and as we drew nearer to it, with some red and some white cliffs; these last in latitude 26° 10′ S. where you will find fifty-four fathom, within four miles of the shore . . .

On 5 August we saw land again, at about ten leagues' distance. This noon we were in latitude 25° 30′ and in the afternoon our cook died, an old man, who had been sick a great while, being infirm before we came out of England.

On 6 August in the morning we saw an opening in the land, and we ran into it, and anchored in seven and a half fathom water, two miles from the shore, clean sand. It was somewhat difficult getting in here, by reason of many shoals we met with: but I sent my boat sounding before me. The mouth of this sound, which I called Shark's Bay, lies in about 25° S. latitude and our reckoning made its longitude from the Cape of Good Hope to be about 87°; which is less by 195 leagues than is usually laid down in our common draughts, if our reckoning was right, and our glasses did not deceive us. As soon as I came to anchor in this bay I sent my boat ashore to seek for fresh water: but in the evening my men returned, having found none. The next morning I went ashore, myself, carrying pickaxes and shovels with me, to dig for water: and axes to cut wood. We tried in several places for water, but finding none after several trials, nor in several miles' compass, we left any farther search for it, and

---

* Whittell thinks these could have been crested terns.

spending the rest of the day in cutting wood, we went aboard at night . . .

There were but few land-fowls; we saw none but eagles, of the larger sorts of birds; but five or six sorts of small birds. The biggest sort of these were not bigger than larks; some no bigger than wrens, all singing with great variety of fine shrill notes; and we saw some of their nests with young ones in them. The water-fowls are ducks (which had young ones now, this being the beginning of the spring in these parts), curlews, galdens,* crab-catchers, cormorants, gulls, pelicans; and some water-fowl, such as I have not seen anywhere besides. I have given the pictures of four several birds on this coast.†

The land-animals that we saw here were only a sort of raccoon,‡ different from those of the West Indies, chiefly as to their legs; for these have very short forelegs; but go jumping upon them as the others do (and like them are very good meat); and a sort of iguana, of the same shape and size with other iguanas I have described, but differing from them in three remarkable particulars: for these had a larger and uglier head, and had no tail: and at the rump, instead of the tail there, they had a stump of a tail, which appeared like another head; but not really such, being without mouth or eyes. Yet this creature seemed by this means to have a head at each end; and, which may be reckoned a fourth difference, the legs also seemed all four of them to be forelegs, being all alike in shape and length, and seeming by the joints and bending to be made as if they were to go indifferently either head or tail foremost. They were speckled black and yellow like toads, and had scales or knobs on their backs like those of crocodiles, plated on to the skin, or stuck into it, as part of the skin. They are very slow in motion; and when a man comes nigh them they will stand still and hiss, not endeavouring to get away. Their livers are also spotted black and yellow: and

---

* Possibly reef herons or mangrove herons.
† Identified by both Whittell and William Sclater as 3, Australian avocet; 4, oyster-catcher; 5, bridled tern; 6, noddy.
‡ Joseph C. Shipman suggests this animal may not have been a kangaroo, but a Dama wallaby or banded hare-wallaby.

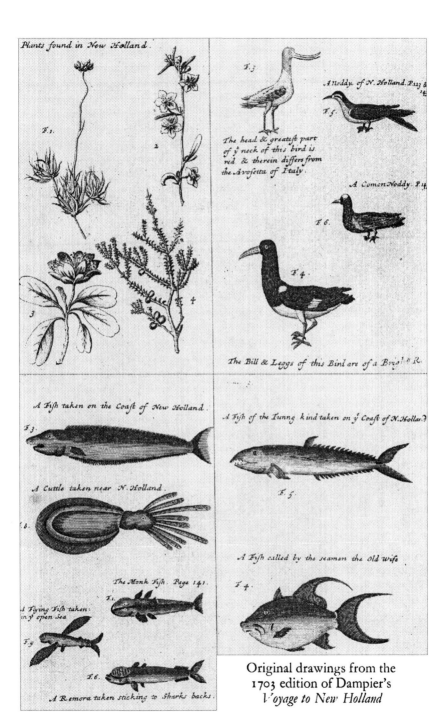

Original drawings from the
1703 edition of Dampier's
Voyage to New Holland

the body when opened has a very unsavoury smell. I did never see such ugly creatures anywhere but here. The iguanas I have observed to be very good meat; and I have often eaten of them with pleasure: but though I have eaten of snakes, crocodiles and alligators and many creatures that look frightfully enough, and there are but few I should have been afraid to eat of, if pressed by hunger, yet I think my stomach would scarce have served to venture upon these New Holland iguanas, both the looks and the smell of them being so offensive . . .

There are also some green turtle weighing about 200 lb. Of these we caught two which the water ebbing had left behind a ledge of rock, which they could not creep over. These served all my company two days; and they were indifferent sweet meat. Of the sharks we caught a great many, which our men eat very savourily. Among them we caught one which was eleven foot long. The space between its two eyes was twenty inches, and eighteen inches from one corner of his mouth to the other. Its maw was like a leather sack, very thick, and so tough that a sharp knife could scarce cut it: in which we found the head and bones of a hippopotamus*; the hairy lips of which were still sound and not putrefied, and the jaw was also firm, out of which we plucked a great many teeth, two of them eight inches long, and as big as a man's thumb, small at one end, and a little crooked; the rest not above half so long. The maw was full of jelly which stank extremely: however I saved for a while the teeth and the shark's jaw. The flesh of it was divided among my men; and they took care that no waste should be made of it . . .

The 21st day also we had small land-breezes in the night, and sea-breezes in the day: and as we saw some sea-snakes every day, so this day we saw a great many, of two different sorts or shapes. One sort was yellow, and about the bigness of a man's wrist, about four foot long, having a flat tail about four fingers broad. The other sort was much smaller and shorter, round and spotted black and yellow. This day we sounded several times, and had forty-five fathom sand. We did not make the land till noon, and then saw it first from

* Bernard Heuvelmans believes this was probably a dugong.

our topmast-head. It bore SE by E. about nine leagues'
distance; and it appeared like a cape or head of land. The
sea-breeze this day was not so strong as the day before, and
it veered out more; so that we had a fair wind to run in with
to the shore, and at sunset anchored in twenty fathom, clean
sand, about five leagues from the bluff point; which was not
a cape (as it appeared at a great distance) but the eastern-
most end of an island, about five or six leagues in length,
and one in breadth. There were three or four rocky islands
about a league from us between us and the bluff point; and
we saw many other islands both to the east and west of it,
as far as we could see either way from our topmast-head:
and all within them to the south there was nothing but islands
of a pretty height, that may be seen eight or nine leagues off.
By what we saw of them they must have been a range of
islands of about twenty leagues in length, stretching from
ENE to WSW and for aught I know, as far as to those of
Shark's Bay; and to a considerable breadth also (for we
could see nine or ten leagues in among them), towards the
continent or mainland of New Holland, if there be any such
thing hereabouts. And by the great tides I met with a while
afterwards, more to the north-east, I had a strong suspicion
that here might be a kind of archipelago of islands,* and a
passage possibly to the south of New Holland and New
Guinea into the great South Sea eastward; which I had
thoughts also of attempting in my return from New Guinea
(had circumstances permitted) and told my officers so. But
I would not attempt it at this time, because we wanted water,
and could not depend upon finding it there. This place is
in latitude 20° 21′ but in the draught that I had of this coast,
which was Tasman's,† it was laid down in 19° 50′, and the
shore is laid down as all along joining in one body or continent, with some openings appearing like rivers; and not
like islands as really they are. This place lies more northerly
by 40′ than is laid down in Mr Tasman's draught; and beside

---

* Now called Dampier Archipelago. The nearest large mainland town
is Dampier.
† The Dutchman Abel Tasman (1603–1659) sailed along this stretch of
coast in 1644. He had discovered Tasmania during the previous year.

its being made a firm, continued land, only with some openings like the mouths of rivers, I found the soundings also different from what the pricked line of his course shows them, and generally shallower than he makes them; which inclines me to think that he came not so near the shore as his line shows, and so had deeper soundings, and could not so well distinguish the islands. His meridian or difference of longitude from Shark's Bay agrees well enough with my account which is 232 leagues, though we differ in latitude. And to confirm my conjecture that the line of his course is made too near the shore, at least not far to the east of this place, the water is there so shallow that he could not come there so nigh . . .

The 30th day, being in latitude 18° 21' we made the land again, and saw many great smokes near the shore; and having fair weather and moderate breezes, I steered in towards it. At four in the afternoon I anchored in eight fathom water, clear sand, about three leagues and a half from the shore. I presently sent my boat to sound nearer in, and they found ten fathom about a mile farther in; and from thence still farther in the water decreased gradually to nine, eight, seven, and at two mile distance to six fathom. This evening we saw an eclipse of the moon, but it was abating before the moon appeared to us; for the horizon was very hazy, so that we could not see the moon till she had been half an hour above the horizon: and at two hours, twenty-two minutes after sunset, by the reckoning of our glasses, the eclipse was quite gone, which was not of many digits.* The moon's centre was then 33° 40' high.

On 31 August betimes in the morning I went ashore with ten or eleven men to search for water. We went armed with muskets and cutlasses for our defence, expecting to see people there; and carried also shovels and pickaxes to dig wells. When we came near the shore we saw three tall black naked men on the sandy bay ahead of us: but as we rowed in, they went away. When we were landed, I sent the boat with two men in her to lie a little from the shore at an anchor, to prevent being seized; while the rest of us went after the three

* A digit here means one twelfth of the diameter of the moon.

black men, who were now got on the top of a small hill about a quarter of a mile from us, with eight or nine men more in their company. They, seeing us coming, ran away. When we came on the top of the hill where they first stood, we saw a plain savannah, about half a mile from us, farther in from the sea. There were several things like haycocks, standing in the savannah, which at a distance we thought were houses, looking just like the Hottentots' houses at the Cape of Good Hope: but we found them to be so many rocks. We searched about these for water, but could find none, nor any houses; nor people, for they were all gone. Then we turned again to the place where we landed, and there we dug for water.

While we were at work there came nine or ten of the natives to a small hill a little way from us, and stood there menacing and threatening of us, and making a great noise. At last one of them came towards us, and the rest followed at a distance. I went out to meet him, and came within fifty yards of him, making to him all the signs of peace and friendship I could; but then he ran away, neither would they any of them stay for us to come nigh them; for we tried two or three times. At last I took two men with me, and went in the afternoon along by the seaside, purposely to catch one of them, if I could, of whom I might learn where they got their fresh water. There were ten or twelve of the natives a little way off, who seeing us three going away from the rest of our men, followed us at a distance. I thought they would follow us: but there being for a while a sandbank between us and them, that they could not then see us, we made a halt, and hid ourselves in a bending of the sandbank. They knew we must be thereabouts, and being three or four times our number, thought to seize us. So they dispersed themselves, some going to the seashore, and others beating about the sand-hills. We knew by what rencounter we had had with them in the morning that we could easily outrun them; so a nimble young man that was with me, seeing some of them near, ran towards them; and they, for some time, ran away before him; but he soon overtaking them, they faced about and fought him. He had a cutlass, and they had wooden lances;

with which, being many of them, they were too hard for him. When he first ran towards them I chased two more that were by the shore; but fearing how it might be with my young man, I turned back quickly, and went up to the top of a sandhill, whence I saw him near me, closely engaged with them. Upon their seeing me, one of them threw a lance at me, that narrowly missed me. I discharged my gun to scare them, but avoided shooting any of them; till finding the young man in great danger from them, and myself in some; and that though the gun had a little frighted them at first, yet they had soon learnt to despise it, tossing up their hands, and crying 'Pooh, Pooh, Pooh'; and coming on afresh with a great noise, I thought it high time to charge again, and shoot one of them, which I did. The rest, seeing him fall, made a stand again; and my young man took the opportunity to disengage himself, and come off to me; my other man also was with me, who had done nothing all this while, having come out unarmed; and I returned back with my men, designing to attempt the natives no farther, being very sorry for what had happened already. They took up their wounded companion; and my young man, who had been struck through the cheek by one of their lances, was afraid it had been poisoned: but I did not think that likely. His wound was very painful to him, being made with a blunt weapon; but he soon recovered of it.

Among the New Hollanders, whom we were thus engaged with, there was one who by his appearance and carriage, as well in the morning as this afternoon, seemed to be the chief of them, and a kind of prince or captain among them. He was a young brisk man, not very tall, nor so personable as some of the rest, though more active and courageous. He was painted (which none of the rest were at all) with a circle of white paste or pigment (a sort of lime, as we thought) about his eyes, and a white streak down his nose from his forehead to the tip of it. And his breast and some part of his arms were also made white with the same paint; not for beauty or ornament, one would think, but as some wild Indian warriors are said to do, he seemed thereby to design the looking more terrible; this his painting adding very much to his natural deformity; for they all of them have the most unpleasant looks and the worst features of any people that ever I saw, though I have seen great variety of savages. These New Hollanders were probably the same sort of people as those I met with on this coast in my *Voyage Round the World*; for the place I then touched at was not above forty or fifty leagues to the north-east of this: and these were much the same blinking creatures (here being also abundance of the same kind of flesh-flies teasing them) and with the same black skins, and hair frizzled, tall and thin, etc. as those were. But we had not the opportunity to see whether these, as the former, wanted two of their foreteeth.

We saw a great many places where they had made fires; and where there were commonly three or four boughs stuck up to windward of them; for the wind (which is the sea-breeze) in the daytime blows always one way with them; and the land-breeze is but small. By their fireplaces we should always find great heaps of fish-shells, of several sorts; and 'tis probable that these poor creatures here lived chiefly on the shellfish, as those I before described did on small fish, which they caught in wires or holes in the sand at low-water. These gathered their shellfish on the rocks at low-water; but had no wires (that we saw) whereby to get any other sorts of fish. As among the former I saw not any heaps of shells as here, though I know they also gathered some shellfish. The lances also of those were such as these had; however they being upon an island, with their women and children, and all in our power, they did not there use them against us, as here on the continent, where we saw none but some of the men under head, who come out purposely to observe us. We saw no houses at either place; and I believe they have none, since the former people on the island had none, though they had all their families with them.

Upon returning to my men I saw that though they had dug eight or nine foot deep, yet found no water. So I returned aboard that evening, and the next day being 1 September, I sent my boatswain ashore to dig deeper, and sent the seine with him to catch fish. While I stayed aboard I observed the flowing of the tide, which runs very swift here, so that our nun-buoy* would not bear above the water to be seen. It flows here (as on that part of New Holland I described formerly) about five fathom: and here the flood runs SE by S. till the last quarter; then it sets rights in towards the shore (which lies here SSW and NNE) and the ebb runs NW by N. When the tides slackened we fished with hook and line, as we had already done in several places on this coast; on which in this voyage hitherto, we had found but little tides: but by the height, and strength, and course of them hereabouts, it should seem that if there be such a passage or strait going through eastward to the great South Sea, as I said one might suspect, one would expect to find the mouth of it somewhere between this place and Rosemary Island,† which was the part of New Holland I came last from.

Next morning my men came aboard and brought a rundlet‡ of brackish water which they got out of another well that they dug in a place a mile off, and about half as far from the shore; but this water was not fit to drink. However we all concluded that it would serve to boil our oatmeal for burgoo [porridge], whereby we might save the remains of our other water for drinking till we should get more; and accordingly the next day we brought aboard four hogsheads of it: but while we were at work about the well we were sadly pestered with the flies, which were more troublesome to us than the sun, though it shone clear and strong upon us all the while, very hot. All this while we saw no more of the natives, but saw some of the smokes of some of their fires at two or three miles' distance.

The land hereabouts was much like the part of New Holland that I formerly described. 'Tis low, but seemingly barricaded with a long chain of sandhills to the sea, that lets nothing be seen of what is farther within land. At high water the tides rising so high as they do, the coast shows very low; but when 'tis low water it seems to be of an indifferent height. At low watermark the shore is all rocky, so that then there is no landing with a boat: but at high water a boat may come in

* A buoy attached to the anchor, marking its position.
† So named by him, but possibly today's Lewis Island.
‡ A barrel with capacity of fifteen gallons.

over those rocks to the sandy bay, which runs all along on this coast. The land by the sea for about five or six hundred yards is a dry sandy soil, bearing only shrubs and bushes of divers sorts. Some of these had them at this time of the year, yellow flowers or blossoms, some blue, and some white; most of them of a very fragrant smell.* Some had fruit like peascods, in each of which there were just ten small peas; I opened many of them, and found no more nor less. There are also here some of that sort of bean which I saw at Rosemary Island:† and another sort of small, red, hard pulse, growing in cods also, with little black eyes like beans.‡ I know not their names, but have seen them used often in the East Indies for weighing gold; and they make the same use of them at Guinea, as I have heard, where the women also make bracelets with them to wear about their arms. These grow on bushes; but here are also a fruit like beans growing on a creeping sort of shrublike vine. There was great plenty of all these sorts of cod-fruit growing on the sandhills by the seaside, some of them green, some ripe, and some fallen on the ground: but I could not perceive that any of them had been gathered by the natives; and might not probably be wholesome food.

The land farther in, that is lower than what borders on the sea, was so much as we saw of it, very plain and even; partly savannahs, and partly woodland. The savannahs bear a sort of thin coarse grass. The mould is also a coarser sand than that by the seaside, and in some places 'tis clay. Here are a great many rocks in the large savannah we were in, which are five or six foot high, and round at top like a haycock, very remarkable; some red, and some white. The woodland lies farther in still; where there were divers sorts of small trees, scarce any three foot in circumference; their bodies twelve or fourteen foot high, with a head of small nibs or boughs. By the sides of the creeks, especially nigh the sea, there grow a few small black mangrove trees.

There are but few land-animals. I saw some lizards; and

---

* Possibly *Crotalaria*.
† Now called *Eurybia dampieri*.
‡ *Abrus precatorius*.

my men saw two or three beasts like hungry wolves, lean like so many skeletons, being nothing but skin and bones. 'Tis probable that it was the foot of one of those beasts that I mentioned as seen by us in New Holland. We saw a raccoon or two, and one small speckled snake. The land-fowls that we saw here were crows (just such as ours in England), small hawks and kites; a few of each sort: but here are plenty of small turtle-doves, that are plump, fat and very good meat. Here are two or three sorts of smaller birds, some as big as larks, some less; but not many of either sort. The sea-fowl are pelicans, boobies, noddies, curlews, sea-pies, etc. and but few of these neither.

The sea is plentifully stocked with the largest whales that I ever saw; but not to compare with the vast ones of the northern seas. We saw also a great many green turtle, but caught none; here being no place to set a turtle-net in; here being no channel for them, and the tides running so strong. We saw some sharks, and parakeets; and with hooks and lines we caught some rock-fish and old-wives. Of shellfish, here were oysters both of the common kind for eating, and of the pearl kind; and also whelks, conches, mussels, limpets, periwinkles, etc. and I gathered a few strange shells; chiefly a sort not large, and thickset all about with rays or spikes growing in rows.

TIMOR

'I had spent about five weeks in ranging off and on the coast of New Holland, a length of about three hundred leagues,' writes Dampier, but this second visit proved no more productive than the first, eleven years earlier, so 'I resolved to steer away for the island Timor, where, besides getting fresh water, I might probably expect to be furnished with fruits and other refreshments to recruit my men, who began to droop, some of them being already to my great grief afflicted with the scurvy, which was likely to increase upon them and disable them.' He arrived at Timor, five hundred miles north of what is now Roebuck Bay, on 15 September. This is the island that Captain Bligh reached in June 1789 at the end of his 3,600-mile voyage in an open boat after being ejected from the Bounty.

The original natives of this island are Indians: they are of a middle stature, straight-bodied, slender-limbed, long-visaged; their hair black and lank; their skins very swarthy. They are very dextrous and nimble, but withal lazy in the highest degree. They are said to be dull in everything but treachery and barbarity. Their houses are but low and mean, their clothing only a small cloth about their middle; but some of them for ornament have frontlets of mother-of-pearl, or thin pieces of silver or gold, made of an oval form, of the breadth of a crown piece, curiously notched round the edges; five of these placed one by another a little above the eyebrows, making a sufficient guard and ornament for their forehead. They are so thin, and placed on their foreheads so artificially, that they seem riveted thereon: and indeed the pearl oystershells make a more splendid show than either silver or gold. Others of them have palmetto caps made in divers forms.

As to their marriages, they take as many wives as they can maintain; and sometimes they sell their children to purchase more wives. I enquired about their religion, and was told they had none. Their common subsistence is by Indian corn, which every man plants for himself. They take but little pains to clear their land; for in the dry time they set fire to the withered grass and shrubs, and that burns them out a plantation for the next wet season. What other grain they have, beside Indian corn, I know not. Their plantations are very mean, for they delight most in hunting; and here are wild buffaloes and hogs enough, though very shy, because of their so frequent hunting.

They have a few boats and some fishermen. Their arms are lances, thick round short truncheons and targets [shields]; with these they hunt and kill their game, and their enemies too; for this island is now divided into many kingdoms, and all of different languages; though in their customs and manner of living, as well as shape and colour, they seem to be of one stock ... They have an inveterate malice to their neighbours, insomuch that they kill all they meet, and bring away their heads in triumph. The great men of Kupang stick the heads of those they have killed on poles; and set them on the tops of their houses; and these they esteem above all their other riches. The inferior sort bring the heads of those they kill into houses made for that purpose; of which there was one at the Indian village near Fort Concordia almost full of heads, as I was told. I know not what encouragement they have for their inhumanity.

SABUDA

From Timor Dampier sailed to the north-west coast of New Guinea and on 14 January 1700 reached the island of Sabuda.

A little after noon we saw smokes on the islands to the west of us, and, having a fine gale of wind, I steered away for them. At seven o'clock in the evening we anchored in thirty-five fathom, about two leagues from an island, good, soft, oozy ground. We lay still all night and saw fires ashore. In the morning we weighed again, and ran farther in, thinking to have shallower water; but we ran within a mile of the shore, and came to in thirty-eight fathom, good, soft, holding ground. While we were under sail, two canoes came off within call of us: they spoke to us, but we did not understand their language, nor signs. We waved to them to come aboard, and I called to them in the Malayan language to do the same; but they would not; yet they came so nigh us, that we could show them such things as we had to truck with them. Yet neither would this entice them to come aboard; but they made signs for us to come ashore, and away they went. Then I went after them in my pinnace, carrying with me knives, beads, glasses, hatchets, etc. When we came near the shore, I called to them in the Malayan language. I saw but two men at first, the rest lying in ambush behind the bushes; but as soon as I threw ashore some knives and other toys, they came out, flung down their weapons, and came into the water by the boat's side, making signs of friendship by pouring water on their heads with one hand, which they dipped into the sea. The next day in the afternoon several other canoes came aboard, and brought many roots and fruits, which we purchased . . .

This island lies in latitude 2° 43′ S., and meridian distance from Port Babao on the island Timor, 486 miles. Besides this island, here are nine or ten other small islands, as they are laid down in the draughts.

The inhabitants of this island are a sort of very tawny Indians, with long black hair; who in their manners differ but little from the Mindanaoans, and others of these Eastern islands. These seem to be the chief; for besides them we saw also shock curl-pated New Guinea Negroes; many of which are slaves to the others, but I think not all. They are very poor, wear no clothes, but have a clout about their middle, made of the rinds of the tops of palmetto trees; but the women had a sort of calico clothes. Their chief ornaments are blue and yellow beads, worn about their wrists. The men arm themselves with bows and arrows, lances, broadswords like those of Mindanao; their lances are pointed with bone. They strike fish very ingeniously with wooden fizgigs,* and have a very ingenious way of making the fish rise: for they have a piece of wood curiously carved and painted much like a dolphin (and perhaps other figures); these they let down into the water by a line with a small weight to sink it; when they think it low enough, they haul the line into their boats very fast, and the fish rise up after this figure; and they stand ready to strike them when they are near the surface of the water. But their chief livelihood is from their plantations. Yet they have large boats, and go over to New Guinea, where they get slaves, fine parrots, etc. which they carry to Gorong and exchange for calico. One boat came from thence a little before I arrived here; of whom I bought some parrots; and would have bought a slave, but they would not barter for anything but calico, which I had not. Their houses on this side were very small, and seemed only to be for necessity; but on the other side of the island we saw good large houses. Their proas are narrow with outriggers on each side, like other Malayans. I cannot tell of what religion these are; but I think they are not Mahometans, by their drinking brandy out of the same cup with us without any scruple. At this island we continued till the 20th instant, having laid in store of such roots and fruits as the island afforded.

* See note on p. 39.

NEW IRELAND

After visiting Sabuda, the Roebuck *rounded the western end of New Guinea, through what is now called Selat Dampir (Dampier Strait), and cruised along the north coast to New Ireland, anchoring between Konos and Silom.*

The mainland, at this place, is high and mountainous, adorned with tall flourishing trees. The sides of the hills had many large plantations and patches of cleared land; which, together with the smoke we saw, were certain signs of its being well inhabited; and I was desirous to have some commerce with the inhabitants. Being nigh the shore, we saw first one proa; a little after, two or three more; and at last a great many boats came from all the adjacent bays. When they were forty-six in number, they approached so near us that we could see each other's signs, and hear each other speak; though we could not understand them, nor they us. They made signs for us to go in towards the shore, pointing that way; it was squally weather, which at first made me cautious of going too near; but the weather beginning to look pretty well, I endeavoured to get into a bay ahead of us, which we could have got into well enough at first; but while we lay by, we were driven so far to leeward, that now it was more difficult to get in. The natives lay in their proas round us; to whom I showed beads, knives, glasses, to allure them to come nearer; but they would not come so nigh as to receive anything from us. Therefore I threw out some things to them, viz. a knife fastened to a piece of board, and a glass bottle corked up with some beads in it, which they took up and seemed well pleased. They often struck their left breast with their right hand, and as often held up a black truncheon over their heads, which we thought was a token of friendship; wherefore we did the like. And when we stood in towards their shore, they seemed to rejoice; but when we stood off, they frowned, yet kept us company in their proas, still pointing to the shore. About five o'clock, we got within the mouth of the bay, and sounded several times, but had no ground though within a mile of the shore. The basin of this bay was above two miles within us, into which we might have gone; but as I was not assured of anchorage there, so I thought it not prudence to run in at this time; it being near night, and seeing a black tornado rising in the west, which I most feared: besides, we had near 200 men in proas close by us. And the bays on the shore were lined with men from one end to the other, where they could not be less than three or four hundred more. What weapons they had, we know not, nor yet their design. Therefore I had, at their first coming near us, got up all our small arms, and made several put on cartouche boxes to prevent treachery. At last I resolved to go out again: which, when the natives in their proas perceived, they began to fling stones at us as fast as they could, being provided with engines for that purpose (wherefore I named this place Slinger's Bay); but at the firing of one gun they were all amazed, drew off and flung no more stones. They got together, as if consulting what to do; for they did not make in towards the shore, but lay still, though some of them were killed or wounded; and many more of them had paid for their boldness, but that I was unwilling to cut off any of them; which if I had done, I could not hope afterwards to bring them to treat with me.

NEW BRITAIN AND BURNING ISLAND

New Britain, thus called by Dampier, was his next landing point. This island, at the eastern end of Papua New Guinea and twice the size of Wales, was one of numerous places in the area to receive, and retain, names given by him. We cannot with certainty identify Burning Island; possibly it is Sakar Island, to the west of New Britain, in what is now known as Dampier Strait. (The other Dampier Strait – Selat Dampir – is off north-west New Guinea.)

I sent ashore commodities to purchase hogs etc. being informed that the natives have plenty of them, as also of yams and other good roots; but my men returned without getting anything that I sent them for, the natives being unwilling to trade with us. Yet they admired our hatchets and axes; but would part with nothing but coconuts; which they used to climb the trees for; and so soon as they gave them our men, they beckoned to them to be gone, for they were much afraid of us. The 18th, I sent both boats again for water, and before noon they had filled all my casks. In the afternoon I sent them both to cut wood; but seeing about forty natives standing on the bay at a small distance from our men, I made a signal for them to come aboard again; which they did, and brought me word that the men which we saw on the bay were passing that way, but were afraid to come nigh them. At four o'clock I sent both the boats again for more wood, and they returned in the evening. Then I called my officers to consult whether it were convenient to stay here longer, and endeavour a better acquaintance with these people; or go to sea. My design of tarrying here longer was, if possible, to get some hogs, goats, yams and other roots; as also to get some knowledge of the country and its product. My officers unanimously gave their opinions for staying longer here. So the next day I sent both boats ashore again, to fish and to cut more wood. While they were ashore about thirty or forty men and women passed by them: they were a little afraid of our people at first; but upon their making signs of friendship, they passed by quietly, the men finely bedecked with feathers of divers colours about their heads, and lances in their hands; the women had no ornament about them, nor anything to cover their nakedness, but a bunch of small green boughs, before and behind, stuck under a string which came round their waists. They carried large baskets on their heads, full of yams. And this I have observed amongst all the wild natives I have known, that they make their women carry the burdens, while the men walk before, without any other load than their arms and ornaments . . .

On the 24th in the evening we saw some high land bearing NW, half W.; to the west of which we could see no land, though there appeared something like land bearing west a little southerly; but not being sure of it, I steered WNW all night, and kept going on with an easy sail, intending to coast along the shore at a distance. At ten o'clock I saw a great fire bearing NW by W., blazing up in a pillar, sometimes very high for three or four minutes, then falling quite down for an equal space of time; sometimes hardly visible, till it blazed up again. I had laid me down, having been indisposed this three days: but upon a sight of this, my chief mate called me; I got up and viewed it for about half an hour, and knew it to be a burning hill by its intervals: I charged them to look well out, having bright moonlight. In the morning I found that the fire we had seen the night before was a burning island; and steered for it. We saw many other islands, one large high island, and another smaller, but pretty high. I stood near the volcano, and many small low islands with some shoals.

On 25 March 1700, in the evening, we came within three leagues of this burning hill, being at the same time two leagues from the main. I found a good channel to pass between them, and kept nearer the main than the island. At seven in the evening I sounded, and had fifty-two fathom fine sand and ooze. I stood to the northward to get clear of this strait, having but little wind and fair weather. The island all night vomited fire and smoke very amazingly; and at every belch we heard a dreadful noise like thunder, and saw a flame of fire after it, the most terrifying that ever I saw. The intervals between its belches, were about half a minute, some more, others less: neither were these pulses or eruptions alike, for some were but faint convulsions in comparison of the more vigorous; yet even the weakest vented a great deal of fire; but the largest made a roaring noise, and sent up a large flame twenty or thirty yards high; and then might be seen a great stream of fire running down to the foot of the island, even to the shore. From the furrows made by this descending fire, we could in the daytime see great smokes arise, which probably were made by the sulphureous matter thrown out of the funnel at the top, which tumbling down to the bottom, and there, lying in a heap, burned till either consumed or extinguished; and as long as it burned and kept its heat, so long the smoke ascended from it; which we perceived to increase or decrease, according to the quantity of matter discharged from the funnel. But the next night, being shot to the westward of the burning island, and the funnel of it lying on the south side, we could not discern the fire there, as we did the smoke in the day when we were to the southward of it. This volcano lies in the latitude of 5° 33′ S., and meridian distance from Cape St George, 332 miles W.

ASCENSION ISLAND AND THE END OF THE ROEBUCK

The Admiralty's choice of the Roebuck *for the voyage to New Holland had hardly been generous. She was designated a fifth-rate ship and, while cruising off New Guinea, began to show ominous signs of deterioration. Repairs had to be undertaken with increasing frequency; on one occasion Dampier directed that timbers be replaced with wedges of salt beef, deeming these virtually impenetrable. He accordingly set sail for England, reaching the Cape without too many alarms.*

On 30 December, we arrived at the Cape of Good Hope; and departed again on 11 January 1701. About the end of the month we saw abundance of weeds or blubber swim by us, for I cannot determine which. It was all of one shape and colour. As they floated on the water, they seemed to be of the breadth of the palm of a man's hand, spread out round into many branches about the bigness of a man's finger. They had in the middle a little knob, no bigger than the top of a man's thumb. They were of a smoke-colour; and the branches, by their pliantness in the water, seemed to be more simple than jellies.* I have not seen the like before.

On 2 February, we anchored in St Helena Road, and set sail again from thence on the 13th.

On the 21st we made the island of Ascension, and stood in towards it. The 22nd, between eight and nine o'clock, we sprung a leak, which increased so that the chain-pump could not keep the ship free. Whereupon I set the hand-pump to work also, and by ten o'clock sucked her; then wore† the ship, and stood to the southward, to try if that would ease her; and then the chain-pump just kept her free. At five the

---

* Jellyfish.

† Steered the ship onto the other tack, bringing the wind round to the stern.

next morning we made sail and stood in for the bay; and at nine anchored in ten and a half fathom, sandy ground. The south point bore SSW distance two miles, and the north point of the bay, NE half N., distance two miles. As soon as we anchored, I ordered the gunner to clear his powder-room, that we might there search for the leak, and endeavour to stop it within board if possible; for we could not heel the ship so low, it being within four streaks of the keel; neither was there any convenient place to haul her ashore. I ordered the boatswain to assist the gunner; and by ten o'clock the powder-room was clear. The carpenter's mate, gunner, and boatswain went down; and soon after I followed them my-self, and asked them whether they could come at the leak. They said they believed they might, by cutting the ceiling; I told the carpenter's mate (who was the only person in the ship that understood anything of carpenters' work) that if he thought he could come at the leak by cutting the ceiling without weakening the ship, he might do it for he had stopped one leak so before; which though not so big as this, yet having seen them both, I thought he might as well do this as the other. Wherefore I left him to do his best. The ceiling being cut, they could not come at the leak; for it was against one of the foot-hook-timbers, which the carpenter's mate said he must first cut, before it could be stopped. I went down again to see it, and found the water to come in very violently. I told them I never had known any such thing as cutting timbers to stop leaks; but if they, who ought to be best judges in such cases, thought they could do any good, I bid them use their utmost care and diligence, promising the carpenter's mate that I would always be a friend to him if he could and would stop it. He said, by four o'clock in the after-noon he would make all well, it being then about eleven in the forenoon. In the afternoon my men were all employed, pumping with both pumps; except such as assisted the car-penter's mate. About one in the afternoon I went down again, and the carpenter's mate was cutting the afterpart of the tim-ber over the leak. Some said it was best to cut the timber away at once; I bid them hold their tongue, and let the carpenter's mate alone; for he knew best, and I hoped he would do his utmost to stop the leak. I desired him to get everything ready for stopping the violence of the water, before he cut any further; for fear it should overpower us at once. I had already ordered the carpenter to bring all the oakum he had, and the boatswain to bring all the waste cloths, to stuff in upon occasion; and had for the same purpose sent down my own bedclothes. The carpenter's mate said he should want short stanchions, to be placed so that the upper end should touch the deck, and the underpart rest on what was laid over the leak; and presently took a length for them. I asked the master-carpenter what he thought best to be done. He replied till the leak was all open, he could not tell. Then he went away to make a stanchion, but it was too long: I ordered him to make many of several lengths, that we might not want of any size. So, once more desiring the carpenter's mate to use his utmost endeavours, I went up, leaving the boatswain and some others there. About five o'clock the boatswain came to me, and told me the leak was increased, and that it was impossible to keep the ship above water; when on the contrary I expected to have had the news of the leak's being stopped. I presently went down, and found the timber cut away, but nothing in readiness to stop the force of water from coming in. I asked them why they would cut the timber, before they had got all things in readiness: the carpenter's mate answered they could do nothing till the timber was cut that he might take the dimensions of the place; and that there was a caulk which he had lined out, preparing by the carpenter's boy. I ordered them in the meantime to stop in oakum, and some pieces of beef; which accordingly was done, but all to little purpose, for now the water gushed in with such violence, notwithstanding all our endeavours to check it, that it flew in over the ceiling; and for want of passage out of the room overflowed it above two foot deep. I ordered the bulkhead to be cut open, to give passage to the water that it might drain out of the room; and withal ordered to clear away abaft the bulkhead, that we might bail. So now we had both pumps going, and as many bailing as could; and by this means the water began to decrease; which gave me some hope of saving the ship. I asked the carpenter's mate what he thought of it. He said, 'Fear not; for by ten o'clock at night I'll engage to stop the leak.' I went from him with a heavy heart; but putting a good countenance upon the matter, encouraged my men, who pumped and bailed very briskly; and, when I saw occasion, I gave them some drams to comfort them. About eleven o'clock at night, the boatswain came to me, and told me that the leak still increased; and that the plank was so rotten, it broke away like dirt; and that now it was impossible to save the ship, for they could not come at the leak because the water in the room was got above it. The rest of the night we spent in pumping and bailing. I worked myself to encourage my men, who were very diligent; but the water still increased, and we now thought of nothing but saving our lives. Wherefore I hoisted out the boat, that if the ship should sink yet we might be saved: and in the morning we weighed our anchor, and warped in nearer the shore; yet did but little good.

In the afternoon, with the help of a sea-breeze, I ran into seven fathom, and anchored; then carried a small anchor ashore, and warped in till I came into three fathom and a half; where, having fastened her, I made a raft to carry the men's chests and bedding ashore; and, before eight at night, most of them were ashore. In the morning I ordered the sails to be unbent, to make tents; and then myself and officers went ashore. I had sent ashore a puncheon, and a thirty-six gallon cask of water, with one bag of rice for our common use: but great part of it was stolen away, before I came ashore; and many of my books and papers lost.

On the 26th following, we, to our great comfort, found a spring of fresh water, about eight miles from our tents, beyond a very high mountain, which we must pass over: so that now we were, by God's providence, in a condition of subsisting some time; having plenty of very good turtle by our tents, and water for the fetching. The next day I went up to see the watering-place, accompanied with most of my officers. We lay by the way all night, and next morning early got thither; where we found a very fine spring on the south-east side of the high mountain, about half a mile from its top: but the continual fogs make it so cold here, that it is very unwholesome living by the water. Near this place are abundance of goats and land-crabs. About two miles south-east from the spring, we found three or four shrubby trees, upon one of which was cut an anchor and cable, and the year 1642. About half a furlong from these, we found a convenient place for sheltering men in any weather. Hither many of our men resorted, the hollow rocks affording convenient lodging; the goats, land-crabs, men-of-war birds, and boobies, good food, and the air was here exceeding wholesome.

About a week after our coming ashore, our men that lived at this new habitation, saw two ships making towards the island. Before night they brought me the news; and I ordered them to turn about a score of turtle, to be in readiness for their ships if they should touch here: but before morning they were out of sight, and the turtle were released again. Here we continued without seeing any other ship till 2 April, when we saw eleven sail to windward of the island: but they likewise passed by. The day after appeared four sail, which came to anchor in this bay. They were His Majesty's Ships the *Anglesey*, *Hastings* and *Lizard*; and the *Canterbury* East India ship. I went on board the *Anglesey* with about thirty-five of my men; and the rest were disposed of into the other two men-of-war.

We sailed from Ascension on the 8th; and continued aboard till the 8th of May:* at which time the men-of-war having missed St Jago [São Tiago], where they designed to water, bore away for Barbados: but I, being desirous to get to England as soon as possible, took my passage in the ship *Canterbury*, accompanied with my master, purser, gunner, and three of my superior† officers.

---

* The day on which Captain Kidd was tried at the Old Bailey and sentenced to death for piracy.
† I.e. senior.

CHAPTER
NINE

A DISAPPOINTING ENGAGEMENT

In June 1702 Dampier was court-martialled for 'very hard and cruel usage towards Lieutenant Fisher'; he was docked his pay for the two-year expedition and stigmatised 'not a fit person to be employed as commander of any of Her Majesty's Ships'. Yet ten months after this apparent disgrace the fifty-one-year-old ex-buccaneer had an audience of Queen Anne, kissing hands on receipt of a Letter of Marque that entitled him to lead a privateering voyage funded by London and Bristol businessmen. He took charge of two ships and set sail at the end of April 1703. Our principal source for the events that unfolded is A Voyage Round the World *by William Funnell, who was mate on the* St George, *captained by Dampier. The mission was a total failure, with dissident members of the two crews, including Alexander Selkirk, regularly disembarking or being put ashore. In the following engagements described by Funnell, Dampier's consort was Captain Thomas Stradling of the* Cinque Ports.

On 29 February 1704, at noon, we saw a sail: so we got on board all our people, got up our yards and topmasts; and, he being pretty near, we clapped our longboat on our moorings, let slip, and got under sail. He, seeing us get under sail, tacked and stood from us; and we made the best of our way after him; and our comrade made what haste he could after us; and about eleven at night we came close up with him, but did not think convenient to engage till day. In this chase our pinnace towed underwater; so we cut her loose. Captain Stradling's boat also broke loose, and in her was a man and a dog.

At sunrise the next morning, being 1 March, we began to engage the said ship, which was a French ship of about four hundred tons, and thirty guns, well-manned. We fought her very close, broadside and broadside, for seven hours; and then, a small gale springing up, she sheared off. As for our consort,* he fired about ten or twelve guns, and then fell astern, and never came up again during the fight. We had nine of our men killed in the fight, and several wounded. We were desirous to have the other trial with him, knowing it would be of dangerous consequence to let him go; for if we did, we were sure he would discover us to the Spaniards, which would be of ill consequence to our whole proceedings: but our captain was against it, saying that at the worst, if the Spaniards should know of our being in those seas, and so should hinder their merchant ships from coming out, yet that he knew where to go and could not fail of taking to the value of £500,000 any day in the year. Upon this we lay by for our consort, who soon came up; and it was quickly agreed between the two captains to let her go. So the enemy stood from us, I suppose very well satisfied that he had disappointed us both: and we were very much dissatisfied that we should suffer ourselves to be so baffled in our first attempt.

CAPTAIN DAMPIER'S VINDICATION

When Funnell's book appeared in 1707, Dampier was so incensed by the portrait of him as a vacillating and timid commander that he immediately published an eight-page broadsheet, a testy and sometimes incoherent tirade which was written in the shadow of impending legal action by his depleted Bristol backers. The prose style gives us strong grounds for believing that his previous works were edited and corrected by others.

SOME SMALL OBSERVATIONS FOR THE PRESENT ON MR FUNNELL'S CHIMERICAL RELATION OF THE VOYAGE ROUND THE WORLD; AND DETECTED IN LITTLE, UNTIL HE SHALL BE EXAMINED MORE AT LARGE.

In the first place, he calls himself my mate: he went out my steward, and afterwards I did make a midshipman of him.

* In this case, accompanying vessel, sister ship.

Indeed he had the advantage of perusing draughts and books, of which he afterwards gave but a slender account, for some he pretended were lost, and others the draughts are torn out of them; especially the draughts of winds, which I greatly suspect him of doing, because he is not the first man that has endeavoured to build upon another man's foundation . . . Though there may be more mistakes that we pass over to abbreviate this matter, as yet, my crew not being wholly here, I mention only the two actions of the voyage, on which depend the miscarriage of the whole, by the men's disorder.

The first of which is the French ship that we engaged, that was coming to the island of Juan Fernandez to whom we gave chase from three in the afternoon, and fetched upon her so fast, that making of her to hull, I found she was an European ship and not a Spaniard, upon which I was not willing to pursue her any further, but the men being (as they pretended) in a desire of engagement, right or wrong, I followed her; and next morning early, we came up with her, and when I saw nothing would disengage them from an insignificant attempt, I encouraged them all I could. By this time my consort had given her a broadside, so I ranged up her other side, and gave her a broadside likewise. Now to show the confusion they were then in, they fired upon our own consort in his falling astern, and hindered his help. Notwithstanding this I came up again, and exchanged three or four broadsides with her, wherein ten of my men suffered, nine killed and one wounded; which dismayed my men so much, they actually run down off the deck, and made nothing of it afterwards, so that when I could have boarded her and carried her, the mate, Clipperton by name, cried 'The men are all gone'; and Bellhash the master, whose office it was to be always upon deck, was gone also; though this gentleman is now a valiant talker to my detriment.

Mr Funnell says the crew were desirous to fight this ship again. Now since they made nothing of it while in my power, what was to be done afterwards?

DAMPIER REBUTTED

Dampier might have done better to leave Funnell's relatively mild criticisms unanswered, for by printing his Vindication *he provoked a retaliatory broadsheet from John Welbe, midshipman on the* St George, *who, in* An Answer to Captain Dampier's Vindication of His Voyage to the South Seas in the Ship 'St George', with Particular Observations on His Ungenerous, False and Barbarous Usage to His Ship's Crew, *subjected him to harsher and more damaging treatment.*

Sincerity is the greatest ornament that belongs to mankind; and he that is not endowed with it, ought to be had in no regard with his fellow creatures. If three and two be five, and matter of fact beyond speculation, I hope this subsequent discourse will induce all gentlemen to believe that what Captain Dampier writes is all scandalous, false, and malicious; and that I am every hour in the day ready to justify it to his face, and stand the examination with him, either before a committee of merchants, or commanders of ships.

First, I can't but smile at the captain's witty (otherwise foolish) phrase, 'Mr Funnell's chimerical relation', not having the least thought of his ferraginous compendium, full of enthusiasms and improbable stuff, such as no man yet could ever understand; no, not even the courageous author himself ... Captain Dampier being in his cabin quite drunk.

He says he mentions only the two actions of the voyage, on which depends the miscarriage of the whole, by the men's disorder.

To which I answer, that the miscarriage of the voyage depends wholly on the want of courage and conduct in the commander. As for the French ship, that we engaged near the island Juan Fernandez, 'tis true, we chased her all the afternoon, and fetched upon her; but taking her to be an European ship (as Captain Dampier says in his own scandalous vindication) he did not care to engage her (he believing that she might have guns on board, to which he always had a natural aversion; and besides, not knowing how to behave himself, or work his ship in time of engagement, as it plainly appeared afterwards). Having chased this ship all night, in the morning our consort came first up with her, and gave her a broadside or two; but finding her to be a ship of greater force than his was, he soon sheared off, and shortened sail, which was the occasion of his falling astern; and now it being left to the courageous Captain Dampier, to dispute the decision of the victory, he, as soon as we came within gunshot of the enemy, thought it convenient to shorten sail; but, by the persuasions of the officers, made sail, and run along her side, often asking his men, whether he was near enough? Captain Dampier is pleased to say in his own vindication, that after we had exchanged several broadsides with the enemy, wherein several of our men were killed and wounded, that his men run down off the deck, and made nothing of it.

To this I answer that none of our men quitted their posts, during the time of engagement, except Captain Dampier himself, who the whole time of engagement, neither encouraged his men, nor gave any regular command, as is usually required from a commander at such times; but stood upon the quarterdeck behind a good barricade, which he had ordered to be made of beds, rugs, pillows, blankets, etc. to defend him from the small shot of the enemy; where he stood with the fusee* in his hand, and never so much as took care to have the quarterdeck guns and paterero† fired. And whereas he says he could have boarded her, and carried her, it is probably true; but he was so far from intending it, that he called out to make sail, for fear the enemy should clap us on board, and take us; which was the first word that I heard him speak during the engagement; and so accordingly we sheered off from her, and lay by, till our consort came up; and then both ships' companies would fain have attacked her again, knowing that if we did not take her, that she would discover our being in the seas to the Spaniards, which would consequently frustrate our designs on the coast of Peru (as accordingly it afterwards happened), but Captain Dampier would not consent to it. And afterwards meeting her the second time off Lima, all our men being in health, and both

* The same as fusil, a flintlock musket.
† A paterero was a small breach-loading swivel gun.

ships' companies willing to fight her again, for the aforesaid reasons, Captain Dampier would in no wise consent to it; but calling for the doctor, asked him if he could make any more men, in case he should engage this ship, and lose any? But the doctor told him that he could not make men; yet he would do his endeavour to preserve those he had, if he should have any wounded. Upon which answer, the captain ordered us to stand to sea, and would in no wise consent to hazard his person in a second engagement. Upon which, one of our men told him to his face he was a coward, and asked him whether he came to those parts of the world to fight, or not? And he replied he did not come to fight; for he knew where to make a voyage without fighting.

THE MANILA SHIP

The Manila ship was the ultimate objective of the St George and Cinque Ports expedition. Dampier had been able to justify to his crew his apparent cowardice in engagements earlier in the voyage by propounding the need to preserve lives and equipment for the big occasion – the attack on the treasure galleon. But, when the moment at last arrived, he once more proved unequal to the task, as Funnell describes:

On 6 December in the morning, being off the volcano of Colima, we saw a sail, and soon came up with her. She proved to be the Manila ship. So we, being all provided, gave her several broadsides, before she could get any of her guns clear. For they did not suspect us to be an enemy, and were not at all prepared for us. Captain Martin was then a prisoner on board us: he advised to lay her aboard immediately, while they were all in a hurry, and that this would be the only way to take her; but if we gave them so much time as to get out their great guns, they would certainly beat us in pieces, and we should lose an opportunity of making ourselves masters of the value of sixteen millions of pieces of eight. And accordingly it happened: for time being delayed in quarrelling, between those of us that would lay her aboard, and those that would not, the enemy got out a tier of guns, and then were too hard for us; so that we could not lie along her side to do her any considerable damage. For our five-pound shot, which was the biggest we had, signified little against such a ship as she was; but any of her shot, which were eighteen- and twenty-four-pounders, if any of them happened to strike us, our ship being very much decayed, it would drive in a piece of plank of three or four foot. So being much damaged, and receiving particularly a shot from the enemy between wind and water in our powder-room; by which we had two foot of plank driven in on each side the stem; the signal was made to stand off from the enemy.

Thus our design being disappointed, all our men grew discontented, and were for going home; knowing we could do no good in these parts, either for ourselves or owners; having provision but for three months, and that very short; and our ship being ready of herself to fall in pieces.

CAPTAIN DAMPIER'S VINDICATION CONTINUED:

As to the Acapulco ship which he mentions. He says, when we came up with the Acapulco ship, we gave her several broadsides before she could get any of her guns clear. To this I answer:

It is false, entirely so; for I no sooner fired on her, but she fired on me, and had her guns out before. Again he says:

That while some of them were quarrelling about laying her on board, and some disputing the contrary, she got out a tier of guns, and then was too hard for us.

Mr Funnell might hear dispute, as he calls it, among the men; THAT WAS NOTHING TO MY COMMAND. They might have taken her, would they have obeyed my advice, which was to ply her with my chase guns, and command her that way: for we had nothing to do alongside, and that I refer myself to all sailors in the world, whether it was right or not. And considering the inequality of our numbers and bulk of ship.

Before the beginning of this action, we were to the wind-ward of her, she standing to the westward, and we bearing away upon her with a flown sheet. I then ordered my officers

to keep enough to be sure to be windward of her: instead of
this, spite of my heart, they edged away, and were so far from
having the power to command and board her, as I intended,
that we lost the opportunity, and were forced to leeward the
first time; after that I tacked, came about, and had her under
my lee-bow: and then I hoped to batter her with my chase
guns, she having no stern-chase to gall us; this I took to be
the best way of disabling her, and this way I could have made
her yield. Instead of this, to show the world how ready my
officers were to board her, or perform their duty, the master
and the mate left the braces, and betook them to the great
guns: so in this confusion neither they nor the private men
(let 'em talk what they will) ever intended boarding her. For
'tis an argument against all they can say, there was not a man
to be assistant to any purpose; no yards braced, not a rope
spliced or knotted in all the action. For the very man at helm
contradicted my orders, edged her away to leeward once
more: *at which I offered to shoot him through the head.* While
things were at this pass, the boatswain being at the braces, I
asked him what they did intend to do? He told me to board
her. *Clap her on a wind then, said I.* But for want of wind by
this time (they being drunk and bewitched) as if all things
had concurred to our wrong, the ship had neither way, nor
would she keep to. Now could I have gotten alongside, they
were so far from being desirous to board her, that the master
went about discouraging of the men: not only that, but he
and another came to me, showing the powder barrels at the
enemy's yardarms. About four in the afternoon, when we
were a great way to the leeward, Clark the mate, who by this
time was potent in liquor, cried 'Board, board her.'

I answered, 'Tonight 'tis impossible, we have a fair day
tomorrow before us, and now no wind to work the ship.'
But to see the nature of these fellows, in the night they
actually lost her in steering directly from her; and for three
days after this, they were frighted, and not dissatisfied, as
they call it, their panic qualms was ever incurable, and they
would not tack about again on any account.

A FINAL BROADSIDE

*Whom should we believe of Dampier, Funnell and Welbe? There is
no means of telling. But we can surely conclude that Dampier lacked
the gift of leadership and alienated most of those he commanded. His
buccaneer past had become too ingrained. John Welbe delivers a final
broadside:*

Likewise he says: that when we first saw the Acapulco ship,
she was standing to the westward: which is a very great mistake of Captain Dampier's; for she came from the Philippine
Islands, which lies to the westward, and was bound for
Acapulco, which was to the eastward of us.

Likewise he says: It was his men's fault, that he did not
take her: which is like the rest of his false stories; for we were
close upon a wind, having our larboard tacks on board,
standing offshore, the wind being easterly. She was about
two leagues ahead of us, a little on our lee-bow, having her
starboard tacks on board, standing in for the shore; and as
soon as she came right head of us, she bore away, and stood
directly to us; and a little before she came within gunshot of
us, which was about ten in the morning, she hoisted her
Spanish ensign, and fired a gun to the leeward, as a friend,
believing us to be a Spanish ship. Upon which, the officers
desired the captain to hoist Spanish colours, and answer her
with a gun to the leeward; but he would not consent to it,
but immediately hoisted an English ensign, and fired a shot
at her. She no sooner perceived that we were an enemy, but
immediately sprung her luff, and hauled close upon a wind,
and so got to the windward of us, and got time to heave all
her boats overboard, and her goods from betwixt decks, and
made a clear ship: and got a tier of guns out from betwixt
deck, she having but two guns upon the upper deck, which
were all the guns that she had clear to fight, when we came
first up with her. After which we tacked, and ran along her
side, the men being resolved to clap her on board; but the
captain was so much against it that when the boatswain
ordered the man at the helm to edge near her, in order to
clap her on board, the captain swore he would shoot the

man at the helm through the head, if he offered to edge near her. After which, we having received several shot under water, one of the men told the captain that our ship was a sinking, and that now was the time to clap her on board. But instead of clapping her on board, the captain cried out, 'Where is the canoe? Where is the canoe?' And was for getting into the boat to save his life, which showed what man of courage and conduct he was. But we, shearing off from her, the carpenter stopped the leaks. After which, the captain ordered us to stand off from her, which accordingly we did: all the ship's company being exceedingly vexed at the captain's ill conduct. We stood about two leagues off from her; and then the captain said, 'Well, gentlemen, I will not say, as Johnie Armstrong said, I'll lay me down and bleed awhile; but I will lay me down and sleep awhile': but he forgot to wake again, till seven or eight o'clock the next morning.* He never so much as left any orders with the officers, what they should do; but set a sentry at his cabin door, that nobody should disturb him. And whereas he says that the men lost him in the night, it is false; for we were in sight of her the next morning, and he ordered us to steer away directly from her. Now, if so be that Captain Dampier would have done as the officers advised him, which was, when we first came up with her, to have hoisted Spanish colours, and fired a gun to the leeward, as a friend, we might have run along her side, she not suspecting us to be an enemy; and then hoisted our English colours, and gave her a broad-size, and a volley of small-shot; which would have been a great surprise to them, and so clapped her on board. In the confusion, we might very easily have taken her.

When we went to take the town of St Mary's [El Real de Santa Maria],† Captain Stradling would have had Captain

---

*   *I'll lay me down and bleed awhile*
             And then I'll rise and fight again
are the dying words of Andrew Barton in the naval ballad named after him. A bonny Scots privateer, he fell foul of the English and was killed at sea in 1511. His countryman Johnie Armstrong, also remembered in heroic song, was hanged near Teviothead in 1529.
† In Darien.

Woodes Rogers, 'the promising young captain'
as Governor of the Bahamas later in his career

Dampier to have given each man a dram of brandy to encourage them. But Captain Dampier answered, 'If we take the town, they will get brandy enough; but if we don't take the town, I shall want it myself'* . . . Captain Dampier's usual treatment to everybody being rogue, rascal, son-of-a-bitch, and other such vulgar expressions, which was the occasion of Mr Bellhash's quarrel last with him.

THE RESCUE OF ALEXANDER SELKIRK

Dampier reached England towards the end of 1707 after a disastrous privateering voyage and his second circumnavigation. He then had Funnell's and Welbe's criticisms to plague him and the prospect of legal action from his Bristol backers. But some of these business-men now planned a similar venture and chose a promising young captain, Woodes Rogers, to lead it; he, in turn, asked for Dampier as navigator, since no man was better qualified. In acceding to his request, they shelved their litigation. The Duke *and* Dutchess *weighed from Bristol on 1 August 1708, their principal quarry being the Manila galleon, which Woodes Rogers aimed to intercept in December 1709. At the end of January 1709 they sighted the Juan Fernández Islands, four hundred miles west of Chile. The description of Selkirk's rescue there has become the best known passage in Rogers's* A Cruising Voyage Round the World *(1712) and is seen as an important influence on* Robinson Crusoe. *Strangely enough, Rogers's manuscript was emended and polished by the Whig pamphleteer George Ridpath, who in 1713 helped trigger Defoe's arrest for high treason.*

On 2 February we stood on the back side along the south end of the island, in order to lay in with the first southerly wind, which Captain Dampier told us generally blows there all day long. In the morning, being past the island, we tacked to lay it in close aboard the land; and about ten o'clock opened the south end of the island, and ran close aboard the land that begins to make the north-east side. The flaws†
came heavy offshore, and we were forced to reef our topsails

* They did not take the town.
† Sudden bursts or squalls of wind.

when we opened the middle bay, where we expected to find our enemy, but saw all clear, and no ships in that nor the other bay next the north-west end. These two bays are all that ships ride in which recruit on this island, but the middle bay is by much the best. We guessed there had been ships there, but that they were gone on sight of us. We sent our yawl ashore about noon, with Captain Dover, Mr Frye, and six men, all armed; meanwhile we and the *Dutchess* kept turning to get in, and such heavy flaws came off the land that we were forced to let fly our topsail-sheet, keeping all hands to stand by our sails, for fear of the wind's carrying 'em away: but when the flaws were gone, we had little or no wind. These flaws proceeded from the land, which is very high in the middle of the island. Our boat did not return, so we sent our pinnace with the men armed, to see what was the occasion of the yawl's stay; for we were afraid that the Spaniards had a garrison there, and might have seized 'em. We put out a signal for our boat, and the *Dutchess* showed a French ensign. Immediately our pinnace returned from the shore, and brought abundance of crawfish, with a man clothed in goatskins, who looked wilder than the first owners of them. He had been on the island four years and four months, being left there by Captain Stradling in the *Cinque Ports*; his name was Alexander Selkirk, a Scotchman, who had been master of the *Cinque Ports*, a ship that came here last with Captain Dampier, who told me that this was the best man in her; so I immediately agreed with him to be a mate on board our ship. 'Twas he that made the fire last night when he saw our ships, which he judged to be English. During his stay here, he saw several ships pass by, but only two came in to anchor. As he went to view them, he found 'em to be Spaniards, and retired from 'em; upon which they shot at him. Had they been French, he would have submitted; but chose to risk his dying alone on the island, rather than fall into the hands of the Spaniards in these parts, because he apprehended they would murder him, or make a slave of him in the mines, for he feared they would spare no stranger that might be capable of discovering the South Sea. The Spaniards had landed, before he knew what they were, and they came so near him that he had much ado to escape; for they not only shot at him but pursued him into the woods, where he climbed to the top of a tree, at the foot of which they made water, and killed several goats just by, but went off again without discovering him. He told us that he was born at Largo in the county of Fife in Scotland, and was bred a sailor from his youth. The reason of his being left here was a difference betwixt him and his captain; which, together with the ship's being leaky, made him willing rather to stay here, than go along with him at first; and when he was at last willing, the captain would not receive him. He had been in the island before to wood and water, when two of the ship's company were left upon it for six months till the ship returned, being chased thence by two French South Sea ships.

He had with him his clothes and bedding, with a firelock, some powder, bullets, and tobacco, a hatchet, a knife, a kettle, a bible, some practical pieces, and his mathematical instruments and books. He diverted and provided for himself as well as he could; but for the first eight months had much ado to bear up against melancholy, and the terror of being left alone in such a desolate place. He built two huts with pimento trees, covered them with long grass, and lined them with the skins of goats, which he killed with his gun as he wanted, so long as his powder lasted, which was but a pound; and that being near spent, he got fire by rubbing two sticks of pimento wood together upon his knee. In the lesser hut, at some distance from the other, he dressed his victuals, and in the larger he slept, and employed himself in reading, singing psalms, and praying; so that he said he was a better Christian while in this solitude than ever he was before, or than, he was afraid, he should ever be again. At first he never ate anything till hunger constrained him, partly for grief and partly for want of bread and salt; nor did he go to bed till he could watch no longer: the pimento wood, which burnt very clear, served him both for firing and candle, and refreshed him with its fragrant smell.

He might have had fish enough, but could not eat 'em for want of salt, because they occasioned a looseness; except crawfish, which are there as large as our lobsters, and very good: these he sometimes boiled, and at other times broiled, as he did his goats' flesh, of which he made very good broth, for they are not so rank as ours. He kept an account of 500 that he killed while there, and caught as many more, which he marked on the ear and let go.* When his powder failed, he took them by speed of foot; for his way of living and continual exercise of walking and running, cleared him of all gross humours, so that he ran with wonderful swiftness through the woods and up the rocks and hills, as we perceived when we employed him to catch goats for us. We had a bulldog, which we sent with several of our nimblest runners, to help him in catching goats; but he distanced and tired both the dog and the men, caught the goats, and brought 'em to us on his back. He told us that his agility in pursuing a goat had once like to have cost him his life; he pursued it with so much eagerness that he caught hold of it on the brink of a precipice, of which he was not aware, the bushes having hid it from him; so that he fell with the goat down the said precipice a great height, and was so stunned and bruised with the fall, that he narrowly escaped with his life, and when he came to his senses, found the goat dead under him. He lay there about twenty-four hours, and was scarce able to crawl to his hut, which was about a mile distant, or to stir abroad again in ten days.

He came at last to relish his meat well enough without salt or bread, and in the season had plenty of good turnips, which had been sowed there by Captain Dampier's men,† and have now overspread some acres of ground. He had enough of good cabbage from the cabbage trees, and seasoned his meat with the fruit of the pimento trees, which is the same as the Jamaica pepper, and smells deliciously. He found there also a black pepper called malagita, which was very good to expel wind, and against griping of the guts.

He soon wore out all his shoes and clothes by running through the woods; and at last being forced to shift without

---

* Thirty-two years later, in June 1741, Commodore Anson, stopping at Juan Fernández during his circumnavigation, came across some of Selkirk's ear-marked goats, still alive.
† In February 1704.

them, his feet became so hard, that he ran everywhere without annoyance: and it was some time before he could wear shoes after we found him; for not being used to any so long, his feet swelled when he came first to wear 'em again.

After he had conquered his melancholy, he diverted himself sometimes by cutting his name on the trees, and the time of his being left and continuance there. He was at first much pestered with cats and rats, that had bred in great numbers from some of each species which had got ashore from ships that put in there to wood and water. The rats gnawed his feet and clothes while asleep, which obliged him to cherish the cats with the goats' flesh; by which many of them became so tame, that they would lie about him in hundreds, and soon delivered him from the rats. He likewise tamed some kids, and to divert himself would now and then sing and dance with them and his cats: so that by the care of providence, and vigour of his youth, being now but about thirty years old, he came at last to conquer all the inconveniences of his solitude, and to be very easy. When his clothes wore out, he made himself a coat and cap of goatskins, which he stitched together with little thongs of the same, that he cut with his knife. He had no other needle but a nail; and when his knife was wore to the back, he made others as well as he could of some iron hoops that were left ashore, which he beat thin and ground upon stones. Having some linen cloth by him, he sewed himself shirts with a nail, and stitched 'em with the worsted of his old stockings, which he pulled out on purpose. He had his last shirt on when we found him in the island.

At his first coming on board us, he had so much forgot his language for want of use, that we could scarce understand him, for he seemed to speak his words by halves. We offered him a dram, but he would not touch it, having drank nothing but water since his being there, and 'twas some time before he could relish our victuals.

He could give us an account of no other product of the island than what we have mentioned, except small black plums, which are very good, but hard to come at, the trees which bear 'em growing on high mountains and rocks.

Pimento trees are plenty here, and we saw some of sixty foot high, and about two yards thick; and cotton trees higher, and near four fathom round in the stock.

The climate is so good, that the trees and grass are verdant all the year. The winter lasts no longer than June and July, and is not then severe, there being only a small frost and a little hail, but sometimes great rains. The heat of the summer is equally moderate, and there's not much thunder or tempestuous weather of any sort. He saw no venomous or savage creatures on the island, nor any other sort of beast but goats, etc. as above-mentioned; the first of which had been put ashore here on purpose for a breed by Juan Fernando, a Spaniard, who settled there with some families for a time,* till the continent of Chile began to submit to the Spaniards; which being more profitable, tempted them to quit this island, which is capable of maintaining a good number of people, and of being made so strong that they could not be easily dislodged.

Ringrose, in his account of Captain Sharp's voyage and other buccaneers, mentions one who had escaped ashore here out of a ship which was cast away with all the rest of the company, and says he lived five years alone before he had the opportunity of another ship to carry him off. Captain Dampier talks of a Mosquito Indian that belonged to Captain Watling,† who, being a-hunting in the woods when the captain left the island, lived here three years alone, and shifted much in the same manner, as Mr Selkirk did, till Captain Dampier came hither in 1684, and carried him off. The first that went ashore was one of his countrymen, and they saluted one another first by prostrating themselves by turns on the ground, and then embracing. But whatever there is in these stories, this of Mr Selkirk I know to be true; and his behaviour afterwards gives me reason to believe the account he gave me how he spent his time, and bore up under such an affliction, in which nothing but the divine providence could have supported any man. By this one may see that solitude and retirement from the world is not such an un-

* In the 1560s.
† John Watling, a buccaneer.

sufferable state of life as most men imagine, especially when people are fairly called or thrown into it unavoidably, as this man was; who in all probability must otherwise have perished in the seas, the ship which left him being cast away not long after, and few of the company escaped. We may perceive by this story the truth of the maxim, that necessity is the mother of invention, since he found means to supply his wants in a very natural manner, so as to maintain his life, though not so conveniently, yet as effectually as we are able to do with the help of all our arts and society. It may likewise instruct us, how much a plain and temperate way of living conduces to the health of the body and the vigour of the mind, both which we are apt to destroy by excess and plenty, especially of strong liquor, and the variety as well as the nature of our meat and drink: for this man, when he came to our ordinary method of diet and life, though he was sober enough, lost much of his strength and agility. But I must quit these reflections, which are more proper for a philosopher and divine than a mariner, and return to my own subject.

SELKIRK NEARLY CHANGES HIS MIND

Edward Cooke, second in command on the Dutchess, *also wrote a book about the expedition, which was published shortly before that by Woodes Rogers, thus introducing Selkirk to the world at large. Cooke's description of the rescue is not as entertaining as Rogers's, but includes a fascinating allusion to Dampier, showing that Selkirk, like Welbe, could hardly be numbered among his admirers.*

He saluted the newcomers with much joy, being satisfied they were English, and they in return invited him aboard; he first enquired whether a certain officer that he knew was aboard; and hearing that he was, would rather have chosen to remain in his solitude, than come away with him, till informed that he did not command. They had much difficulty to persuade him to venture himself on board, so great was the aversion he had conceived against the officer aforesaid.

THE MANILA SHIP AGAIN

The climax of the voyage arrived on 22 December 1709. During the previous day, 'to our great and joyful surprise', a large ship appeared on the horizon off Cabo San Lucas, at the southern tip of Baja California. The Duke *and* Dutchess *began to manoeuvre into attack positions, with the* Marquiss, *taken off Ecuador, in reserve, anchored in Bahia San Lucas. Back in January 1686, with Captain Swan, Dampier had missed the Manila galleon, 'which would have enriched us beyond measure'. In December 1704, as commander himself, he failed to stop the great ship. Would he be luckier a third time? The encounter is described by Woodes Rogers.*

We made a clear ship before night, had everything in a readiness to engage her at daybreak, and kept a very good lookout all night for the boat's false fires, which we saw and answered frequently. At daybreak we saw the chase* upon our weather-bow, about a league from us, the *Dutchess* ahead of her to leeward near about half as far. Towards six our boat came aboard, having kept very near the chase all night, and received no damage, but told us the *Dutchess* passed by her in the night, and she fired two shot at them, but they returned none. We had no wind, but got out eight of our ship's oars, and rowed above an hour; then there sprung up a small breeze. I ordered a large kettle of chocolate to be made for our ship's company (having no spiritous liquor to give them); then we went to prayers, and before we had concluded were disturbed by the enemy's firing at us. They had barrels hanging at each yardarm, that looked like powder barrels, to deter us from boarding 'em. About eight o'clock we began to engage her by ourselves, for the *Dutchess* being to leeward, and having little wind, did not come up. The enemy fired her stern-chase upon us first, which we returned with our fore-chase several times, till we came nearer, and when close aboard each other, we gave her several broadsides, plying our small arms very briskly, which they returned as thick awhile, but did not ply their great guns half

---

* In this instance, the quarry; below, the word refers to the various cannon fielded by the galleon.

so fast as we. After some time we shot a little ahead of them, lay thwart her hawse* close aboard, and plied them so warmly, that she soon struck her colours two thirds down. By this time the *Dutchess* came up, and fired about five guns, with a volley of small shot, but the enemy, having submitted, made no return. We sent our pinnace aboard, and brought the captain with the officers away, and having examined 'em, found there was another ship came out of Manila with them, of a bigger burthen, having about forty brass guns mounted, and as many patereroes; but they told us they lost her company three months ago, and reckoned she was got to Acapulco before this time, she sailing better than this ship. This prize was called by the long name of *Nuestra Señora de la Incarnación Desengaño*, Sir John Pichberty† commander; she had twenty guns, twenty patereroes, and 193 men aboard, whereof nine were killed, ten wounded, and several blown up and burnt with powder. We engaged 'em about three glasses,‡ in which time we had only myself and another man wounded. I was shot through the left cheek, the bullet struck away great part of my upper jaw, and several of my teeth, part of which dropped down upon the deck, where I fell; the other, Will Powell, an Irish landman, was slightly wounded in the buttock. They did us no great damage in our rigging, but a shot disabled our mizzenmast. I was forced to write what I would say, to prevent the loss of blood, and because of the pain I suffered by speaking.

23 December: After we had put our ships to rights again, we stood in for the harbour, which bore north-east of us, distant about seven leagues. Our surgeons went aboard the prize to dress the wounded men.

24 December: About four yesterday afternoon we got to an anchor in Port Segura in twenty-five fathom water, found the *Marquiss* in a sailing posture, and all the company much overjoyed at our unexpected good fortune. In the night I felt

---

* The hawse is the part of the bow that lies between the ship's head and the anchor.
† Le Sieur Jean Pichberty, a French chevalier of Scottish descent in the service of Spain.
‡ I.e. one and a half hours.

something clog my throat, which I swallowed with much pain, and suppose it's a part of my jaw bone, or the shot, which we can't yet give an account of. I soon recovered myself; but my throat and head being very much swelled, have much ado to swallow any sort of liquids for sustenance.

A SECOND ENCOUNTER

On 26 December, a larger Manila galleon hove into view. 'By midnight', writes Woodes Rogers, 'we were pretty well up with them.'

In the morning as soon as 'twas day, the wind veering at once, put our ship about, and the chase fired first upon the *Dutchess*, who by means of the wind's veering was nearest the enemy; she returned it smartly: we stood as near as possible, firing as our guns came to bear; but the *Dutchess* being by this time thwart the Spaniard's hawse, and firing very fast, those shot that missed the enemy flew from the *Dutchess* over us, and betwixt our masts, so that we ran the risk of receiving more damage from them than from the enemy, if we had lain on her quarters and cross her stern, as I designed, while the enemy lay driving. This forced us to lie alongside, close aboard her, where we kept firing round shot, and did not load with any bar or partridge,* because the ship's sides were too thick to receive any damage by it, and no men appearing in sight, it would only have been a clog to the force of our round shot. We kept close aboard her, and drove as she did as near as possible. The enemy kept to their close quarters, so that we did not fire our small arms till we saw a man appear, or a port open; then we fired as quick as possible. Thus we continued for four glasses, about which time we received a shot in the mainmast, which much disabled it; soon after that the *Dutchess* and we firing together, we came both close under the enemy and had like to have been all aboard her, so that we could make little use of our guns. Then we fell astern in our berth alongside, where the enemy threw a fireball out of one of her tops, which, lighting upon our quarterdeck, blew up a chest of arms and cartouche

* Bar or partridge: missiles, such as sticks or stones and pieces of iron.

boxes* all loaded, and several cartridges of powder in the steerage by which means Mr Vanbrugh, our agent, and a Dutchman, were very much burnt; it might have done more damage, had it not been quenched as soon as possible. After we got clear of each other, the *Dutchess* stood in for the shore where she lay braced to, mending her rigging, etc. The *Marquiss* fired several shot, but to little purpose, her guns being small. We were close aboard several times afterwards, till at last we received a second shot in the mainmast not far from the other, which rent it miserably, and the mast settled to it, so that we were afraid it would drop by the board, and brought to, making a signal to our consorts to consult what to do; in the interim we got ordinary fishes† for support to the mainmast, and fastened it as well as we could to secure it at present. Captain Courtney and Captain Cooke came aboard with other officers, where we considered the condition the three ships were in, their masts and rigging being much damnified in a place where we could get no recruit; that if we engaged her again, we could propose to do no more than what we had already done, which was evident did her no great hurt, because we could perceive few of our shot entered her sides to any purpose, and our small arms availed less, there being not a man to be seen above-board; that the least thing in the world would bring our mainmast, and likewise the *Dutchess's* foremast by the board, either of which by its fall might carry away another mast, and then we should lie a battery for the enemy, having nothing to command our ships with; so that by his heavy guns he might either sink or take us: that if we went to board her, we should run a greater hazard in losing a great many men with little hopes of success, they having above treble the number aboard to oppose us, and there being now in all our three ships not above 120 good men fit for boarding, and those but weak, having been very short of provisions a long time. Besides we had the disadvantage of a netting-deck‡ to enter upon, and a ship every

* Boxes containing cartridges for muskets.
† Two long pieces of hard wood, convex on one side and concave on the other, bound opposite to each other to strengthen the masts.
‡ A netting extending fore and aft to prevent an enemy from boarding.

other way well provided; so that if we had boarded her, and been forced off, or left any of our men behind, the enemy by that means might have known our strength, and then gone into the harbour and taken possession of the prize in spite of all we could do to prevent it: besides, our ammunition was very short, having only enough to engage a few glasses longer. All this being seriously considered, and knowing the difficulty we should have to get masts, and the time and provisions we must spend before we could get 'em fitted, 'twas resolved to forbear attempting her further, since our battering her signified little, and we had not strength enough to board her: therefore we agreed to keep her company till night, then to lose her, and make the best of our way into the harbour to secure the prize we had already took. We engaged first and last about six or seven hours, during all which time we had aboard the *Duke* but eleven men wounded, three of whom were scorched with gunpowder. I was again unfortunately wounded in the left foot with a splinter just before we blew up on the quarterdeck, so that I could not stand, but lay on my back in a great deal of misery, part of my heel-bone being struck out, and all under my ankle cut above half through, which bled very much, and weakened me, before it could be dressed and stopped. The *Dutchess* had about twenty men killed and wounded, three of the latter and one of the former were my men. The *Marquiss* had none killed or wounded, but two scorched with powder. The enemy's was a brave lofty new ship, the Admiral of Manila, and this the first voyage she had made; she was called the *Bigonia*, of about 900 tons, and could carry sixty guns, about forty of which were mounted, with as many patereroes, all brass; her complement of men on board, as we were informed, was above 450, besides passengers. They added, that 150 of the men on board this great ship were Europeans, several of whom had been formerly pirates, and having now got all their wealth aboard, were resolved to defend it to the last. The gunner, who had a good post in Manila, was an expert man, and had provided the ship extraordinary well for defence, which made them fight so desperately; they had filled up all between the guns with bales to secure the men. She kept a Spanish flag at her main topmast-head all the time she fought us; we shattered her sails and rigging very much, shot her mizzenyard, killed two men out of her tops, which was all the damage we could see we did 'em; though we could not place less than 500 shot (six-pounders) in her hull. These large ships are built at Manila with excellent timber, that will not splinter; they have very thick sides, much stronger than we build in Europe.

SAFE HAVEN

The Duke, Dutchess *and their prizes returned home in October 1711 after sailing round the world – Dampier's third circumnavigation. Despite their failure to take the larger Manila galleon, the expedition was an overwhelming financial success, with net profits of £150,000. As 'Pilot for the South Seas', Dampier, now aged sixty, was entitled to one per cent – £1,500 – sufficient of a nest egg to keep him in comfort for the remaining four years of his life.*

Litigation among the backers prolonged payment for four years, but financiers were happy to advance credit. So, at the age of sixty, Dampier at last swallowed the anchor and retired. 'An old man driven by the Trades to a sleepy corner', he was looked after, at a house in Coleman Street, in East London, by his cousin Grace, until his death three and a half years later in March 1715.

*William Dampier's diversity and extraordinary range of achievements have won admirers from many spheres of human endeavour. The greater geographer Admiral James Burney wrote in his impos-*ing Chronological History of the Voyages and Discoveries in the South Sea (*1819*):

It is not easy to name another voyager or traveller who has given more useful information to the world; to whom the merchant and mariner are so much indebted; or who has communicated his information in a more unembarrassed and intelligible manner. And this he has done in a style perfectly unassuming, equally free from affectation and from the most distant appearance of invention.

As we have noted earlier, his appeal was also felt by the poet John Masefield:

When one considers his busy life of action, one is surprised that Dampier should have found time to write the three books of voyages by which he is remembered today. But when one considers that the man's literary life was spent among pirates, lumber-men, and drunken and ignorant sailors, one is surprised that he ever wrote a word. It is pathetic to think of him ('a man,' as Coleridge says, 'of exquisite refinement of mind'), writing up his journal, describing a bunch of flowers, or a rare fish, in the intervals between looting a wine-ship and sacking a village. Of ease and leisure, during the years of his literary production, he knew nothing. His best book was written aboard a buccaneer cruiser, amid the drunkenness and noise of his shipmates. He must have gone without sleep many times (a sailor will appreciate this sacrifice) in order to 'take a survey,' or drawing, of the coast. When he went ashore, he did not follow his mates into the rum-shops, to taste the 'fine Rack', or curious 'Boshee Drink', of their hearts' desires. He examined the natives and the country, and jotted down every detail of every bird, beast, tree, and fruit which he chanced to see.

For nearly two hundred years after Dampier's death there existed no memorial to him, since we do not normally erect monuments to buccaneers. But in 1908 St Michael's, East Coker, where he was baptised, grasped the nettle and put up a magnificent brass plaque depicting him with two of his ships. Mincing no words, its opening lines proclaim:

To the memory of

WILLIAM DAMPIER

Buccaneer, Explorer, Hydrographer

In this same church, the ashes of T. S. Eliot were interred on Easter Saturday 1965. Though neither born nor resident in the village, the

Nobel Laureate wished to be buried there because of a distant family connection. His own plaque is across the aisle from Dampier's. Such juxtaposition would have tickled both their fancies.

LIST OF SOURCES

(All by Dampier unless otherwise stated. See Bibliography for further details).

Chapter One: From *The Campeachy Voyages*, except 'The Great Storm of June 1676', from *A Discourse of Winds*.

Chapter Two: From *A New Voyage Round the World*, except 'Dampier to the Rescue', from *A Discourse of Winds*.

Chapter Three: From *A New Voyage Round the World*, except 'Chock-full', from *A Discourse of Winds*.

Chapter Four: From *A New Voyage Round the World*.

Chapter Five: From *A New Voyage Round the World*.

Chapter Six: From *A New Voyage Round the World*, except 'A Voyage to Tonquin' and 'The People of Tonquin', from *A Voyage to Tonquin*.

Chapter Seven: From *A Voyage to Tonquin*, except 'The Painted Prince', 'The Death Ship', 'Hodmadods', 'Zebra' and 'St Helena', from *A New Voyage Round the World*.

Chapter Eight: From *A Voyage to New Holland*.

Chapter Nine: 'A Disappointing Engagement' and 'The Manila Ship', from William Funnell's *A Voyage Round the World*; *Captain Dampier's Vindication of His Voyage to the South Seas in the Ship 'St George'*; John Welbe's *An Answer to Captain Dampier's Vindication of His Voyage to the South Seas in the Ship 'St George', with Particular Observations on His Ungenerous, False and Barbarous Usage to His Ship's Crew*; 'The Rescue of Alexander Selkirk', 'The Manila Ship', 'A Second Encounter', from Woodes Rogers's *A Cruising Voyage Round the World*; and 'Selkirk Nearly Changes His Mind', from Edward Cooke's *A Voyage to the South Sea and Around the World*.

BIBLIOGRAPHY

Dampier, William   *A New Voyage Round the World* (London, 1697)
Voyages and Descriptions (London, 1699)
A Voyage to New Holland (London, 1703, 1709)
Captain Dampier's Vindication (London, 1707)

Defoe, Daniel   *A General History of the Robberies and Murders of the Most Notorious Pyrates* (London, 1724)

Exquemelin, A. O.   *The Buccaneers of America* (Amsterdam, 1678)

Funnell, William   *A Voyage Round the World* (London, 1707)

Heuvelmans, Bernard   *On the Track of Unknown Animals* (London, 1958)

Ringrose, Basil   *The Buccaneers of America, Part IV* (London, 1685)

Rogers, Woodes   *A Cruising Voyage Round the World* (London, 1712)

Sclater, W. L.   'William Dampier as an Ornithologist', in *Ibis*, Series 14, No. 4

Shipman, Joseph C.   *William Dampier, Seaman–Scientist* (Kansas, 1962)

Wafer, Lionel — *A New Voyage and Description of the Isthmus of America* (London, 1699)

Welbe, John — *An Answer to Captain Dampier's Vindication* (London, 1707)

Whittell, Hubert Massey — *The Literature of Australian Birds* (Perth, 1954)

INDEX

Printed in the United Kingdom
by Lightning Source UK Ltd.
121213UK00001B/13-48